RELUCTANT
BEDFELLOWS

RELUCTANT BEDFELLOWS

Feminism, Activism, and Prostitution in the Philippines

Meredith Ralston and Edna Keeble

Kumarian Press
An Imprint of Stylus Publishing

Reluctant Bedfellows

Published in 2009 in the United States of America by Kumarian Press, 22883 Quicksilver Drive, Sterling, VA 20166 USA.

The text of this book is set in 10/12 Janson Text.

Editing and book design by Joan Weber Laflamme, jml ediset.
Proofread by Beth Richards.
Index by Robert Swanson.

Printed in the United States of America by Thompson-Shore. Text printed with vegetable oil-based ink.

∞ The paper used in this publication meets the minimum requirements of the American National Standard for Information Sciences—Permanence of Paper for printed Library Materials, ANSI Z39.48–1984

Library of Congress Cataloging-in-Publication Data

Ralston, Meredith L.
    Reluctant bedfellows : feminism, activism and prostitution in the Philippines / Meredith Ralston and Edna Keeble.
        p. cm.
    Includes bibliographical references (p.) and index.
        ISBN 978-1-56549-269-1 (pbk. : alk. paper)
    1. Social work with prostitutes—Philippines—Angeles. 2. Women in community development—Philippines—Angeles. 3. Prostitution—Philippines—Angeles. 4. Feminism—Philippines—Angeles. I. Keeble, Edna. II. Title.
    HQ415.R35 2009
    363.4'408209599—dc22
                                                                        2008036909

18 17 16 15 14 13 12 11 10 09   10 9 8 7 6 5 4 3 2 1   First Printing 2009

Contents

For Scott and Roy

Preface

This has been a book in progress for several years, and, in addition to the wonderful staff at Smitty's in Halifax, there are so many people to thank. First and foremost are the two people without whom this project would never have happened: our original project director, the late Marietta Suarez, and Edna's mother, Lydia Roasa Ward, who both paved the way for our introductions in the Philippines. Once up and running, the project in the Philippines would never have flowed as smoothly as it did without the amazing talents of our subsequent Filipino project director, Edda Flores, and our project manager, Maureen Woodhouse. Both of them kept us and the project going and provided a warm, efficient, and rewarding working environment. Other irreplaceable partners in the project include Lou Ayuyao, Carmen Brooks, Richard Devlin, Agnes Espiritu, Fely Flores, Pearlie Flores, Raquel Frye, Puring Gilbore, the late Justice William Grant, Cecil Lazatin, Francine McIntyre, Donna Melchor, Dulce Natividad, Babes Pascual, Stephen Perrott, Aida Santos, Reynaldo Suarez, Linda Tullao, and the late Ely Yap. We would never have accomplished as much as we did without them. We thank our respective universities for providing such wonderful moral and financial support for us and the project. Before this ever became a CIDA-funded project, it was fully supported by Saint Mary's University and Mount Saint Vincent University. We particularly want to thank our editor at Kumarian Press, Erica Flock, for her support of the project from the very beginning and for her invaluable comments and suggestions along the way. Our research assistant, Jolani Rhodenizer, kept the bibliography current, kept Meredith organized, and dealt with all our technical and formatting issues. We also thank all our colleagues who helped shape the arguments in this book, particularly Lorraine Code, who led us to Sonia Kruks's work on acting on one's privilege and Kathy Davis's work on transnational feminism; Mary Delaney, who told us about transversal politics; and Sue Campbell, for her sensitive reading of Chapter 2.

Edna wants to thank her family: her mother, Lydia, mentioned above, who has lived her life to "facilitate" all that is good; her children, Kelli and Brett, who bear witness to inequalities and believe that they, as individuals, have a responsibility to act; and her husband, Roy, who has taught her more than he'll ever know, just because he has always lived, acted, and loved (her) as only a liberal cosmopolitan feminist could. Mostly, I want to thank Meredith for not only shaping and influencing my feminist views intellectually and practically through many years of friendship and collaboration, but also for leading and believing that what we have to say is important, necessary, and shared, and that we can make a difference by writing about what we've experienced, what we've learned, and what we've determined to be our guideposts in acting as engaged scholars and ethical individuals.

Meredith wants to thank Edna for being such a wonderful friend and colleague and for living all the principles outlined in this book for collaborative and respectful dialogue. She wants to thank her partner, Scott MacMillan, for his love and encouragement, and reading and debating every word of this book. She thanks the Howies, particularly Kristine, Robert, and Adam, for being such good companions and helpers at the cottage. She especially wants to thank her parents, Norman and Lynn Ralston, and tell a story about their lifelong modeling of "doing something," which has become the theme of this book.

When I was about ten years old, my younger sister and I were being driven home by our father in the backseat of an old Dodge. It was snowing heavily in wintry New Brunswick, and the roads were very slippery. As we came to an intersection, an older man was trying to cross the street and had stumbled over a large snow bank trying to get to the other side. In the midst of traffic and beeping cars, my father stopped in the middle of the intersection, got out of the car and helped this old man up and over the snow bank. All the cars and the beeping stopped—respectfully, it seemed to me—to let this happen. My father got back into the car, and we drove away.

Meredith doesn't remember him saying a thing about it but the moral to us is clear: when someone in need is in your path, you do something. It is a lesson we take with us everywhere, whether locally or globally. *When someone is in your path and needs your help, you help.* The following chapters examine why this seems to have become so difficult recently and how we need to encourage people to care about others now more than ever.

Abbreviations/Acronyms

AUCC   Association of Universities and Colleges of Canada

AUF   Angeles University Foundation

AWAN   Aboriginal Women's Action Network

BNA   British North America

CATW   Coalition Against Trafficking in Women

CATW-AP   Coalition Against Trafficking in Women-Asia Pacific
                (the Coalition)

CIDA   Canadian International Development Agency

COYOTE   Call Off Your Old Tired Ethics

FGM   female genital mutilation

GAATW   Global Alliance Against Trafficking in Women

GABRIELA   General Assembly Binding Women for Reforms, Integrity, Equality, Leadership, and Action

HDI   Human Development Index (U.N.)

ILO   International Labour Organization

NAC   National Action Committee on the Status of Women
                (Canada)

NCRFW   National Commission on the Role of Filipino Women

NWSA   National Women's Studies Association

ODA   official development assistance

OFW   Overseas Filipino Workers

PNP   Philippine National Police

TWMAEW   Third World Movement Against the Exploitation of
                Women (the Movement)

UPDC   University Partnerships in Cooperation and Development

USAID   United States Agency for International Development

VFA   Visiting Forces Agreement

WEDPRO   Women's Education, Development, Productivity and Research Organization

WHWC   Women Helping Women Center

RELUCTANT
BEDFELLOWS

PART I

THEORETICAL CHALLENGES

1

"You've Got to Do Something"

The Project

Tenured university professors, particularly in Western countries, lead professional lives that few have the privilege to experience. Even fewer have the opportunity to take their work beyond their classrooms or disciplinary conferences and other traditional academic venues and to become part of state-funded efforts to address global injustices rooted in gender inequalities. These efforts are not without controversy, grounded as they are in North-South realities and the power of donor states over recipient ones, but as one of the tools to address the challenges of poverty-stricken countries, official development assistance (ODA) in its many forms can prove helpful in the creation of small-scale, incremental change, particularly when individuals from the recipient state emerge to champion a specific issue.

How two Canadian feminist academics from Halifax, Nova Scotia, became involved in a development project on prostitution in the Philippines is part of the story we want to tell. Our involvement speaks not only to the sort of scholars we are, but also to the kind of ethical individuals we seek to be. The phrase *scholarship of engagement* comes from the work of Ernest Boyer, in which he not only built on his earlier work on broadening the definition of scholarship but also called for a renewed commitment to public service in the work of universities, particularly in the United States. Variously referred to as the *scholarship of application*, *engaged scholarship*, and *public scholarship*, the scholarship of engagement is connected to the civic renewal of universities and, accordingly, a rethinking of what the service role means in the trinity of academic work.[1] This type of scholarship is "scholarly activity generating new knowledge through academic reflection on issues of community engagement. It integrates research, teaching, and service. It does not assume that useful knowledge simply flows outward from the university to the larger community.

It recognizes that new knowledge is created in its application in the field, and therefore benefits the teaching and research mission of the university."[2]

Understanding scholarship in this way necessitates seeing communities and groups outside of the academy as an integral part of the production of knowledge. They are not merely or primarily recipients in the application of knowledge coming from universities. This is a challenge to the "ivory tower" mentality of scholarly work both in terms of *who* scholars are—they alone are not the producers or generators of knowledge—and in terms of *what* scholars do—they are not disengaged or detached from the world in which they live, thus ensuring that their work is not only relevant but also accessible to the public generally. Relevance and accessibility are crucial components in university-community collaborative research and public education partnerships; relevance is about addressing contemporary problems that affect people's lives, and accessibility is about disseminating knowledge not simply in traditional scholarly venues, such as academic journals, which are often read only by fellow academics. Academics already do this as teachers by making knowledge and expertise accessible to students, but being engaged scholars means taking it outside of the classroom. The scholarship of engagement carries with it a commitment to the public arena, and that is why it is crucial to the civic renewal of universities.

Committed to the scholarship of engagement, the authors brought together two different areas of expertise. Meredith had worked with homeless, prostituted women in Canada, and her work was engaged at the grassroots level. Edna had worked on international security policies, incorporating a feminist component, and her work was engaged at the governmental level. In 1995, we traveled to Manila for the first time and met with academics and activists who were working with women in the sex trade. We quickly discovered that there was not a great deal of research being done by academics on the sex trade and that most of the known prostitution, as chronicled by local and regional women's service and advocacy organizations, was occurring in a place called Angeles City, about sixty miles northwest of Manila. Angeles City had been the site of the Clark Air Force Base from the end of World War II until Mt. Pinatubo erupted in 1991, subsequently destroying much of the base and surrounding areas. Given the association of military bases and rest and recreation, it is not surprising that an active sex trade had developed around the base.[3] When we arrived in 1995, the Americans had been gone for just over three years, and the base was a dust bowl. With buildings gutted and looted, and what looked to us like tumbleweeds flowing down the once-active runways, it was hard to imagine what Clark had looked like in its heyday. The people of Angeles had been hard hit by the American troop withdrawal, and many citizens lamented the decision of the national government not to extend the contract of the U.S. bases at either Clark or Subic Naval Station in nearby Olongapo. The sex trade was, however, beginning to make a comeback with the bars and discos surrounding the former Clark Base being bought by retired Americans, Australians, Swedes, and other foreigners. Military prostitution was fairly quickly replaced by sex tourism.

While in Angeles City for the first time we met with several individuals representing women's groups, and we toured the various prostitution areas. Prostitution is technically illegal in the Philippines, but it is regulated by the municipal government, so there is a slightly schizophrenic reaction to the sex trade in Angeles; that is, much denial of the problem on the one hand, and real economic benefits on the other. At the time of our first visit the community was still reeling from the American withdrawal and the question of what to do with all the bar girls and entertainers who had worked at the bars, discos, and karaokes surrounding the base. Moreover, many bar girls from Olongapo were traveling to Angeles for work because the mayor of Olongapo had cracked down on prostitution and converted bars to "legitimate" businesses, forcing the women to find new jobs or other bars. Given the challenges and downturns of the Philippine economy, the problems of finding alternative livelihoods became even more acute for once-employed entertainers. It was in this environment that we arrived to gather materials for research in 1995. To a person, the women with whom we met—no matter what their groups' ideology or position on prostitution happened to be—wanted us to do more than just research and study the problem. They argued that there was a huge problem, and something had to be done. "You've got to do something" became the refrain of that first trip. Meredith also went to the 1995 United Nations Fourth World Conference on Women in Beijing immediately after that trip and, from that experience, came back even more convinced of the necessity of building a global women's movement founded on local issues and initiatives, regardless of the ideological problem of neo-colonialism, which was gaining ground at that time.

If the original intent of our trip was to develop research ideas to study and "know" the problem, our interactions with women's organizations and activists caused us to reflect on what transnational feminist work means. Although as feminists we knew that we could never be detached observers and were fully aware of the perils and pitfalls of Northern researchers going into Southern communities, the demand that we "do something" resonated with us. Fortunately, we belonged to two universities with institutional missions committed to community outreach and internationalization, and we soon discovered potential funding that enabled academics to engage in development work. Funded as a partnership program of the Canadian International Development Agency (CIDA)—the Canadian equivalent to the United States Agency for International Development (USAID)—the University Partnerships in Cooperation and Development (UPCD) program provides opportunities for Canadian professors to initiate and direct a development project in their research area. The UPCD program is geared toward capacity building and human resource development for organizations (so this is not traditional research funding), and it provides five-year (now six-year) funding for universities. In 1999, after several more trips to the Philippines and after continuing communication with the women's organization that would become our primary Filipino partner, we were successful in obtaining funding for our project, entitled "Sex Trade in the Philippines: A Multi-level Gender-Sensitive Approach to Human Resource Development." Awarded a total funding of $1.1 million from 1999 to 2004, the project was based in Angeles City and it brought together two Canadian universities, Saint Mary's University and Mount Saint Vincent University in Halifax, Nova Scotia, and five very diverse Filipino groups as partners in the project.

Because of the nature of the funding arrangement, the project was primarily focused on institutional capacity building; the overall goal was to increase the ability of the Filipino partners to understand, and help to alleviate, the problem of prostitution in their city. We also wanted to raise the awareness of people in Angeles about the young girls and women in their midst who, as Angelenos always reminded us, were "not from here." The bar girls were situated as outsiders in Angeles, coming from the poor southern provinces. They were cast by the locals of Angeles as poor, immoral individuals who traveled to the city to make a living and to look for a rich foreign husband. The women were looked down on by the locals, when their presence was acknowledged at all, being seen as interlopers who brought shame to the city. Although the project was not about the disbursements of aid monies directly to the prostitutes in Angeles City, we worked directly with the prostituted women through our Filipino partners. On their advice, we decided to work with groups that dealt directly with the bar girls in various capacities to help them deal in a more gender-sensitive fashion with the sex workers. We helped the Filipino partners to make connections between sex tourism and military prostitution and to develop culturally appropriate feminist critiques of prostitution and violence against women in order that members of the groups might carry out training programs within their particular organizations and eventually to the broader community. The project tried to alleviate the hardships of bar girls—legally, financially, and socially—by directing attention to an exploitative group of bar owners and clients, an unsympathetic community, and an insensitive court system.

Two of our Filipino partners were governmental organizations: the Supreme Court of the Philippines and the Philippine National Police (PNP). Both are important actors in the treatment of the bar girls through the enforcement of the law. Because of the tenuous position of prostitution in the Philippines and the fact that only women can be convicted of being prostitutes, it was crucial to involve the judiciary, who interpret the laws, and the police, who enforce them. Not surprisingly, one of our five partners was a local university, Angeles University Foundation (AUF), and it sought to institute both curricular changes within the university and further community outreach, particularly to the prostituted women. We had fellow academics involved on the Canadian side who undertook training and development for the community groups, police, judiciary, and university. We also had additional partners from Canada, namely, Stepping Stone, a Halifax-based service organization advocating for the rights of prostitutes, and the Halifax Regional Police, two organizations that had historical enmity because one saw the other as a barrier to helping women in prostitution. Interestingly, one of the women's groups in the Philippines with whom we had partnered had this sort of hostility with the PNP, while the other women's group had a close working relationship with the police.

These two women's groups, respectively, were the Women's Education, Development, Productivity and Research Organization (WEDPRO) and Soroptimist International of Angeles City. These are two very different kinds of women's groups. Beginning with the latter, the Soroptimists are part of a national and international network of professional, mainly privileged, upper-middle-class women. Dedicated to the concept of women helping women, the Soroptimists are key players in the Angeles community. They have historically raised funds and given resources to those women less privileged in their community. Particularly important to our project, the Soroptimists also initiated the creation of, and continued to support, the Women's Desk of the Philippine National Police. WEDPRO is part of the Coalition Against Trafficking in Women–Asia Pacific (CATW-AP) and, as we soon found out, one of the most radical women's advocacy groups in the Philippines. It started as a dynamic grassroots organization composed of dedicated activists and survivors of the sex trade, and became a research and advocacy network. The members of WEDPRO have worked very hard researching the lives of prostituted women in Angeles City and elsewhere in the Philippines. We were specifically told by Ermelita Valdeavilla, then executive director of the National Commission on the Role of Filipino Women (NCRFW) in the Office of the President, that the partnering of the Soroptimists and WEDPRO was "a challenging but clearly commendable and original part of the project."[4]

The Problem

The challenges were evident from the very beginning. Although four of our Filipino groups saw Canadians as partners in creating change and welcomed our presence in the Philippines, "do something" turned out to have a very strong ideological component in the mind of our fifth partner. Grounded in post-colonial feminist precepts, "do something" to WEDPRO demanded that we, as Northerners, begin by embracing post-colonial discourse that Northern countries, like Canada, are in their economic positions of wealth, and thus are privileged donor states, precisely because of the historical and continuing exploitation of Southern countries, like the Philippines. Moreover, WEDPRO argued, there is a sense of racial or cultural superiority that underpins Northerners wanting to "do something" in the South. Not only do Canadian partners assume that they have skills or knowledge to share—WEDPRO argued that Filipinos, specifically members of their organization, could train the judges, police, and community in gender sensitivity about the plight of prostituted women—but also Canadians have not looked at their own situation because prostitution is as rampant and as exploitative in Canada as anywhere in the South, including the Philippines. In other words, Canadians should "do something" in their own country and leave the efforts in the Philippines to Filipinos. By using our privilege (even for "good" purposes) we were simply reinforcing our superiority. In terms of our specific project, they argued, we should give the monies for human resource development to WEDPRO, which would then take care of the training of the other four Filipino partners, irrespective of the fact that the partners did not want to be trained by, and indeed were initially hostile to, WEDPRO. Leaving aside the arguments that this was an unrealistic and unreasonable proposal, given it was a Canadian-funded project, WEDPRO's view was both damning of the value of outsiders and, as was brought home to us many times subsequently, reflective of current academic feminist theorizing in the West about the neo-colonial aspects of development projects.

In the middle of our involvement in the project we attended the National Women's Studies Association (NWSA) conference in Las Vegas, Nevada, in June 2002 to present our work on prostitution in the Philippines. Like other academics, we cherish the opportunity to attend conferences to present our ongoing work because it allows us to receive feedback from colleagues about our ideas and claims. Attending conferences also compels us to reflect on the privileged nature of scholarly life, certainly far removed from the bars and brothels of Angeles City in the Philippines that had become a focus of study and action for us. Moreover, the NWSA conference's theme—Deconstructing Sin City—had a special appeal to us because our own work was centered in Angeles City, a known site of military prostitution and sex tourism. During our presentation, which was a descriptive look at our development project and the preliminary results from our participatory video component, two (white) female colleagues sat at the back of the room clearly displeased with what we were saying. As the session progressed, it became evident that the women had three fundamental problems with our presentation, reflecting the problems we were having with WEDPRO:

1. Why was the goal of our project not to eliminate prostitution?
2. Why would we presume to know anything about these women's lives, not being sex trade workers ourselves (and in the case of one of us, not even Filipino)?
3. Why were we allowing ourselves to be co-opted by a state-funded development project?

After our presentation the conversation proceeded in the following way, beginning with our response to the first question, which was about the goal of the project. We explained that the goal was to work with community groups and governmental organizations who worked with prostituted women in the Philippines so they would deal more sympathetically with them in the future and not treat them like social outcasts or criminals. Seemingly aghast at the limited (and naive) nature of our ambitions, one of the women told us that she didn't think much of any project on prostitution that did not start with the ultimate goal of its eradication and how that made our project a sham from the very beginning. We responded that we felt a moral and political responsibility to "do something" once we were in the Philippines as we were confronted with the daily living conditions of the women and the exploitation they faced. Similarly appalled, the other woman asked who we were to think that we could maternalistically *help* these women. What does that say about our neo-colonial mentality? We attempted, to no avail, to address our awareness of the dangers inherent in cross-cultural, international development work, and to point out that we had been asked by local community groups to "do something" rather than simply researching them and leaving, never to return. Not good enough, they responded, because development work is inherently a co-optation of community groups by the state, and all we were doing was perpetuating the globally unjust status quo.

As we reflected on these and other experiences, and as we continued to defend our project theoretically, we were able to clarify our own perspectives on these important issues. We came to believe that the positions taken by one of our Filipino partners and the women at the NWSA meetings were ultimately self-defeating, because the logical consequences of these positions cannot be sustained. Do we really need to be a sex worker to know that sex workers deserve human rights protections? Do we really need to be a person of color to know that racism is wrong? Do we not abdicate our responsibilities to others when we simply leave the Filipinos to deal with their problems while we in the West deal with our own—especially when they are not solely responsible for those problems? What are the possibilities for political action and coalition building when feminists become more concerned with silos of differences than with similarities and common political concerns? Can we not work with others respectfully and self-reflectively in order to create social change even if we know that the change is incremental rather than revolutionary? Can we, in fact, use our privileges to create change, and not indulge in white or male or Western guilt for those privileges?

This book is our attempt to address the dilemmas of development work and political action, in all their complexities, at a particular historical juncture when attempts at social change in another place are considered neo-colonial and ethnocentric. Embraced by some Southern women's groups like WEDPRO, there is an impasse in feminist theorizing, which can only be called analysis paralysis, because the polarizing debates between post-structuralist, post-colonialist, and so-called identity feminists have led to a hesitation in individual women and women's groups in Western countries to act politically for fear of being labeled ethnocentric, neo-imperialist, or worse. What was once common sense (that women's studies is the academic arm of the women's movement) has become increasingly problematic in academic feminist theorizing and has led to the current paralysis. This obviously has many negative consequences for women's organizations and other rights-seeking groups, specifically in countries like Canada and the United States. Continuing to witness gendered inequalities not only in their own societies but even more so in other societies throughout the developing or post-colonial world, they (like so many of us) want to act to change the world.

Fundamentally, we believe that social change is a moral and political responsibility of individuals, not just groups, and that worthwhile, valuable change can come about through individual and attitudinal changes, not just through revolutionary group action. We want to show through our work on a development project in the Philippines how the emphasis on differences in feminist theory today limits our ability to "do" feminist politics. We assert that while feminists clearly need to be cognizant of differences, they should not be immobilized by hierarchies of oppression, cultural relativism, and feminist ideologies that tell us we cannot do anything without paralyzing soul searching. While feminists and other progressives argue about who is responsible for what, and who can presume to know anything about anything, millions of people around the world live in utter poverty, destitution, and misery. Many of those who are impoverished are women, and despite the feminist movement teaching us that women working for and with other women have made a difference in the lives of women around the world, many academics, particularly those who happen to live in the West, do not seem to want to take any personal responsibility for creating change.

We want to change that. We believe that we all have a responsibility to make a difference, in our own way, no matter how seemingly small. We are not so naive as to think that privilege is simply a purview of the West, because differences are as evident within societies as between them. The wealthy neighborhoods of Manila would rival any in New York or Los Angeles, but the impoverished conditions throughout the Philippines and elsewhere in the developing world are simply unequalled, if not unimaginable, in the West. Martha Nussbaum, Peter Singer, Thomas Pogge, and Kwame Anthony Appiah have compellingly outlined the responsibilities of those of us living in rich countries.[5] Through public and private giving, states and individuals in rich countries can take responsibility for making a difference in the lives of those who live in the developing world as well as for the poor in their own countries. As Hurricane Katrina demonstrated, there is a mass of humanity in the United States (mainly poor and African American) that is marginalized and disadvantaged in a way that is shameful for a wealthy, developed country, let alone the only superpower left in the world. Much more has to be done locally and globally to make this world a fair, just, and equitable society for all peoples. Our call to action comes from the very specific experiences of two privileged female academics, who, in wanting to better the lives of prostituted women in Angeles City, Philippines, found ourselves accepting that the elimination of prostitution, although perhaps laudable, is an unrealistic goal at this point in history; that we can (and sometimes should) speak for others if we are mindful of our own prejudices and understandings; and that state donor agencies can be useful partners in the creation of change.

To that end, we also want this book to further the debate between feminist activists and academics. We argue that we must go back to the roots of the feminist movement, again, with an eye on politics, not just theorizing. As Sara Evans aptly argues:

> The brilliant creativity and the longevity of feminism in the late twentieth century is grounded in the breathtaking claim that the personal is political. At the same time, this confluence of personal-private and public-political contained the seed of the movement's repeated episodes of fragmentation and self-destruction. On the one hand, the "personal is political" empowered both individuals and groups to challenge inequities that the culture defined as natural. . . . On the other hand, the linkage of the personal and political

led some to a search for purity, for "true" feminism in the realm of ideas and the formula for a perfectly realized feminist life. The pursuit of perfection made it difficult to entertain complexity, sliding easily into dogmatism. Differences of opinion and lifestyle betrayed the "true faith" and could not be tolerated. Thus, this is a history rife with contradiction: growth and fragmentation, innovation and internal conflict.[6]

We believe that this dogma and fragmentation undermines the work of feminists all over the world and particularly demoralizes young people who are currently struggling not only with the issue of gender but also with issues of race, globalization, and poverty. Nowhere is this more evident than in our own university classrooms.

Teaching is a principal component in the lives of academics, and in the troika of scholarly responsibilities (research, teaching, and service), teaching along with service is often undervalued as many universities subscribe to a "publish or perish" mentality. Over a decade ago Shelley Park, undertaking a feminist analysis of the tenure and promotion policies of universities, pointed out that the devaluing of teaching and service in the work of the professoriate stems from seeing these activities as "women's work," whereas research is seen as "men's work."[7] Fortunately, in large part due to the movement broadening the definition of scholarship marked by the publication of Ernest Boyer's *Scholarship Reconsidered*, not only has the integration of research, teaching, and service become more evident in the ways academics do their work, but the incorporation of public or community aspects in the production and dissemination of knowledge is beginning to receive due recognition. Referred to as the scholarship of engagement, this defines the kind of work that the authors do. From the teaching side, students want to be engaged—they want to connect theory to practice—but have found themselves, just as we have, in a quandary, given the rise of identity politics in universities.

Can a man teach feminist political theory? Can a white woman teach African American history? The link between identity and credibility has been manifested in the university classroom through challenges that disciplinary knowledge is no longer sufficient to confer professional authority. As Katherine Mayberry highlights, the "debate over identity-based credibility (teaching what you are versus teaching what you're not) is currently the most visible expression of identity politics in higher education."[8] Although progressive intellectuals have been at the forefront of opening up the university canon through the inclusion of feminist, anti-racist, and lesbian and gay literature in existing disciplines, such as political science and sociology, as well as through the establishment of multi-disciplinary and interdisciplinary programs, such as women's studies, African American studies, or queer studies, these same progressive intellectuals are finding themselves as the "them" in an "us versus them" scenario based on their gender (if they are male), race (if they are white), or sexual orientation (if they are heterosexual). Faced with questions whether he, as a male professor, could properly teach feminist political theory, J. Scott Johnson compellingly stated: "The identities of readers and writers, teachers and students, are clearly germane to many classroom discussions, but only to the extent that such discussion furthers the consideration of ideas. If the discussion of identity degenerates into ad hominem attacks as a way of avoiding ideas and critical thought, then no one is learning."[9] Credibility comes from knowing and reflecting on the privileges and prejudices that we as professors bring to the classroom, not from the static identity markers that are often thrust upon us by colleagues or students. The problem, however, is that dominant theoretical paradigms in academic feminism seem to preclude the transcendence necessary to think and act beyond one's identity, leaving many students confused about what feminism is all about. For example, one of our master of arts (MA) students in women's studies doing work in Yemen summarizes it well when she states that she no longer knows right from wrong because of the mixed messages she has received from feminist theory: feminism is about making life better for women, but don't do anything for women who are not just like you. This student has basically given up in her attempt to look at Yemeni women's experiences and has chosen to do a self-reflective thesis on herself and her attempts to fit into a foreign culture because she has been told by some of her professors that it would be illegitimate for her to write about (speak for) the women of another culture. For similar reasons, we have had to justify our involvement in the Philippines, particularly because one of us is not Filipino.

Accordingly, we argue, in the search for ever-expanding theoretical complexity, some forms of contemporary feminism seem to have become an academic critique of itself, not a critique of male domination and inequality in all its forms. Rather than finding solutions for the many problems women still face in the United States and worldwide, such as lack of adequate health care, shaky reproductive rights, domestic and sexual violence, double day, less pay, unequal participation in politics, and so forth, academics tend to use their theoretical critiques to tell us that there is no category of "woman" with which to begin. As much as we may understand theoretically why post-structuralist philosophers insist upon deconstruction, we look at the women we know in Canada and the Philippines and say it should not be an intellectual exercise when we are dealing with people's lives. How do we tell the poor woman on assistance who does not have access to birth control or abortion, or the woman who is being sexually harassed at work, or the single mother looking for affordable child care while looking after her elderly parents, or the six-teen-year-old bar girl supporting her entire family through prostitution that there is no such category as "woman," that she is not oppressed because she is a woman? As much as categories need to be deconstructed and problematized, there must still remain some common denominator for women, politically, and for other rights-seeking groups.

The larger question is how do we revive the feminist movement? How do we mobilize diverse groups of women (and men) within and outside the academy? There are some hopeful indications that this may just be a stage in the development of feminism. In dialectical terms the early years of the second wave of feminism (the thesis) were in some ways a naive view of a universal, global sisterhood. It came at a time when the recognition of sameness was necessary to make change and bring women together. The more recent antithesis of this naive sisterhood can be seen at the time period we are in today, with its similarly necessary recognition of differences and critique of sisterhood. The necessary synthesis, however, needs to address the fundamental problems with identity politics in feminism and become a social movement that addresses both sameness and difference and that operates both locally and globally to achieve a truly global feminism and global citizenship.

As an example of these historical dialectics, we can look briefly at the National Action Committee on the Status of Women (NAC) in Canada. NAC had its beginnings in 1971 and was the main umbrella group for the women's movement in Canada. The group had many successes over the years, including the inclusion of equality rights clauses in the Constitution Act, 1982, and the striking down of abortion legislation by the Supreme Court in 1988. In the 1990s, however, the group turned inward and became so focused on criticizing itself, its foremothers, and the mainstream women's groups who made up the heart of its membership, that it destroyed itself. This time period also corresponded with a loss of government funding, but without the support of the member organizations and with too much emphasis on an (albeit necessary) critique of "white" feminism, it did not do anything but critique, and the organization has all but folded. It is a shadow of its former self and now basically runs a website. Was the demise of the NAC just the natural passing of a group that had outlived its usefulness, or was it the self-destruction of a national organization due to the narrowness of its agenda, its refusal to work within the system, and its critique of more mainstream women's groups?

We believe our work raises several important epistemic and empirical questions: How has this impasse within feminism occurred? Why do so many academics prefer to critique rather than offer solutions? Why is there such an ambivalence in academia about "doing something"? How does social change actually occur? How do different theoretical

perspectives address social change? What are feminist strategies for social change? Why is development work an important component of social change? How can our work on prostitution in the Philippines help
to illuminate the importance of development work and of how social
change occurs?

In the end, we believe that individuals have an ethical responsibility
to act, as well as to critique—and we will explore a more practical form
of transnational feminism that highlights not only individual responsibility, particularly for those of use who live in the privileged West—but
also the absolute necessity of doing so, if global social change is ever
going to occur. We point out that far too many academic feminists in the
West, even those who have emigrated from the post-colonial South, take
themselves out of the possibility of creating change of any sort because
of their theoretical pronouncements. Although their goals are laudable—
not wanting to be "elitist" by appropriating voice or appearing to be the
"expert"—they inadvertently end up shunning any sort of action and
thus allowing inequalities to perpetuate. We need theoretical constructs
that bring the individual—and action—back into the forefront of feminist thinking. Our goal in writing this book is to address and reject the
three assumptions raised earlier by our skeptical colleagues at the NWSA
conference: that change cannot or should not happen incrementally; that
only insiders can or should know about their own situations (and that
outsiders have nothing to contribute); and that development work is not
a worthwhile avenue for global social change.

Methodology

Because the authors were an integral part of the development project
that serves as a foundation for the arguments and insights in this book,
we invariably become two key informants in the illumination and discussion not only of the project but also of the reactions to our very involvement in the project. In the first instance, we were in many ways
participant-observers because we experienced the project firsthand as
co-project directors, traveling to and from the Philippines and, in turn,
bringing Filipino partners to Canada for training workshops in such areas as gender sensitivity, community development, and university-community relations. In the second instance, we were indeed participants,
and in that way we were being observed by others, whether our Filipino
partners or fellow academics, who in reaching certain judgments or conclusions about our involvement in the project and the project generally,
informed us about what is meant by *feminism*, *activism*, and *prostitution*,
particularly in the Philippines. In addition, we delved into the literature
to make sense of the resistance to action predominant in feminist and

development circles as well as to outline general understandings of prostitution in order to situate the specific case of the Philippines.

This book is not written in a detached or traditionally academic manner because it is deliberately crafted to be accessible to a broad audience. One of the principal reasons for this is that we see this book taking as its point of departure a documentary film based on the lives of several bar girls in Angeles City. Entitled *Hope in Heaven*, aka *Selling Sex in Heaven*, the film tells the story of sex tourism in Angeles City. The documentary was made as part of our development project because one of our goals was public education. It was written, directed, and produced by one of the authors, Meredith, who is also a film maker. A forty-two-minute film cannot capture the complexities of our development project, nor can it deal with the kinds of issues that the project raised in terms of feminist politics and development work. This book is our attempt to expand descriptively about the project and analytically about Western feminists doing development.

At the same time, the film production was crucial from a methodological perspective because it allowed us to conduct formal interviews with our project partners—WEDPRO, the Soroptimists, and the PNP—who work directly with the prostituted women in Angeles City as well as with several bar girls and their customers. For the film we used standard qualitative interview techniques with the requisite ethics approval and guidelines. The bar girls and customers were informed of what we were doing, that this was a film on bar girls in Angeles, and they were asked to participate. We interviewed the bar girls about their lives, why they became bar girls and what they liked and disliked about their job. We interviewed sex tourists about what they liked and disliked about Angeles and why they were there. The bar girls and customers were not part of our development or training activities, so the director was a film maker to them, not a co-participant. The men had no problem talking to us, answering all of our questions, but they refused—to a man—to be filmed talking about their experiences. Their motivation is not entirely clear, but they were all fascinated by why we Westerners were there, particularly the white woman, and what we were doing. The men were very happy to talk to us, sometimes in a justificatory way, no doubt, about what they were doing in that "cesspool."

We interviewed our partners in the project, and those interviews will be used to illustrate the changes that came about because of the project, to show some of the problems with development work, and to support our claims that change can occur incrementally. Some of our project partners were supportive; some were not. Thus, despite our positions as co-project directors, our Filipino partners in the project did not seem to be unduly influenced to respond in any particular way. We received permission from our respective university ethics review boards to do interviews, and the results of these interviews with our partners, bar girls, and customers are found in the text.

We are using those interviews along with our own observations to assess the successes and failures of the project. We want to bring out the sorts of changes that occurred not only in the situation of the women in the bars, but also in the attitudes and behaviors of community members. Thus, in addition to the interviews of bar girls and their customers, there were five main informants representing the Filipino partners. We are not arguing that these voices officially represent WEDPRO, the PNP, or the Soroptimists, but rather that they reflect the ideologies, concerns, and values of their respective groups. Their voices are crucial in helping us present the nuances and details of the project. Just as we do for the three bar girls—Anna, Josie, and Liza—we use pseudonyms for our five project partners in the attribution of statements. Even though all of our interviewees gave written permission for their names and likenesses to be used in the film and book, out of respect for the fact that their words are, of course, subject to our interpretation, we made the decision to change their names in print.

Katerina, who was the executive director of WEDPRO when we started the partnership, is highly educated, middle class, and extremely passionate about the plight of the women. She is a researcher and community educator from Manila and has strong ideological convictions about the harm being done to the bar girls by the customers and the community. She comes from a Marxist background of organizing against the Marcos regime and can be categorized as a post-colonial feminist. WEDPRO's (and Katerina's) position on prostitution reflects its CATW roots as it is strongly abolitionist. Prostitution is a violation of women's human rights and should be eradicated.

Perla, who was part of WEDPRO Angeles, is an older Filipino community worker from Angeles who works directly with the bar girls on Fields Avenue. She is a former bar girl and mamasan, so she has the confidence of the bar girls. She has very little formal education and no particular perspective on prostitution, except for harm reduction and the need for alternative livelihoods. She lives in a squatter community with her four children and is heavily involved with her community of bar girls and former entertainers.

Carmela, who was also part of WEDPRO Angeles, is a social worker, and she, too, works directly with the bar girls on Field Avenue. She is hardworking and dedicated to community causes and has worked for other nongovernmental service and advocacy organizations in Angeles. Her abolitionist view on prostitution is mitigated by her firsthand knowledge of and work with the bar girls. She is a single mother who, in her personal life, has faced many of the gendered challenges evident in many of the traditional customs in the Philippines.

Davida, a senior inspector with the PNP, heads the Angeles City PNP Women's Desk. She has a strong law-and-order background but is a compassionate advocate for the bar girls and casa workers. She was transformed personally throughout the project from a shy woman who could not look anyone in authority in the eye to one of our strongest trainers. Her ideological position on prostitution is pragmatic, but that changed as well—from seeing the women as criminals to seeing them as victims. The PNP have had problems working with WEDPRO in the past because of WEDPRO's criticism of the police and the rumored involvement of the PNP in prostitution.

Maria, who was the president of Soroptimist International of Angeles City, took over as the Filipino project director after the untimely death of the initial head of the Soroptimists. Maria is a wealthy businesswoman who is involved in many philanthropic organizations and is committed to the good of the local community. She is well connected and influential in the Angeles community. Her perspective can be categorized as strongly Christian and conservative. She gives a great deal of time and money to local organizations and believes helping the prostituted women is her moral and religious duty.

In addition to these five Filipino partners and three bar girls, there are, of course, two others: ourselves. Meredith, professor of women's studies and political studies at Mount Saint Vincent University in Halifax, Nova Scotia, was one of the Canadian co-project directors. She is a white woman of Scottish descent who has lived in Atlantic Canada most of her life and is a tenth-generation Canadian. Her academic work has always been linked to her activism, and she has worked with the most marginalized women in society. Meredith became a film maker, in part, to humanize those who have been labeled and stereotyped as "others" and as unlike "us." Focusing on similarities (although not discounting differences) has always seemed to her to provide the necessary empathy needed to make those important human connections. As unlikely as it might seem, given the vast differences in their respective circumstances, Meredith made connections with several bar girls that were life changing.

Edna, professor of political science at Saint Mary's University in Halifax, Nova Scotia, was also one of the Canadian co-project directors. She is a visible minority woman of Filipino descent who has lived in Halifax for over two decades after moving to Canada from the United States when she married a Canadian. Although her involvement in this project came about partly because of her ethnic roots, and indeed her contributions to the project's successes were in part because she is a Filipino Canadian, Edna would have relished any opportunity as an academic to work on an international development project, particularly one that addressed the most marginalized members of a society by those who have the capacity to act. That she became involved in this project was a professional and personal experience that she cherishes.

Meredith and Edna have been friends and colleagues for their entire academic careers. We met when we were doctoral students at Dalhousie University, where we shared an office. This book is in many ways a culmination of a partnership that began when it was brought home to us how similar we are. On August 7, 1995, during our first trip to the Philippines, we were sitting in the Ermita Police Station, interviewing a senior inspector of the Western Police District Command of the PNP who had told us incredulously at one point: "Don't you get it? It's a crime for women to *be* prostitutes, not for men to *go* to them." The senior inspector had all of his subordinates in the room, and we were surrounded by police officers, all male, when the lights went out. This brownout, the term used by Filipinos to describe the loss of electricity that regularly occurred, lasted only a few minutes, but in those few minutes we reached out for each other's hands in the dark, knowing intuitively the vulnerability we both faced and the fear and sense of helplessness we both had. It did not matter that we were Westerners. It did not matter that we were professors. It did not matter that Meredith was white and Edna was brown. What mattered was that we were both women. That is why we deliberately use "we" in this book as we describe, analyze, and reflect on ideas and events. It is not in deference to traditional academic writing, but to make a political statement about our feminist identities that, despite our apparent differences, particularly in terms of ethnicity and race, we are women.

Structure of the Book

Chapter 2 looks at the nature of the analysis-paralysis dilemma by examining the debates among identity, post-structuralist, and post-colonialist feminists and by showing the practical and negative consequences of these debates for activists and academics. We look at the ambivalence of academics about "doing something" and the problems of (not) speaking for others. We show how the lack of solutions for social problems leads to confusion and apathy and creates a hesitation to act on the part of many feminists. We look at the many valuable contributions of post-colonial theory, in particular, but see a problematic pattern emerging. Early development work, though perhaps well meaning, was ethnocentric and perhaps came from a missionary or superior attitude. The idea of the "white man's burden" had to be criticized, and it was. The critique, though, has become just as problematic, and we argue that the synthesis of these two ideas must happen to make possible critical, self-reflective development that combines the desire to change the world with the necessary awareness of self and other to accomplish this by doing no harm.

Chapter 3 looks specifically at the many feminist strategies for social change with regard to prostitution—the ways in which feminists have tried to take action on a specific issue found to be problematic. We look at the four main ways prostitution has been theorized and include examples from scholars and feminist organizations that advocate for the eradication of prostitution; those who advocate for it as a job like any other; those who believe it is a moral or criminal issue; and those who see it as a social-welfare issue. Some argue that regardless of women's choice or agency, or the economic benefits for a community, prostitution remains a human rights violation, while others argue that the stigma surrounding prostitution is what causes most of the problem for sex workers. We examine our partners' views of prostitution and situate them within this framework. This chapter, therefore, looks at feminist responses to prostitution and charts how the sex trade has been problematized in order to show the theoretical complexities surrounding just one feminist issue and the dilemmas of working with groups that could not agree on a theoretical framework.

Chapter 4 elaborates our explanations for prostitution in the Philippines. We show how a variety of interrelated forces have created the current situation regarding the sex trade in the Philippines. We examine the history of colonization by both the Spanish and the Americans, from the sixteenth to mid-twentieth centuries, the effects of the Roman Catholic Church on women; the creation of the Madonna/whore syndrome (if you are not a "good" girl, you are irredeemably "bad"); the double standards of morality in the Philippines and the general level of acceptance of prostitution and "minor wives" for males; the Philippines' location within the global economy as well as class relationships within the society; and the contradictions within the laws that allow prostitution to be illegal and yet regulated by the government. This chapter locates the Philippines within Southeast Asia and shows its unique historical, cultural, and colonial features. It is often said that the Philippines has had four hundred years in the convent and one hundred years in Hollywood, and we look at the effects of such a unique colonial history. We also outline the history of military prostitution in the Philippines, specifically in Angeles City; the development of Clark and Subic after World War II; and the strategic importance of the Philippines. We locate the roots of sex tourism partially in the effects of twentieth- and twenty-first-century globalization and partially on the unique socioeconomic and cultural factors of the place itself. The point of this chapter is to show the complexity of the problem and how fixing one aspect of it will not necessarily fix the whole.

Chapter 5 describes sex tourism and prostitution in the Philippines. The Philippines has a rather unique hybrid model because prostitution is officially illegal (prohibitionist) but regulated by the government in terms of licensing and health checks (regulationist). This makes the system one of the worst for the women involved because of this double bind. We look at the meaning of sexual exploitation and choice in the context of the sex trade in the Philippines, specifically Angeles City, by including the stories of several women and girls working in the sex trade. We describe the many types of prostitution in the Philippines and examine the sex tourists themselves and why they come to Angeles. The point of this chapter is to set up the complexities of the specific context of the Philippines and show how many of the solutions of prostitution theory and praxis will not work in the Philippines—and, consequently, why we took on one small part of the problem (as described in the next chapter).

Chapter 6 outlines the various elements of our five-year development project and the ways in which we attempted to create change and make a difference. We worked with several governmental and nongovernmental organizations, and we argue that the individuals themselves became the agents of social change: the judges, police, Soroptimists, and community workers. By working with such diverse groups with such different ideologies we were able to build a coalition that worked with the particular strengths of the individual groups. WEDPRO contributed the research on bar girls in Angeles but was not able to deliver its message effectively. The judges, police, university professors, and Soroptimists were able to deliver WEDPRO's message more effectively to the community. We look at the difficulties in any development project and specifically one as ambitious as ours in trying to work with such disparate groups with such different ideologies, goals, and experiences. This chapter also examines the different theoretical perspectives on social change and development, including radical or revolutionary change—that nothing is worth doing if it does not immediately eradicate a problem, or is so hopeless and co-opting we do nothing. We look at the liberal view that changes occur gradually and incrementally through structural, behavioral, and attitudinal change, and we show how difficult it is to bring about social change. Finally, we explore how change was created in this project by creating champions in Angeles City who cared enough about the bar girls to educate others in the community about the issues, to build a shelter for women leaving the bars, and to help change the laws regarding prostitution in the Philippines.

Chapter 7 is not about conclusions per se, but rather about focusing on the need for action. "Do something" tells us about the necessity of taking responsibility for the injustices that we witness and the inequalities that we see. In the end, if individuals who have the capacity to act do not, they are abandoning the ethical personas that make us all human. In that way they become part of the problem as opposed to the solution. We reflect back on the three questions posed by our colleagues at NWSA and demonstrate how we have addressed their concerns: change can and does happen incrementally (and we need critical left scholars to feel an obligation to help provide solutions, even if they resist reform-oriented prescriptions); privileged outsiders are important in making change (and in some cases absolutely crucial for change to occur); and development is a worthwhile (and sometimes necessary) avenue for social change.

Despite all our differences, we were able to create social change—individually, collectively, and structurally—in the Philippines. Our hope is to advocate for a renewed global citizenship that allows recognition of and respect for differences while motivating people to act to eradicate (at least some of) the exploitation and oppression all around them. We tentatively defend the notion of cosmopolitan feminism because it is predicated on the belief that people have moral and political responsibilities to one another (because we are all human) but also recognizes that women have separate interests and issues that need to be dealt with through women's organizations. To develop a true transnational feminism, therefore, we need to pursue the *ideals* of philosophical cosmopolitanism as well as concepts from feminists such as Maria Lugones, Nira Yuval-Davis, and Kathy Davis (on the importance of dialogue, friendship, empathy, and seeing through the eyes of others), and particularly Sonia Kruks (on using our privilege strategically and responsibly to make change), and these principles are elaborated in the final chapter.

Philosophically, we conclude that we do not have to be sex workers to understand their problems any more than we need to be from the Third World to understand that we have responsibilities to others beyond our borders—and that it is a huge failure of imagination to think that we can't understand. We can and must transcend (not erase) our particular identities in order to forge strategic alliances with others in the face of the many problems the world currently faces. Therefore, and most important, our privileges, in whatever form they take—whether male privilege or white privilege or class privilege or Western privilege—can be used on behalf of others when done with reflection and care. Our basic theme, and one that is reiterated throughout the book, is that action should not be discouraged and that privilege should not preclude action.

2

The Problem of Analysis Paralysis

Gender, Race, and the Famous Five

The contributions of feminist theorizing are evident in the ways that we identify and understand the multiplicity of identities that define each one of us that go beyond our material differences. If the academic left in liberal-democratic societies, like Canada and the United States, has historically been associated with Marxist or socialist precepts centered on the notion of class, the establishment of women's studies programs within universities has necessarily shifted the focus to the idea of gender. However, whereas class is an identity marker that places academics in the sphere of privilege (that is, academia is composed of middle-class and, in some cases upper-class professionals), gender is an identity marker that brings out that some (males) are more privileged than others (females). In the past two decades, however, our feminist identities have become associated less and less with our gender and more with our race or other difference.

The advancement of women's rights is a hallmark of the modern world, and particularly in the Western context, gender equality is an accepted, if not always practiced, ideal. This, of course, has not always been the case, and there have been historical milestones and individual champions in Western feminism that capture how far women have come in the pursuit of equality. In Canada's case, five of these individual champions—Henrietta Muir Edwards, Emily Murphy, Nellie McClung, Irene Parlby, and Louise McKinney, referred to as the Famous Five—made history in 1929 when they successfully challenged the definition of *persons* as referring only to men in Canada's founding constitutional document, the British North America (BNA) Act or the Constitution Act, 1867. The 1929 decision by the Judicial Committee of the British Privy Council, then Canada's highest court, to declare constitutionally that women were persons not only allowed women to sit in the Senate, but also signaled the continuing recognition of women's rights in the public sphere. Years earlier (some) women had gained the right to vote in federal elections in 1918, and the first woman, Agnes McPhail, was elected to the House of Commons in 1921.

Given the historical significance of what is referred to as the "persons case," it would seem reasonable that when Calgary volunteer Francis Wright decided to establish a foundation in 1996 to raise funds to commemorate the Famous Five with statues both in Alberta, the home province of the five women, and in the nation's capital on Parliament Hill in Ottawa, that it would be relatively uncontroversial. This was not the case. Some opponents, namely REAL Women of Canada, a conservative women's group, argued that this initiative was the action of "a handful of feminists," a "special interest group" unrepresentative of the interests of the majority of Canadian women. The group claimed parliamentarians, including members of the right-wing Reform Party at the time, had been essentially deceived and as a result had agreed to place a statue on Parliament Hill "reserved only for the Fathers of Confederation, former prime ministers and kings and queens."[1] Moreover, REAL Women invoked arguments that other commentators have made that the Famous Five were hardly paragons of egalitarianism because they held classist, ablist, and racist views.[2] They were upper-class, white, privileged women extraordinaire, whose commemoration was questionable, given the nature of contemporary society. Indeed, when the decision was made by the Bank of Canada to place the Famous Five on the new $50 bill in 2004 to commemorate the seventy-fifth anniversary of the "persons case," journalist Deborah Yedlin wrote that "to put them on the back of a banknote that passes through our multicultural society . . . legitimizes racism and xenophobia, and ultimately taints the bill."[3]

Multiculturalism has become a crucial element of modern Western societies. Due in the last three or four decades to the large influx of immigrants, primarily from developing countries, to areas of the more industrialized world, such as Canada and the United States, the demographic face—literally, in terms of race, ethnicity, and color—has changed in the West. This does not mean that race and ethnicity have not been a factor historically, whether in terms of the long history of African Americans since slavery times or in terms of the presence of Asian Americans and Asian Canadians since the nineteenth century, but rather that the emergence of multiculturalism has been concomitant with the rise of anti-racism and the legitimization of ethno-racial identities. Although the multicultural mosaic of Canada has often been contrasted with the melting pot of the United States in order to illustrate the differences in the integration of minority groups by each society, there are in reality more similarities than differences between the two countries. Like many European countries, Canadian and American societies have dealt with the integration of immigrant groups largely from non-European or non-Western backgrounds in the context of racial and post-colonial understandings that are indicative of the progression of Western thinking. Unfortunately, many progressive groups, particularly many academic feminists, have equated multiculturalism with anti-racism, along with the singular prominence of ethno-racial identities, to the point that they retreat from the possibilities of a united feminist voice that would demand changes—action—based on the discrimination against, if not the oppression of, women qua women. As the opposition to Canada's Famous Five demonstrates, the most effective way to delegitimize what the Famous Five accomplished is to label the five women living in the early years of the twentieth century as racist.

At the same time, the opposition to the commemoration of the Famous Five was mainly coming from conservative circles, and although largely unsuccessful, the efforts of REAL Women of Canada are instructive about the wherewithal of less progressive forces to operate in the political arena, both nationally and internationally. When academic feminists not only retreat from dealing with the practical realities of our globalized world, but also resort to diminishing the efforts of those who want to make a difference, even if it is incremental or small scale, they end up either silencing critics from the very beginning or, if voiced, driving those critics to conservative outlets that, not surprisingly, see value in the Western, capitalist way of life. The dominant ideas in academic feminism are rooted in fundamentally anti-Western and anti-capitalist stances that translate to the questioning, if not rejection, of any idea or action that may be construed as either Western based or coming from racial or economic privilege. These, in the end, preclude any action for fear of propping up the oppressive global status quo. This chapter explores some of the dominant theoretical precepts of academic feminism that have led to what we have referred to as analysis paralysis.

Is the Messenger the Problem?

Analysis paralysis is not a new term. Many feminist scholars have attempted to analyze or describe this challenge, labeling it "paralysis," "impasse," "crisis," or "rift."[4] It tends to take on one of two, and sometimes both, of the following characteristics: an ambivalence in academia about doing something, both theoretically and politically, outside one's own backyard; and a hesitation to speak or act for anyone but (literally) one's self, what Nancy Fraser calls a "disengaged academic feminism."[5] Unfortunately, this type of feminism results in an increasingly fragmented world view, with privileged individuals in particular afraid to be seen as "othering" others, thus actively discouraging outsiders from acting and in effect undermining possibilities for global humanitarianism. For instance, Susan Moller Okin writes of her "trepidation" about bringing up "the subject of Western academic feminism's hesitant or ambivalent approach to the issue of violations of women's rights in other cultural contexts" because of accusations of cultural imperialism. Consequently, "many feminists (whether First or Third World, but especially the former) might have felt more than somewhat inhibited about writing anything, especially about Third World women."[6]

How do we go beyond trepidation and inhibition to develop constructive solutions? How do we go beyond giving credence only to insiders when in fact outsiders can make a difference? Kriemild Saunders argues that "wrestling with such issues often entails a moment of *aporia*; a paralysis, a quandary, a condition in which one does not know where to go—the ordeal of the undecidable."[7] We need to be able to carve a space that recognizes the contributions of feminist critical theorists, particularly from post-structuralist and post-colonial perspectives, while also demanding that academics themselves be engaged, particularly because their theorizing points to global and societal inequalities and injustices. We need to be able to highlight the importance of giving voice to those who are marginalized, exploited, or defenseless in society while also recognizing that it is a theoretical and political dead end to argue, for example, that only Filipinos can study and speak about the situation in the Philippines, or that only sex workers can study and speak about exploitation in the prostitution industry. They alone are not responsible for changing their circumstances of marginalization, exploitation, or defenselessness in society, pointing to the necessity of those in privileged positions to act to change such unequal and unjust circumstances.

Let us begin with the difficulties inherent in wanting to "do something." There appears to be a tension in academic theorizing because what may make compelling sense in theory may be difficult to realize in practice. For example, the exploitative nature of female prostitution as practiced in many parts of the developing world, such as the Philippines, may lead one to believe that this is indisputable empirical evidence that prostitution is inherently about female oppression which means that it must be eliminated. However, the realities of organizing or making change require some compromise on the timelines for change and some recognition that short-term goals are needed to reach the overarching goal of, in this case, the elimination of prostitution. This is the crucial dilemma for academics. Can we do something in a reform-oriented manner when the goal is the eradication of some overarching institution or activity? If we feel we cannot, are we not abdicating our responsibility to other peoples, cultures, and social problems by ignoring these issues other than by merely theorizing about them?

Similarly, "doing something" or "helping" has also received condemnation. Helping others appears to belong in bygone days, and the notion of helping has been dissected at length by scholars from different ideological persuasions. Helping has been criticized because it arguably places one party in the dominant position, making the other subordinate or even dependent. Further, since it is only necessary to help others because of historical inequalities, usually caused by the so-called helper, it brings up fundamental questions about the motivations of those who want to help. Unfortunately, this usually leads to the following tautology: The United States has more resources than the Philippines, so it should help the Philippines. However, the United States has more resources because it belongs to the dominant North (and Americans should feel guilty about having the resources to help), and therefore, it would be a form of neo-colonialism for Americans to use their privilege and to do anything. This places Americans, and other Westerners, in the classic double bind: damned if you do, damned if you don't. Helping has been pejoratively referred to as rescuing, colonizing, imperialistic, moralizing, condescending, pitying, homogenizing, neo-colonialist, oversimplified, essentialist, generalizing, totalizing, naive, "the white man's (or more commonly in feminist critiques, white woman's) burden," ethnocentric, stereotypical, and patronizing.[8] A common attitude is the following: "we cannot approach other women from a position of wanting to 'help' them . . . which is *always* tainted with a certain kind of condescending, know-it-all attitude."[9] In this world view, then, helping is automatically condescending and problematic. This might explain some of the responses we have received, as we outlined at the beginning of Chapter 1, when we were perceived as neo-colonialist because we wanted to help prostituted women in the Philippines. With this sort of prevalent attitude in academia, it is little wonder that "doing something" is considered so problematic that it discourages many from doing any type of development work.

Another problem that illustrates the ambivalence within academia and the tension between theory and practice is the issue of who can speak or act for another. Leroy Sievers, a journalist who has reported very movingly on Rwanda, writes that what allowed him to deal with the traumatic nightmares of living through the horrors of the Rwandan genocide was being reminded in a talk by Elie Wiesel that the "role of the journalist is to speak for those who have no voice. That was it. That's what we were trying to do. That's what we had to do . . . anywhere man was doing the worst that he was capable of."[10] Sievers states that although journalists are limited by stereotypes and prejudices, and the media industry too often driven by sensationalism and profit, it is still a powerful tool for change and that journalists sometimes need to speak for others. We recognize that speaking for others is not a popular notion in academic circles these days, and to do so can lead one to be labeled condescending, imperialistic, "arrogant, vain, unethical and politically illegitimate."[11] There are, of course, good reasons to be careful with our speech. As Linda Alcoff has stated, "Though the speaker may be trying to materially improve the situation of some lesser-privileged group, the effect of her discourse is to reinforce racist, imperialist conceptions and perhaps also to further silence the lesser-privileged group's own ability to speak and be heard."[12] This argument is made by very prominent feminists, including Alison Jaggar, who states, "Regardless of the speakers' motivations, the structure and context of their discursive interventions may have the consequence of positioning the subjects of their discourse as less than equal."[13] What Sievers was doing, it could be argued (though probably not intended by Alcoff or Jaggar), was reinforcing racist stereotypes of Rwandans and, in effect, silencing their suffering because it was reported only through the eyes of a Western journalist. The question is, if Sievers, or other Western journalists, or for that matter Western military commanders, such as former Major-General Romeo Dallaire, did not report on the atrocities that occurred in Rwanda, then who would?

The other practical (and again unintended) consequences of these well-meaning warnings for feminists are, however, silencing and paralysis of their potential (privileged) allies. We are not arguing that Alcoff and others are saying not to act politically—Alcoff writes explicitly that to "retreat" from speaking up totally is to be politically irresponsible. We are arguing that what gets *heard* and acted upon in practice are not her very sophisticated rules for speaking for others, but rather, don't speak for others who are not like you. We mentioned in Chapter 1 the dilemma of one student who was not allowed to do a thesis on Yemeni women because it would be "speaking for them"; this is unfortunately not an isolated phenomenon. Another MA student was told that she could not "study down" in her research to avoid speaking for others with less privilege, and a colleague doing work on women's history was berated at a Canadian Women's Studies Association meeting on the grounds that she could not possibly know what it was like to be a single mother in the 1920s and therefore could not presume to speak for them. These are professors twisting Alcoff's valuable message; the situation is much worse in women's organizations.[14] What we want to do in this chapter is point out the negative practical consequences of these theoretical positions in the hopes that theorists might eventually take more positive positions on people's ability to act outside their own contexts.

What Alcoff and others do not allow for, fundamentally, is the ability to transcend or go beyond (not erase) our particular locales and identities (particularly if we are privileged in some way). This is unfortunately the norm, ironically, for both identity or standpoint theorists, like Alcoff, and anti-essentialist theorists, like Judith Butler. Quoting Alcoff again:

> Where an individual speaks from affects both the meaning and truth of what she says and thus she cannot assume an ability to transcend her location. In other words, a speaker's location . . . has

an epistemically significant impact on that speaker's claims and can serve either to authorize or de-authorize her speech. . . . The second claim holds that not only is location epistemically salient but certain privileged locations are discursively dangerous.[15]

That is to say, those who speak from a position of privilege, whether male privilege or white privilege or class privilege or heterosexual privilege or Western privilege, could be silenced from speaking at all because their privilege is dangerous to the less dominant group. Although we deal with this more in Chapters 6 and 7 in terms of strategies for change, wouldn't the better tactic be to let people speak and then engage them in (perhaps heated) dialogue, particularly if we disagree with their assessment? Rather than see them as dangerous, maybe we should be encouraging conversation rather than inhibiting dialogue. Otherwise, we see how problematic it makes action for our "privileged" students and other potential male, white, Western allies. We will come back to this problem of transcendence in the final chapter.

Wanting to help by educating others about injustices in the world is an important motivator for people to make change. Because some theorists are not interested in short-term change or in the psychology of why people want to make change, they sometimes rely on seeing the problem as the messenger—blaming the feminists who report on "bad things," rather than the bad things themselves. A particularly egregious example of "shooting the messenger" (and silencing the privileged outsider in the process) is reported by Alison Jaggar in her article about how we might justify the exclusion of outsiders as a strategic goal (albeit in the short term) to promote global feminism:

> One especially bitter controversy arose around an article co-authored by two Australian women, an anthropologist of European descent and a "traditional" Aboriginal woman. This article exposed *astronomical rates* of violence and rape, including frequent gang rape, committed by Aboriginal men against Aboriginal woman. The *truth of the allegations was undisputed*, but some Aboriginal women objected that it was inappropriate for this topic to be broached by a white woman, even in collaboration with an Aborigine.[16]

This is an extremely troubling example of politics trumping the painful truth that must be faced. However, it will be familiar to those who have studied feminist theorizing. It is commonplace now to hear that only black women can study the black community, that only native women can study the native community, and that white women should stick to their own communities. These attitudes are explained partly by the fear that white, Euro-centric assumptions will be considered universal, partly by the need to protect communities from outside criticism, and partly by the worry of fueling racist attitudes against men of color. But does it make sense to direct criticisms, not at the "astronomical rates" of gang rape in Aboriginal communities, but at the white feminist who pointed it out? Does it not seem that we have lost all direction in terms of what academics do? And why would we think that knowledge can only be advanced by insiders commenting on insider problems? There are many examples when social problems were dealt with only after outsiders pointed out something that the locals did not see. Moreover, in the context of development issues, this goes both ways: North and South. Southerners can, and do, point out problems that Northerners do not see. Societies are constantly evolving, and more inclusive categories of rights, anti-discrimination laws, and ideas of social justice are becoming more evident. The reciprocal nature of insider/outsider arrangements is crucial to the development of ideas and solutions.

Another example of the unintended negative consequences stemming from feminist theorizing is found in Uma Narayan's otherwise invaluable discussion of the Indian practice of *sati* and her critique of the positions of Western feminists on the issue.[17] Instead of criticizing the practice of widow-burning outright, Narayan criticizes the lack of "contextual variations" and generalizations made by Western feminists. It may be that *sati* happens rarely or occurs only within certain castes or is a sign of fundamentalism, and that some women do it voluntarily and some do not, and that some are drugged and some are not. It may indeed be the case that historically British colonial masters used the practice as a way of demonstrating the uncivilized nature of Indian society; using Gayatri Chakravorty Spivak's famous phrase, it was a prime example of "white men saving brown women from brown men."[18] The point, though—surely—is that it is a problem in whatever "contextual variation" is described. The recognition of racial and colonial oppression could never make this an acceptable practice, and by not clearly condemning it, discussions like this inadvertently contribute to paralyzing relativism by making it sound as though Western feminists, not widow burning itself, are the problem.

Our credibility as feminist activists, as researchers, and especially as teachers requires us to recognize and highlight problems, whatever and wherever they might be. Widow-burning is a problem; domestic violence is a problem; female genital mutilation (FGM) is a problem; rape is a problem; child sexual abuse is a problem; honor killings are a problem; keeping women locked up as sexual slaves is a problem; pay differentials between men and women are a problem; less that 50 percent of politicians being women is a problem. Western feminists pointing out the problems is *not* the problem. These misogynistic cultural, political, social, and economic phenomena are the problem. Let us name these problems and then look for solutions. That is when all the critiques can be helpful. We need to know which particular women need help; we need explanations; we need to know what can be done, how to mobilize, and how to educate other women (and men). Only then will women collectively be able to solve our problems. But until we face the fact that it is not feminists who are the problem, the movement will be fragmented, divided, and internally oppressed; it will be fighting the wrong enemy; and it will not be as effective as we can, and must, be.

To Deconstruct the World?

How did this paralysis in feminist theorizing come about? The problems, as we see it, are threefold: First, identity politics and standpoint theory have created the idea that some groups of women are differently placed and differently oppressed than others, specifically white middle-class women, which creates competitive and multiple hierarchies of oppression. Second, post-structuralism, in trying to escape the "essentialism" of identity politics, has problematized the subject to such an extent that it makes it very difficult to justify doing politics, regardless of whether individual post-structuralists actually manage to get out and "do something." Third, post-colonialism paints most development work as inherently neo-colonialist. Therefore, feminists (and many others) doing development or who want to "help" are, by definition, colonialist. Most important, neither post-structuralism nor post-colonialism is particularly helpful at suggesting concrete solutions for what to do about the very real problems in the world.

The original culprit in the development of analysis paralysis can arguably be traced to the emergence of identity politics in the mid to late 1980s with the publications of several important books that rang the death knell for Robin Morgan's "sisterhood is powerful" concept.[19] In these works the concept of difference enters into feminist theorizing so that the important and necessary critique of the concept of woman begins: What kind of woman are we referring to? What are the differences among women? How does the life of a working-class woman compare to the life of a middle-class woman? How are black women's experiences different from white women's experiences? Are some women more oppressed than others? In what ways can we begin to address the differences among groups of women? Does it make sense to speak about women at all, or do we need to refer to different types of women who are oppressed differently? At the same time, the rise of feminist standpoint theory brought concepts from Marxism to feminist theory, particularly the notion that one's particular location will allow one a better or worse view of reality.[20] This essentially resulted in the coupling of oppression and knowledge; that is, the more oppressed one is, the more knowledge-able one could be of the situation. Although this was a vital and neces-sary component in the development of the politics of recognition, feminist standpoint theory had the unfortunate effect of creating silos of differ-ence.

This is the situation that Christina Hoff Sommers and Daphne Patai write about in their forays into the NWSA conferences and women's studies departments in the late 1980s—ideological fights over who is more oppressed than whom and factions of smaller and smaller groups of women looking for recognition of their victimization and difference, such as black, lesbian, disabled women against black, lesbian mothers on welfare.[21] Although both Sommers and Patai represent what feminist academia refers to as anti-feminism, they were both successful in bring-ing out—and some would argue unfortunately publicizing—the divisive and counterproductive elements of feminist theorizing. Standpoint theory also meant that differences became more important than similarities, because the focus was on how groups of women differed from other groups. Recognizing the hierarchies of oppression arguably was initially about the need to identify the sources of victimization of different wom-en, but it quickly became all about one's specific victimization and who can speak for whom. From here, it became apparent that, for example, only Filipinos can speak for Filipinos, and only sex workers can speak for sex workers. Underpinning the development of hierarchies of oppres-sion was the identification of white feminists as a source of victimiza-tion, and the very divisive critique of feminism as merely a white, middle-class phenomenon began to take root.

Identity politics was, of course, recognized as a problem, but the so-lutions have been just as problematic. As feminists fought over who was more oppressed than whom, post-structuralism began to gain ground, problematizing the very subject of woman. The debate evolved from questions about which group of women is more oppressed than another to what a woman is in the first place. Consequently, much of feminist theorizing in the past decade has been concerned with the essentialism of the category woman, with post-structuralism in the forefront of this critique. The challenge posed by post-structuralism has to do with the very possibility and validity of knowledge, as post-structuralism tends to focus on difference, fragmentation, discourse, and language. Howard Gardner writes:

> Arising principally in France in the 1960s, deconstruction . . . ques-tions the possibility of developing a coherent explanatory account of any phenomenon, or of arriving at agreement about what a text means. According to the literary critic and philosopher Jacques

Derrida, all texts carry within them contradictions that undermine their apparent claims. As a reader or analyst the most that one can do is to bring out these contradictions. Social constructivism begins with the unexceptional claim that all knowledge must be constructed . . . but it rapidly escalates to the far bolder claim that science is itself a social invention which reflects no more than a momentary consensus based on considerations of power and authority. On this view, one scientific explanation cannot be shown, on any objective basis, to be superior to others. There are simply rival accounts that are adopted or not, depending on contingencies like conventional wisdom and the influence of the adopters.[22]

In terms of feminism, post-structuralism has deconstructed and destabilized gender-related concepts to the point that it can appear to leave no subject at all. And it has meant that "some parts of what might constitute global feminist inquiry are made to look naive or downright foolish."[23]

Lisa McLaughlin contends that, on the one hand, feminism is at the "vanguard of postmodernism in questioning the master narratives of Western knowledge and distinguishing between their democratic ideals and exclusionary effects." On the other hand, feminism, because of its origins, remains rooted in the modern, offering a critique of knowledge from the standpoint of social movements. Since the "feminist movement's representational politics has necessitated the articulation of a stable subject ('women'), the feminist subject appears to be discursively constituted by the very political system that is supposed to facilitate its emancipation." This, she writes, corresponds to the difficulty within feminism of how to avoid speaking for others when interpreting their experiences—"the politics of representing the other."[24]

Judith Butler is one of the most widely known and oft-quoted theorists of feminist post-modernism/post-structuralism. She has been at the forefront of the debate between theorizing and action. Butler argues that "categories like butch and femme are not copies of a more originary heterosexuality, but show how the so-called originals—men and women within the heterosexual framework—are similarly constructed and performatively established." In describing why and for whom she wrote *Gender Trouble*, Butler asserts that she wanted to expose the rampant heterosexism of feminist theory and, just as important, to give recognition to those people who do not live according to traditional gender norms. "There were many who asked whether they were women—some asked it in order to become included in the category and some asked it in order to find out whether there were alternatives to being in the category." She claims that theory itself is transformative, but she realizes that it is not "sufficient for social and political transformation. Something besides theorizing must take place: interventions at social and

political levels which involve actions, sustained labor, and institutionalized practice, which are not quite the same as the exercise of theory."[25]

However, Butler has distanced herself from the label of post-mod-
ernist. While this might be partly because she does not want to be labeled (in true postmodern fashion), it is also because "there were and are
several ways of questioning the category of 'the subject.' But to question
the category is not to do away with it. And it is not to deny its usefulness
or even its necessity."[26] This is a problem. She recognizes that people
criticize and sometimes dismiss her work as postmodern because they
use the label to dispute the political relevance of her work. At the same
time, she does not seem to realize that her words carry tremendous weight
and that authors have a responsibility for their words and the effects of
their pronouncements. Perhaps they can theorize one way and live another, but their readers, followers, and adherents look to them for guidance about solutions and strategies. When these are not forthcoming, or
worse, when the efforts of others are labeled imperialist, neo-colonialist,
and naive, it has a devastating effect on people's ability and desire to "do
something." It is clear that Butler does not believe this or simply does
not realize her political influence. Butler states:

> Do we really think that we must decide on a common methodol-
> ogy before we can march in the street together? I doubt it. I think
> that we could have several engaged intellectual debates going on at
> the same time and find ourselves joined in the fight against vio-
> lence. I think we could disagree on modernity and find ourselves
> joined in asserting and defending the rights of indigenous women
> to health care, reproductive technology, decent wages. . . . And if
> you saw me on such a protest line, would you wonder how a
> postmodernist was able to muster the necessary "agency" to get
> there?[27]

Unfortunately, it is important that we ask the question because we see
this separation of theory and practice resulting in very confused students
and even colleagues who do not know how to act because the subject of
knowledge has been so compromised. We end up either ignoring the
logical conclusions of her theoretical work or taking a dead-end relativist position. This may not be her intention (and there are good grounds
to argue that it is not), but the problem remains. A pertinent analogy
might be the ways in which Roman Catholics deal with the conservative
pronouncements of their church. Members can either pick and choose
what rules they personally will ignore, although ignoring such rules undermines the project and authority of the church, or they can choose to
reject all the pronouncements and thus the church itself.

This dilemma of theorizing one way and acting another politically perhaps offers some context to the nasty debate between American philosopher Martha Nussbaum and several enraged readers of her review of Judith Butler's work in *The New Republic* in 1999. Although this is also an example of the (unfortunately not uncommon) name-calling within academia, it is a good illustration of what happens when members of one ideological group criticize another, and the silencing that can occur because of it. Nussbaum's main point, it seems to us, is that Butler's work is not responsible to its readers and to the realities of political life, and it is therefore dangerous—it simply glorifies its own clique, language, and concepts. Though perhaps Nussbaum could have used less emotionally laden language in her critique—stating that Butler's work is not all that original and "collaborates with evil"—her point remains that authors have responsibilities to their audiences and that Butler does not seem to take these responsibilities seriously. The response of Butler supporters—to what must have appeared to them as a personal attack—was to attack back. The review was "matronizing," vicious, abusive, and Nussbaum was on a "civilizing mission," according to Gayatri Spivak; disingenuous, vituperative, and authoritarian, according to Seyla Benhabib, Nancy Fraser, and Linda Nicholson; Manichean, moralist fundamentalism, according to Joan Scott; and a simplistic, facile, ad feminam attack, according to Drucilla Cornell and Sara Murphy.[28] The vitriolic nature of the attacks might help to explain why some feminists are hesitant to speak out about dominant ideas in feminist theorizing. That Nussbaum was pointing out the dangers of Butler's work and the political ramifications of postmodernism has been highlighted by many others. As Sandra Whitworth has asserted, postmodernism's continued "back-pedalling and disclaimers are not only politically unacceptable, they are, more importantly, politically irresponsible."[29]

Perhaps in response to Nussbaum and others, Butler has reevaluated postmodernism and her association with it. She admits that, in terms of *Gender Trouble*, she "probably wrote [it] too quickly and whose future [she] did not anticipate at the time." She is also more open about solutions now and writes that "it is a question of developing, within law, within psychiatry, within social and literary theory, a new legitimating lexicon for the gender complexity we have always been living."[30]

As Butler reflects on the consequences of postmodern theorizing and sees the importance of creating change within the complexities that we all live, we see intersections with what liberals, like Nussbaum, have always asserted: we can make change incrementally through changing laws, norms, behaviors, and attitudes. Butler argues specifically against relativism and states that we are "compelled to speak of the human, and of the international and to find out in particular how 'human rights' do and do not work in favor of women, of what 'women' are and what they are not." She recognizes that humanity is about having responsibilities to others and to our collective future, and uses language very much like Nussbaum in her discussion of the "liveable life." According to Butler: "When we ask what makes a life livable, we are asking about certain normative conditions that must be fulfilled for life to become life. . . . We must ask . . . what humans require in order to maintain and reproduce the conditions of their own livability. And what are our politics such that we are, in whatever way is possible, both conceptualizing the possibilities of the livable life and arranging for its institutional support?" Her answer is to be part of a "critical democratic project" which understands how "human" has been used in the past, that "not all humans have been included within its terms, that the category of 'women' has been used differentially and with exclusionary aims, and that not all women have been included within its terms, and that women have not been fully incorporated into the human and that both categories are still in process, under way and unfulfilled." But how is her call for all genders to be recognized as "human" different from the goals of a liberal humanist? As Butler beautifully states: "What might it mean to . . . be willing, in the name of the human, to allow the human to become something other than what it is traditionally assumed to be?"[31] We completely agree and, we suspect, so would Nussbaum.

The two areas where we do not agree, and which we will take up in the final chapter, are Butler's concept of agency and her views on political action, as specifically outlined in her debate with Seyla Benhabib. According to Fiona Webster, "Butler criticizes Benhabib for offering an account of agency which implies that subjects are at some point capable of action which transcends the limitations of the situation or context from which they act and, most significantly through which they are constituted." This indicates that Butler does not think that people can transcend their circumstances, as similarly problematized by Alcoff. In terms of political action, Butler "disagrees with any project which seeks to set out the norms or requirements of political life in advance of political action. These norms and requirements, she claims, only come to be articulated in and through political action." It is not altogether clear if Butler has a program of action for feminist politics, and indeed Webster finds in her work a "reluctance to address explicitly the questions of how it is that individuals in practice resist determination by dominant gender norms and how such norms might be actively contested in the context of a feminist political movement. Until such issues are addressed, accounts such as Butler's risk providing a theoretical framework for feminism which bears little relation to the practical political issues it faces."[32]

In the final analysis, it may be that post-structuralism cannot offer solutions for feminist activism. McLaughlin writes that instability, difference, and fragmentation do not lend themselves "to developing the collective action and solidarity that are necessary preconditions for oppositional social movements to emerge, thrive and survive."[33] Jane Duran argues that there is no way out of this conundrum and that we have to accept that

> although feminists have sometimes been accused of failing to see the difference in the positions that "women" have in various societies, there can be little dispute about the fact that the overwhelming majority of the world's illiterate and poorly educated are women, and a disproportionately high number of infant mortalities and serious illness occur to females. All of these facts lend credence to our contention that the global status of females is worthy of investigation, even in this postmodern era.[34]

Post-colonialism is arguably another form of identity politics, criticizing the essentialism of white Western feminists but making the silos of difference even greater with regard to women in the developing world. In addition, it is not altogether clear what sorts of solutions are offered in post-colonialist critiques because these, too, rest on many assumptions coming from the postmodern turn in feminist theorizing. As Christine Sylvester has so aptly put it when discussing the tensions between traditional development studies and post-colonialism: "Development studies does not tend to listen to subalterns and postcolonial studies does not tend to concern itself with whether the subaltern is eating."[35] Gayatri Spivak, probably one of the best known and most quoted post-colonialist theorists, is known primarily for her writings on the subaltern, as captured in the title of her famous article, "Can the Subaltern Speak?" In this and in much of her subsequent work Spivak attempts to explain what she means both by the term *subaltern* and how subalterns are silenced by research done *on* them, not *with* them. Many theorists use these concepts and they now have become commonplace. For example, Deborah Stienstra writes: "Women in the North have "Othered" women in the South, making them into objects of study by those from the North who can 'more clearly see' the problem."[36] And Ilan Kapoor has argued even more directly: "Working in development inevitably positions us within 'a development discourse,' where the North's superiority over the South is taken for granted, and Western-style development is the norm. Our encounters with, and representations of, our 'subjects' are therefore coded or framed in terms of an us/them dichotomy in which 'we' aid/develop/civilise/empower 'them.'"[37]

Spivak's work is important because it addresses the issue of difference within mainstream feminist thought and brings attention to the plight of the most disadvantaged people in a society, specifically those not benefiting from globalization or urbanization. As important as her work is, however, the logical extension of her insights is problematic because she does not offer solutions to the problems of Westerners doing development, except to argue that they should not do it. Spivak appears to find particularly problematic work such as that on India done by Martha Nussbaum, as evident in her defense of Judith Butler and her scathing comments on Nussbaum in other works. In addition, Spivak's critiques of "woman-centered philanthropy" exist alongside her own work in rural Indian schools.[38] We might ask the question: how different is Spivak's work, in terms of volunteering to teach local teachers and running local schools, from the work of Nussbaum, who in addition to doing research has done extensive volunteer work in India? Without making clear what she means by dismissing "woman-centered philanthropy," Spivak comes dangerously close to saying that only people from a particular country should be engaged in development work there. If there are non-Indian people whom she thinks could do acceptable research in India, then we need to hear her criteria. Unfortunately, she loses us when she critiques Nussbaum unfairly. Spivak, who calls Nussbaum colonizing, imperialistic, and so forth, also characterizes Nussbaum's work as a "holier-than-thou effort. No, I'm not Martha Nussbaum. I'm not reading Dickens with them."[39] Whatever apparent personal and philosophical problems Spivak has with Nussbaum, we would like to think that she can respectfully acknowledge Nussbaum's long-standing work in the developing world.

It is irrelevant that individual post-structuralists or post-colonialists are involved in grassroots activism because it contradicts their theoretical pronouncements and because separating theory and praxis is problematic. Spivak, who is one of the biggest critics of Westerners doing anything in the South, runs and volunteers at a village school in India. We think that she should be applauded for "doing" something, that she should publicize her acts of generosity, and that she should write about it theoretically, but when asked about her generous work in India, she states that she does not want to be known for that; she wants to be known only for her theoretical work: "But if I talk about these places . . . I think I would get the kind of approval from your readership which I would much rather earn because of my theoretical work. You know, there is a certain kind of benevolent approval which I really resist."[40] From a charitable perspective, we might admire her humility. From a less charitable perspective, we might point out that she knows such work goes against everything she theorizes about, unless she can somehow justify why it is acceptable for her to do this work and not for others. Again, it seems to us that these well-known theorists do not realize the influence that they have over others and the effects of their contradictory positions on such important issues. Students read Spivak's words and pick up her problems with Nussbaum, leaving the impression that the problem with Nussbaum is that she is not Indian. This translates to the conclusion that people who are not Indian should not be doing research or volunteer work in India. Students who read Nussbaum see clear guidelines and justifications for women's rights, in line with the United Nations Platform for Action. Nussbaum's work, like that of Spivak, is well researched and compelling, but students are confused about to whom they should be listening and, in effect, to whom they should give epistemic privilege. Spivak wins on that account because she happens to be from India. She may be a privileged woman at a privileged Ivy League college, like Nussbaum, but her status as a woman from the South gives her the edge. Unfortunately, what she gives the students looking for moral and political guidance about what to do in the world is, if not more confusion, then certainly a justification not to act for fear of being seen as colonialists.

Without giving solutions, Spivak simply describes gender-development programs as "matronizing and sororizing" and another "way of silencing the subaltern," who is oppressed by "second-class cultures."[41] She rejects working with the United Nations, seeing that as co-optation, because "U.S.-based UN feminism works in the interest of global financialization, a.k.a. development."[42] Spivak's criticisms extend to women-centered development programs funded by national and international donor agencies regardless of the involvement of women from the developing world. She states: "In this phase of capitalism/feminism, it is capitalist women saving the female subaltern. WID—Women in Development—is a subsidiary of USAID and WEDO—Women in Environment and Development Organization—is a generally North-controlled international nongovernmental organization with illustrious Southern spokeswomen."[43] Spivak does not allow for mixed motivations in wanting to help those in the developing world; for her, development is always an assertion of power by the privileged. As Kapoor states:

> Spivak's point is to underline that our representations of the Third World/subaltern cannot escape our institutional position and are always mediated by a confluence of diverse institutional interests and pressures. . . . If professional motives dictate, at least to a degree, what and how we do (in development), we cannot pretend to have pure, innocent or benevolent encounters with the subaltern. To do so . . . is to perpetuate, directly or indirectly, forms of imperialism, ethnocentrism, appropriation.[44]

Why is it that individuals and institutions cannot be driven by imperatives that are both self-interested and benevolent?

Spivak may not give us solutions, but she certainly leaves clues to how she is thinking. When she discusses the problem of child labor, in particular a case of organizing a boycott of a company on the basis of its use of child labor and how it did more harm than good, she makes the following disclaimers: "It is about the easy goodwill of boycott politics. It is about the lazy cruelty of moral imperialism. . . . It is about finding in this a justification for a permanent involvement in a country's affairs through foreign aid." What then would she do about it? What is she willing to do about it? It is so easy to critique what others try to do but very difficult to come up with solutions. Perhaps she is worried about how easily her solutions will be critiqued as well. The most she will say, in terms of solutions, seems to be the need for the "recognition of the agency of the local resistance."[45] She has also promoted in the past (though now apparently distances herself from) the notion of "strategic essentialism," and we encourage her to develop this concept more fully so that her readers will have an idea of what concrete forms of action she advocates as well as the theoretical basis to use such a concept in making social change.

To Change the World?

Unfortunately, devising concrete forms of action is not likely to happen since Spivak's dismissal of women-centered philanthropy also illustrates the implicit and unrealistic vision of social change underlying much post-colonialist thought. What might be the problem with, let us say, women in the North raising money for a shelter for women in the South to a post-colonialist? First of all, Spivak might object to the giving itself—what will small sums of money do for anyone other than the few individuals who will benefit from the shelter? She might object to the piecemeal approach of the giving—it is not focused on large-scale structural change, just on changing the lives of a few individual women. She also might object to who is doing the giving—privileged Westerners who benefit from the structural inequities in the world (and who are trying to make themselves feel better) without making any real change in their own lives. Spivak has argued that "such noble and altruistic claims are never just that: knowledge is always imbricated with power, so that getting to know (or 'discursively framing') the Third World is also about getting to discipline and monitor it to have a more manageable Other; and helping the subaltern is often a reaffirmation of the social Darwinism implicit in development, in which 'help' is framed as 'the burden of the fittest.'"[46] Finally, and of course the biggest objection Spivak might have, is that women-centered philanthropy does nothing to address the real problem in the world, which is the global capitalist system. And that is where the real problem lies. How do we overthrow the global capitalist system? Is it even possible or desirable to overthrow a whole system? How does one act on a day-to-day basis when one is trying to overthrow a system, and still show compassion for those worst affected by it?

Spivak's theoretical and apolitical stance resonates well with the current climate in progressive academia. Questions about appropriating voice and speaking for others are not only pertinent to relations between North and South, but also between ethno-cultural minorities and mainstream majorities in Western societies. The debate over FGM is an interesting case study of the different, and polarizing, views of feminist academics and feminist activists, and the resulting (albeit inadvertent) paralysis and frustration surrounding the issue. While some feminist academics believe that FGM should be equated with "equally offensive Northern traditional practices" and that we should fight equally hard against them in order not to be ethnocentric, we believe that the particularly heinous nature of the cutting and the fact that it is done on non-consenting children, cannot be said to be the same as, for example, cosmetic surgery, child sexual abuse, or anorexia.[47] These last two are said by Deborah Stienstra to be "traditional" practices in the North but, though unfortunately still common, they are by no means practices accepted by the community. They are illegal acts, in the case of child sexual abuse, or are classified as a mental illness, as in the case of anorexia, and they are certainly not acts condoned by religious, legal, or political leaders or by the community itself, as FGM has continued to be in most countries where it is practiced. The other problem for feminists, once a practice has been condemned, is what to do about it. In the case of FGM, although we definitely perceive it to be a human rights violation of the worst kind, it would not be appropriate to go into a Gambian village, stand in front of a group of elders, and tell them what we think of it. We would work with the local community and local women's groups who think the same way, and we would assist them in developing culturally sensitive delivery modes to help make the change in legal status (first of all) and in attitudes and behaviors (secondarily). We might use the well-known drama troupes in the Gambia to get the messages across, and we would not ourselves be delivering these workshops on such culturally sensitive issues. Would it be clear what our perspective is? Yes. Would it be foisted on another culture? Not at all.

There is no question that feminists and activists in countries where FGM is practiced are best placed to deal with ensuring that the practice is made illegal, but the idea that Western feminists don't have the right to claim that it should be seen as a human rights violation and lobbied against at the United Nations, for instance, seems wrongheaded. Practically, if we can't say FGM is wrong, what can we claim that is not hopelessly relativist? This means abdicating our responsibility for what happens in other parts of the world, and contributes to the apathy about what is happening "over there." Moreover, FGM is a practice that is apparently being done in some immigrant communities throughout the Western world, so that it appears to be happening "right here." Even if the interest in FGM is sensationalized by the media or even if the reason students are interested in the issue is because of their "othering" of a foreign culture, whether in a faraway land or within their own country, the issue arouses strong feelings and makes them want to act, whether by giving money, lobbying their own governments, or becoming interns in a development project. People need personal interests in issues to make them relevant. And most women (and men) intuitively know that the horror of holding down a little girl and cutting off her genitals is a human rights violation of the worst kind. Why should we be hesitant about saying that? Why do we allow this type of cultural relativism for issues surrounding the rights of women and girls, and why do we fear being called ethnocentric?

Do Spivak and others just represent extreme cases of cultural relativism—meaning that one country or culture cannot be judged by the standards of another? Do they really believe that all Westerners are just ethnocentric—a belief that one set of standards is superior to another and usually the standards are of the dominant culture? Both ideas seem problematic to us. Cultural relativism means that any code of conduct is acceptable as long as it is part of the culture of a population, but this raises questions about genocide and slavery and violence against women, among others.[48] The dilemma then becomes how to reconcile "the rights and realities of local cultural diversity with . . . the need to authorize some common values on which humanity as a whole takes an official stand"—universal standards for human rights, for instance.[49]

Susan Moller Okin and other respondents to Okin's original essay address the issue of cultural relativism in *Is Multiculturalism Bad for Women?* Okin deals with the issues of religion and culture, and she concludes that group rights which allow for sex discrimination due to culture or religion are incompatible with the individual right to be free of sex discrimination. She is particularly critical of the notion of silencing others when she deals with feminism's incompatibility with many oppressive religious practices:

> Am I the silencer of such voices, in taking into account that hundreds of millions of women are rendered voiceless or virtually so by the male-dominated religions with which they live? Or are the silencers those feminists who downplay the patriarchy of many variants of their religions, but who enjoy every moment of their own lives freedoms that are unthinkable to those "Others" whose voices they think I am drowning out?[50]

Okin's words have become particularly pertinent in the post-9/11 era as Western societies have necessarily become focused on differences not only with Muslim-majority countries, particularly in the Middle East, but also with their own Muslim minorities. Haideh Moghissi's critique of cultural relativism and postmodernism is very convincing in its indictment of Islamic fundamentalism and the subsequent limits of postmodern analysis. Moghissi argues that postmodernism and anti-imperialism turn a "blind eye to the consequences" of confusing principles of recognition with "unprincipled tolerance for oppressive political and cultural practices" in Muslim countries. She writes against both Orientalism in the West and Islamic fundamentalism and she does not see it as an either/or proposition because she argues that we can be against both. Moghissi points out the ironic similarities between fundamentalism and postmodernism: "an unremitting hostility to the social, cultural and political processes of change, originated in the West, known as modernity."[51]

Moghissi is particularly critical of Western tolerance of cultural relativism:

"Cultural sensitivity" and "cultural tolerance" provide an excuse to Western governments to conveniently put to bed their much advertised concerns about women's rights, lack of democracy and freedom of expression in Islamic societies. ... If the treatment of women in Iran, Afghanistan and Sudan is contrary to all internationally recognized (and signed) conventions, it is because *their* cultural beliefs, practices and ways of doing things are *different*; "they" have *their* ways, "we" have *ours*. We should be "more accepting" of practices which are unacceptable *here* but admissible *there*.[52]

This she rejects as "abandoning women to [the] iron rule" of fundamentalist regimes. She scoffs at the "intellectual acrobatics" needed to turn harems and veiling into "an empowering experience for women."[53] But to

oppose Western imperialist interests in Islamic states ... should not mean supporting the fundamentalists' self-serving, anti-Western perspectives in the name of anti-imperialism; nor does criticism, however sharp, of the manifold failures of Western "modernity" ... require celebration of the "primitive." ... Islamic societies cannot advance by relying on pre-industrial cultural values and ideas."[54]

Modernity is, after all, responsible for the enhanced status of women in the West.

The legal, social and cultural rights women enjoy in the West as compared with their sisters elsewhere, are a consequence of the recognition of women's full citizenship status . . . their materialization . . . was closely associated with the recognition in the West of individual rights, separation of church from state, and the rule of law rather than the rule of the divine—all of which originated from the political ideas and political institutions central to the Enlightenment, universalism and the project of modernity.[55]

However, with the strength of post-structuralist and post-colonial critiques, the fruits of the Enlightenment project do not dominate feminist academic theorizing. The complexities of the feminist project in the post-9/11 world where Western countries, led by the United States, have gone to war against Muslim-majority countries have become more evident. By highlighting efforts to end gender oppression, particularly by dismantling the Taliban-led regime in Afghanistan, or by working toward gender equality by maintaining a moderate Islamic state in a post-Hussein Iraq, Western governments have recast their self-interested reasons to attack militarily states that harbor terrorists or promote terrorism to more benevolent justifications centered on concerns for gender equality. "The uncritical assertion that Muslim women are veiled, passive and utterly dominated by Muslim men has been used as a rationale for military interventions in Afghanistan and Iraq. The argument is that a significant benefit includes 'liberating the women.' This smacks of a new imperialism reminiscent of the old colonial model of the civilizing benefits of intervention and occupation."[56] Many academic feminists have taken an antiwar stance and are rightly suspicious of government rationales about "liberating the women," but they are finding themselves in a defensive position precisely because many women in many Muslim-majority countries *are* oppressed. As Christina Hoff Sommers has argued:

The women who constitute the American feminist establishment today are destined to play little role in the battle for Muslim women's rights. Preoccupied with their own imagined oppression, they can be of little help to others—especially family-centered Islamic feminists. The Katha Pollitts and Eve Enslers, the vagina warriors and university gender theorists—these are women who cannot distinguish between free and unfree societies, between the Taliban and the Promise Keepers, between being forced to wear a veil and being socially pressured to be slender and fit. Their moral obtuseness leads many of them to regard helping Muslim women as "colonialist" or as part of a "hegemonic" "civilizing mission." It disqualifies them as participants in this moral fight.[57]

The criticisms made by Sommers highlight the continuing tendencies of Western academic feminists to retreat from the political space because of the dominance of post-structuralist and post-colonial critiques, but this has meant that conservative forces end up dominating the political arena. Sommers, labeled an anti-feminist, is a resident scholar at the conservative American Enterprise Institute, but her criticisms are compelling precisely because of the tendencies of moral equivalencies, emanating from cultural relativism, often evident in the critical left. Sommers has been joined by Ayaan Hirsi Ali, the Somali-Dutch politician turned activist, who is also a vocal critic of cultural relativism. Ali writes passionately about not excusing fanaticism and the oppression of women by saying it is "their" culture: "My central, motivating concern is that women in Islam are oppressed. That oppression of women causes Muslim women and Muslim men, too, to lag behind the West. It creates a culture that generates more backwardness with every generation. It would be better for everyone—for Muslims, above all—if this situation could change."[58] Although very unpopular in academia, Ali uses the concepts of better and worse freely and rejects cultural relativism outright. Western nations are "better" than countries dominated by Islam, politically, economically, and socially. Ali's anti-Islam stance can be mitigated, ironically, by Sommers's discussion of Islamic feminism with its "celebrated adherents, among them the Moroccan sociologist Fatima Mernissi, the Iranian Nobel laureate Shirin Ebadi, and the Canadian journalist and human rights activist Irshad Manji."[59] The problem, of course, is that Islamic feminism is no more a singular entity than is Western feminism. For example, Irshad Manji is rejected by many Canadian Muslims, both male and female, who argue that she does not speak for them. This highlights a further problem of identity politics, because there are indeed communities within communities, making it virtually impossible to discern who really speaks for whom.

Post-colonialism, Duran asserts, allows us to see how "non-European cultures have been viewed through European lenses, frequently to the detriment of the former." However, there is a paradox here. Post-colonialists also tend to believe that any generalizations made "about non-Western groups is itself an instance of Western colonialism and hegemony."[60] What are the consequences of such a stance? Does it mean that only members of a particular group can study that group? Can we not move past the characterization or stereotype that all third-world women are homogeneous, victimized, and living truncated lives by applying self-reflection, critical thinking, empathy, rigorous empirical studies, *and* action? Spivak, Narayan, and others warn us about the dangers of the oversimplification, generalization, and naivety of Western analyses of the situation of women in the Third World. However, as Duran also argues, "the situation demands that one address it. That is, feminists from around the globe—including the industrialized and European countries—can either choose to work on issues of interest to women around the world or deem themselves unfit to work on such projects by virtue of their having been participants in the hegemonic structure."[61]

We chose to work on a particular interest of ours: the sexual exploitation of women and girls in the Philippines. We believe that localized, specific, contextualized action can make a difference, and this determined in part the (limited) parameters of our work. We were not trying to eradicate prostitution or get women out of prostitution. We tried to make their lives better within their particular contexts. In the next chapter we begin to examine our specific case study by showing how difficult it is to make small-scale, incremental change, let alone eliminate an entire system, when even the idea of it is contested. Feminist views of prostitution and prostitution policy offer opportunities to explore these issues in greater detail because prostitution is an emotionally debated issue and middle-ground perspectives are not particularly evident because it is usually seen as a human rights violation or an issue of sexual autonomy. We hope to show that there is a middle ground through our work in the Philippines and argue that we are up against a strong tenet in feminism that believes that prostitution must be eradicated, just as many critical-left scholars believe global capitalism must be eliminated. We do not believe that either idea is possible in reality, and we examine the consequences of taking an "all or nothing" approach to making social change and therefore of doing nothing.

PART II

PRACTICAL CHALLENGES

3

Philosophical Issues of Prostitution

At the United Nations Fourth World Conference on Women, held September 1995 in Beijing China, hundreds of women representing sex-trade workers, advocates for those in prostitution, shelter workers, researchers on sex trafficking and government policymakers gathered to debate what to do about prostitution. Should sex work be legalized or decriminalized? Should prostitution be seen as a human rights violation? Should U.N. documents refer only to "forced" prostitution or "child" prostitution? How is prostitution simply work like any other, and how is it different? Should sex work be condemned as sexual exploitation of all women or celebrated as sexual liberation for women? The debates were heated and the underlying and conflicting beliefs and ideologies about women's sexuality, equality, exploitation, work, and traditional roles became clear. What was also clear, however, was how deeply committed every participant, regardless of perspective, was to the issues of violence against women in prostitution, the poverty of women and lack of economic choices that result in prostitution, eliminating the condemnation of women in the sex trade, and most important, the necessity to alleviate the working conditions of sex workers. It is from this perspective that we delve into the heated debates among feminist groups about the philosophical issues of prostitution—issues that have only gotten more complicated and divisive in the decade and a half since Beijing.

For many citizens, particularly in the middle and upper classes throughout the world, to discuss female prostitution is to deal with an issue that they do not know about firsthand—or *claim* not to know about firsthand. The social stigma surrounding prostitution is such a powerful, historical, cross-cultural phenomenon that it helps to explain why the "world's oldest profession," the exchange of sex for money, does not affect the everyday lives of "decent" people and is allowed to continue whether prostitution is legal or illegal. People of "decency" are deliberately contrasted with those who are not (such as prostitutes), and state action on prostitution and other activities around sex and sexuality is to keep such activities from the public eye. As long as prostitution is kept

49

away from "decent" people, it is allowed to flourish, whether in the ubiquitous red-light districts of the Netherlands, the numerous escort services of the United States, or the countless bars in the Philippines. It matters little whether states legalize, regulate, prohibit, abolish, or criminalize prostitution as long as the lives of "decent" people are left untouched.

These days, due to the strength of women's rights movements worldwide, there is some credence to the argument that the welfare of women in prostitution is no longer a marginal consideration of the state. Debates about what constitutes prostitution revolve around what is best for the women, so it is argued. This chapter deals with three ideological considerations in understanding prostitution: prostitution as a social ill; prostitution as a form of violence against women; and prostitution as work like any other. And it advocates a fourth: prostitution as an economic necessity and often the only choice (and hope) for women in poverty.

As we systematically discuss each understanding of prostitution, we look at how different states have dealt with prostitution and how this has affected the lives of women in prostitution. Far from solely giving facts, we try to dispel some myths in order to provide a nuanced understanding of prostitution that, we argue, must recognize the different contexts in which prostitution operates. Fundamentally, notions of choice and consent so characteristic of the (in general) urbanized, individualistic, post-material societies where so much of the wealth is concentrated may be less relevant to the lives of women coming from primarily poor, rural, collectivist, family-oriented, religious households where the state does not have social-support programs to help women with their education and employment requirements, with their physical and mental health-care needs, and with other supports to ensure real equality in the society.

In retrospect, we realize that we could not have tried to tackle a more divisive topic or a more difficult issue around which to build a working coalition than prostitution. Compromise between opposite ideologies can become impossible or perceived as impossible by one or more of the coalition. Prostitution is one of the most divisive issues in feminism today, and we describe in this chapter some of our challenges in working on such a problematic and emotional topic. Sometimes we wondered if the philosophical, let alone the practical, issues of prostitution could ever be resolved.

The debates about prostitution are angry and passionate. The religious right speaks against prostitution for moral reasons: sex outside marriage is against family values. Many feminists are against buying sex because they claim it is a form of male power and control over, and violence against, women. Libertarians and so-called pro-sex feminists argue in favor of prostitution for reasons of liberty and equality: we should celebrate our sexuality and all forms of it and not be such prudes. Sex-trade workers themselves want respect and dignity, and basic workers' rights. How to reconcile these very different points of view is the focus of this chapter. How do we create public policy that will alleviate the violence and health issues of women and men working in the sex industry? How do (or should) we differentiate between the choice issues and exploitation of the trafficked teen in Nepal and the independent call girl in Los Angeles? How does the context of prostitution help us decide whether prostitution should be accepted and legalized, de-criminalized, or abolished? Is prostitution really work like any other? Should sex workers be regulated, licensed, and taxed like any other employee? Are brothels and red-light districts the answer to our tough public-policy questions? In this chapter we examine how prostitution has been theorized about and why it is such an explosive issue. We will bring together the perspectives of four diverse groups working for the rights of prostitutes in an attempt to see whether these philosophical issues can be resolved. Can policy ever be enacted to assist sex-trade workers without legitimizing the work or penalizing some aspects of it, since it seems that these are the only two options given by the pro- and anti-prostitution lobbies?[1]

Different views and ideologies of prostitution were evident in our project, as they are in most debates about prostitution. Some residents of Angeles, for instance, say that life in Angeles was better with the American presence: more employment, better health care, more money for infrastructure and development. They believe that prostitution is a necessary evil for "fallen women" and sexually insatiable men. Others argue that regardless of women's choice or agency, or the economic benefits for a community, prostitution remains a human rights violation. Most of the groups we worked with saw prostitution as a moral, legal, and/or human rights dilemma.

From the beginning there were differences of ideology, language, goals, and strategies between and among the Canadian and Filipino groups. The Filipino group, WEDPRO, whose world view is clearly influenced by its membership in CATW-AP (or the Coalition) was strongly in favor of the eradication of prostitution in Angeles; its members saw it as a form of violence against the women. As post-colonial feminists, they objected to our "first-world" language in the funding proposal when we identified a "sex-trade" problem and referred to the bar girls as "sex-trade workers." To WEDPRO, the women needed to be addressed and referred to as prostituted women, making their beliefs clear that all the women were victimized, regardless of whether they chose to work as bar girls. For the police, the women were criminals because prostitution is illegal in the Philippines. The judges, Soroptimists, and university professors saw the women as morally deficient and working for "easy money" as they often put it. Ironically, given the problems we subsequently had, the Canadians were more in line with WEDPRO's point of view in the beginning.

In terms of agency or choice, the groups also strongly diverged. To the more conservative members of our partnership, the bar girls clearly had a choice: they could have chosen to work in factories or have set up independent BBQ stands or have partaken in the many alternative-livelihood programs run by groups like the Soroptimists to become seamstresses or manicurists. That the women had these alternatives and still chose to be bar girls was a further indication of their moral deficiencies and interest in easy money and a foreign husband. There was definitely recognition of the poverty and lack of opportunity in the Philippines for many poor families, but a strong undercurrent of blame ran through the discourse of the partners. WEDPRO had the opposite view, in line with its post-colonial feminism: because of the global position of the Philippines in relation to the industrialized world and the history of colonization by the Americans, the bar girls had no choice but to do what they did, to support their families and themselves. There was no blame of the women but intense condemnation of the foreign and local men who used the bar girls, national and local government officials, globalization, wealthy Filipinos, and the Roman Catholic Church. Building a coalition around such a divisive issue, particularly when the members held opposing ideologies of prostitution was, to put it mildly, a challenge. We outline the characteristics of and debates among the three main perspectives below.

Prostitution Is a Social Ill

The first ideological position we had to deal with in Canada and the Philippines is the one that has been the most prevalent view of prostitution historically and that continues to influence public policy around the world about what to do about the public selling of sex. Though academics generally and feminists in particular will think of this notion as a quaint relic of the past, the idea that prostitution is a moral issue is still popular with the general public in the United States, Canada, and the Philippines. Prostitutes are stigmatized, shunned, and viewed as moral failures. They are not allowed into some churches in the Philippines and are condemned for trying to make "easy money." Streetwalkers in the United States and Canada are considered public nuisances and neighborhoods campaign to have them driven out of their areas—the NIMBY (not in my backyard) syndrome. Historically, women have been criminalized, not men, because they were faulted for luring men into sin. A prostitute can signal her sexual availability and weaken any man; his urges will simply come alive because of her tempting ways. As we mentioned in Chapter 1, the police in the Philippines were genuinely horrified at the idea that men were doing anything wrong. They believed it was clearly women's fault for tempting the innocent men.

Prostitution is a social ill, then, because of a collective understanding of what we mean by something "bad" for society, thus predicated on normative assumptions. Prostitutes break the sorts of norms that exist in the society that are often culturally understood and where culture may be based on religious codes of ethics. Unfortunately for women, who determines what is "bad" and what is "good" for society is based on who holds the power, and the decision makers are often men, usually wealthy, heterosexual, and able-bodied men. Similarly, family-values proponents argue that family, the institution of marriage, and monogamy within marriage are the foundation of any society because of their role in the cycle of life and the propagation of society. Prostitution is a social ill because it undermines the family by taking away from sexual intimacy and ultimately monogamy. In many ways, then, there is a conservative element in characterizing prostitution as a social ill in this way. There is also a definite double standard in the treatment of women and men; historically, it has been women who have been stigmatized and punished, and it is street prostitution or visible prostitution that has been targeted by law enforcers.

The popular culture images of the prostitute have changed over time, but they reproduce the double standards as well. Movies such as *Pretty Woman, Unforgiven,* and *Leaving Las Vegas* reflect the idea of the hooker with a heart of gold or fallen women in need of rescue; other movies depict prostitutes as gold-diggers who need their comeuppance *(Whore, Mona Lisa, Crimes of Passion)*. Films such as *Monster* and *Dirty Pretty Things* portray prostitutes as dirty, polluted, and addicted, reflecting the idea of sex as danger. The Broadway play "The Best Little Whorehouse in Texas," which was originally produced in 1977, shows the centrality of community outcry and double standards in precipitating the state to act against prostitution. Made into a 1982 film of the same name, starring Dolly Parton and Burt Reynolds, this is the story of the Chicken Ranch, a legendary Texas brothel that existed from the 1840s to 1973. Although a part of the community for over a century and a quarter, and a place frequently visited by politicians and other notables alike, the Chicken Ranch was forced to shut down when members of the community, charged up by a sensationalist-seeking conservative television broadcaster, demanded that the brothel, called a place for "loveless copulation," be eliminated from their midst. Decent people, after all, would never knowingly allow such a place to exist. There was no consideration of the women in the brothel or of Miss Mona, the proprietress of the Chicken Ranch, who was once one of the working girls and now the owner, except to identify them as whores to be shunned and women to be treated as outcasts, separate from the society and the community.

So what is wrong with this picture? Why is the blame placed on the women in prostitution? Why is there no blame placed on the men? Why do women in prostitution have to be "saved" but not the men? Why have women been the ones to be stigmatized and demeaned? The notion of the "fallen woman" is an important historical and religious construct that has been crucial to the view of prostitutes as dirty (carriers of disease), immoral (using their sexuality for money rather than love), promiscuous (double standard of sexuality), and disposable (of literally no worth). One only has to look at the horrible fate of the missing women of the Vancouver Downtown Eastside to see that these are throwaway women. Upwards of sixty-five women had to go missing before police started an investigation that finally resulted in a pig farmer being accused of killing twenty-six of them and being convicted of killing six.

Unfortunately, the stigmatization of prostitution is still prevalent, even for women who were sexually abused in their families or who are drug addicts or who started in sex work while they were still children—those who in the past might have been labeled as the deserving poor. There is an incredibly strong blaming tendency in society about even these women. When we first started publicizing this project, we got very hostile responses in letters to the editor in the local papers and to call-in radio shows, outraged that taxpayers' money was going to be used to help prostitutes. The women were blamed for all their own problems, viewed as criminals, and held to be not worthy of support. Many organizations dealing with prostitution will work only with women who are on the streets through "no fault of their own," because they find it very difficult to raise funds for any programs dealing with drug addiction or with women who have chosen to be prostitutes. This is not just an unfortunate developed-world "blame the victim" mentality. We will profile two organizations in the Philippines that also help only those women who want to leave the trade and are willing to train as manicurists, seamstresses, or domestics. Both of these organizations are explicitly Christian, and proselytizing is part of the curriculum.

Double standards are also in play, not just in terms of male and female sexuality, but also in terms of prostitution policy itself. As stated, men historically have not been criminalized in regard to their role in prostitution as customers. And women have faced harassment if even presumed to be involved in prostitution because of ambiguous interpretations of notorious vagrancy laws, disease prevention acts, and the fact that it was a crime to be a prostitute, not to go to one. Vagrancy laws, in particular, are a particularly egregious use of state and police power. Because the Philippines does not have anti-solicitation rules, the police can only guess at who is plying the trade and who is simply standing on a street corner waiting for a bus. Therefore, the police make assumptions, "using possession of condoms as evidence of prostitution or arresting them for 'vagrancy' without any evidence of prostitution."[2] In some ways, however, vagrancy laws are an improvement over the previous situation in the Philippines, where the only way to convict a woman of prostitution was to get her to perform a sex act, pay her for it, and then arrest her after she was done! Other ways of making clear the double standards of sexuality and treatment of prostitutes are the so-called social-hygiene clinics put in place by the Americans to prevent their servicemen from becoming infected with sexually transmitted diseases. There has never been a system that we are aware of where the male customers have to go for medical checks before frequenting a brothel or escort service, further stigmatizing the women and contributing to the idea that prostitutes are dirty and have to be kept clean for the men.

The Canadian government, with the help of many women's organizations, recognized the double standard at work when in 1972 it repealed its vagrancy law. According to the vagrancy law, a woman had to be able to account for her presence on the street or risk being prosecuted as a prostitute. Again, nothing was done to the customer. Canada's criminal code was changed again in the 1980s so that its laws prevented soliciting and later on "communicating" for the purpose of prostitution, not prostitution itself—in order to get around the very uncomfortable idea of police officers having sex with prostitutes before arresting them. And it allowed the criminalization of customers as well as the prostitutes. In Canada, therefore, prostitution itself is not illegal but along with laws prohibiting being in, or operating, a common bawdy house and procuring or living off the avails of prostitution, Canada's criminal code criminalizes the activities of prostitutes and johns (and of course pimps and other third-party individuals or groups). In the United States prostitution (the buying *and* selling of sex) is still illegal in forty-eight of the fifty states, with some counties of Nevada legalizing brothel prostitution and Rhode Island allowing indoor prostitution, though still criminalizing street prostitution. The United States has anti-solicitation laws in forty-four states to prevent the abuse of women as noted above, but that leaves four states that still prosecute on the basis of vagrancy and loitering.[3]

Another problem with both the United States and Canada is that the enforcement of prostitution offenses is primarily in regard to street prostitution. Indoor venues, like escort services and massage parlors, are often left alone by the police. Governments, therefore, tolerate a great deal of prostitution as it currently exists in North America. "This has resulted in a two-tiered system of enforcement; while those who are poorer, less well organized, and more likely to be abused and subject to violence who are working on the streets are subject to arrest, more affluent buyers and sellers engage in prostitution with relative impunity."[4] In that way, what seems to matter is not women being unduly harmed by prostitution, but the degree of visibility of prostitution to the community. Unlike street prostitution, escort services and other indoor venues are largely invisible to "decent" Americans, though still technically illegal. Like women in prostitution generally, women in indoor venues are also abused and subject to violence by johns and pimps, but because they are engaged in illegal activities, they find themselves ignored, if not harassed, by enforcement authorities. The position, therefore, that prostitution is a social ill and moral issue (and that prostitution activities should be criminalized) is still very much in evidence in both countries and is a significant barrier to bettering the lives of prostitutes.

Prostitution Is Violence against Women

The second ideology surrounding prostitution that we dealt with in the project was the idea that prostitution is inherently a form of violence against women and hence a human rights violation. According to this view, the women are not criminals or morally bankrupt, but rather are victims of male power and control. Until recently, this was the most popular view among feminists, because it links radical-feminist analyses of men's control over women's sexuality and reproduction with the particular harm done to women working in prostitution. Groups taking this ideology include CATW, based in New York but with branches all over the world, and the Aboriginal Women's Action Network (AWAN) based in British Columbia. In a perfect example of this ideology AWAN recently wrote rejecting the idea of a proposed brothel in Vancouver: "Prostitution is inherently violent, merely an extension of the violence that most prostituted women experience as children. We should aim not merely to reduce this harm, as if it is a necessary evil and/or inescapable, but strive to eliminate it altogether."[5] Groups and individuals with this ideology refuse to call prostitutes "sex-trade workers," as though it is merely another form of work, and insist on calling them "prostituted women," just as our partners did in the Philippines, in order to indicate that all women are harmed by prostitution and that no woman does it by choice. They oppose the legalization of prostitution because it would constitute a normalization of men buying sex from women. AWAN states that legalization "would in fact be harmful, would expand prostitution and would promote trafficking, and would only serve to make prostitution safer and more profitable for the men who exploit and harm prostituted women and children."[6]

It seems clear why this position is an improvement from seeing prostitution as a moral or criminal issue. It recognizes the real harm done to women in prostitution, the lack of choice many of them face, and the need for eliminating the worst aspects of the industry. For instance, how many women freely choose sex work in Canada or the Philippines? In looking at issues of poverty and prostitution within the Canadian context, the Canadian Advisory Council on the Status of Woman put it this way: "Can a person of minimal education and financial well-being be said truly to choose a way of life that is stigmatized by much of society, that is physically dangerous at times, that leaves her little control over her earning power and that can cause her considerable legal complications?"[7] A Filipino study stated that "prostitution is one of the most alienating forms of labour," that the Filipino women carried out their work "with a heavy heart," and that the women "were conscience-stricken because they still considered sex with customers a sin."[8]

An increasing number of ex-prostitutes' survivor groups educate the public and feminists about the harm done to women in prostitution. In response to the proposed Vancouver brothel, a group called Ex-Prostitutes Against Legislated Sexual Servitude claim that prostitution, rather than being "normal work that simply needs to be better regulated," is in fact harmful. "We oppose any measure that would put more power in the hands of the men who abused us by telling them that they are legally entitled to do so. This proposal does not speak for us, would not have affected our level of safety in a way that matters and would not have spared us the harm that is inherent in prostitution."[9] Women Hurt in Systems of Prostitution Engaged in Revolt (WHISPER), based in Minneapolis, advocates for survivors of street prostitution and work in conjunction with CATW to argue that all forms of prostitution are harmful to women and that prostitution is equivalent to other forms of male oppression, like pornography, sexual harassment, and rape.[10]

There is no denying that many women suffer exploitation before, during, and after their experiences of prostitution. CATW has found that women in prostitution in the Philippines have been victims of incest and abuse and have suffered violence at the hands of clients, bar owners, casa owners, and pimps. In its five-country study (which included the Philippines), funded by the Ford Foundation, CATW stated that most of the 146 women in prostitution interviewed did not want prostitution legalized because they saw it as humiliating work that is prone to violence. Not one woman interviewed, according to the CATW study, wanted her children, family, or friends to have to earn money by entering the sex-trade industry.

Violence is often done to women in prostitution not just because laws do not protect women or that work conditions are not what they should be but because men's prostitution use of women and the acts carried out are sexual enactments of a culture and system of subordination of women. Therefore, violence and degradation, even when not acted out, are inherent conditions of prostitution sex. For one thing, the possibility of violence is always present, for another, sex mediated by money means power to dictate what sex will happen. A client encountering refusal of a particular sex act or even condomless sex by a prostitute will merely hire another woman who may be needier and will accept his demands. Harm will therefore be inflicted to another more vulnerable woman.[11]

Seeing prostitution—like wife battering, sexual abuse, pornography and incest—as yet another form of violence against women, Sweden passed a law that went into effect in January 1999 that criminalizes only the buying of sexual services. According to the Swedish model, women who sell their sexual services are clearly prostituted women, exploited, coerced, and forced to sell their bodies by pimps, procurers, or circumstance, whether poverty or dependence on illegal drugs. The change in discourse is deliberate here, too: no longer "prostitutes" but "prostituted women."

Canada considered decriminalization but ultimately rejected it: "Decriminalization or regulation would send a message of endorsement of prostitution when there is much evidence of the victimization of its (female) participants."[12] Indeed, prostitution diversion programs—"john schools" (first launched in Toronto in 1996 and modeled after San Francisco programs)—were meant to target men explicitly. Instead of going through the criminal justice system, men (once arrested) would enter programs to change their (harmful) behavior. Thus, Canada continues to criminalize activities surrounding prostitution, and although both parties (prostitutes and johns) are subject to arrest, the Canadian government seems to recognize, in part, that women are unduly harmed. The United States has been even more reluctant to consider decriminalization because advocates "run up against a wall of public opposition and policy makers are almost universally opposed to the idea, making it a non-starter in any serious discussion of policy alternatives."[13]

Women in prostitution in Canada and the United States, however, like those in Sweden, the Philippines, and even the Netherlands, where prostitution is legal, remain socially stigmatized. Marieke van Doorninck doesn't think that the moral "attitude of the Dutch population today differs very much from that of people in any other country. I don't think our ideas about prostitution and selling sex for money are any different from anyone's else's. Prostitutes and sex workers have the same stigma attached to them as in any other country."[14] So-called decent people, where notions of decency are not merely culturally but also class bound, should be aware of the stigma we attach to prostitutes because it prevents us from really understanding the situation of prostituted women and may even lead us to attack their choices because "they" are not like "us." This continuing stigma is why sex-workers' rights group are gaining popularity as they aim not just to tolerate prostitution but to make it legitimate service work and address the lived experience of prostitutes who have chosen this work as work.

Prostitution Is Work Like Any Other

The third strand in prostitution theory (and practice) is the idea that prostitution is work like any other and should be legitimized. Though we engaged with this idea throughout the project, it was not a popular notion in the Philippines as the partners considered prostitutes criminals, moral failures, and/or victims. There are no sex-workers' rights groups in the Philippines, and our main feminist partner was a member of CATW, which takes a strong position on prostitution as a human rights violation. A recent scan of sex-worker groups in Asia show groups working out of Australia, New Zealand, Thailand, Hong Kong, Taiwan, Japan, and India, but no groups in the Philippines. Regardless, this is an idea that must be addressed because it is so central to feminism and to the idea that the actual experiences of women in prostitution matter. Though an unpopular notion in the Philippines, we did meet women who had chosen to work in the bars, and though *enjoyed* probably would be too strong a word, they wanted to be there. And we have both met women in North America and Europe who freely chose work in the sex industry and claim it is work like any other. Norma Jean Almodavar from COYOTE (Call Off Your Old Tired Ethics), whom we have both met, is an eloquent proponent of the sex-work-as-work argument.

Advocates of prostitution, particularly prostitutes' organizations or collectives, argue that criminalization (as in the United States) only "contributes to the stigma that prostitutes bear, making them more vulnerable to hate crimes, housing and employment discrimination, and other violations of their basic rights."[15] Prostitution is not a social ill, according to this perspective, because there is nothing wrong with selling sex and women should be able to choose freely to engage in sex work. Sex workers are also not all victims because many women choose to work as prostitutes. The reason prostitution continues to be stigmatized is because of outdated sexual attitudes predicated on male control over female desire. Some prostitutes like to compare themselves to sex therapists, educators, and entertainers. They are, they argue, merely performing a service.[16]

Proponents of this view are many and increasing. There are sex-workers' rights groups all over the world, including the Network of Sex Workers Project in London; the Asia Pacific Network of Sex Workers, Sex Workers Outreach Project, and Scarlet Alliance, all in Australia; the Global Alliance Against Trafficking in Women and EMPOWER in Thailand; TULIPS in Taiwan; Stella, Beaver, and Maggies, all in Canada; PONY and COYOTE in the United States; Davida in Brazil; Durbar Mahila Samanwaya Committee of India; SWEAT of South Africa; and the list goes on. All of these groups promote the idea that it is not sex work that is the problem but rather the stigmatization and illegality of it that causes all the problems. They advocate for workers' rights for prostitutes; that is, for sex workers to be included under normal provisions of health, safety, and labor laws. They work to decriminalize prostitution in all its forms and actively promote prostitution as an occupation. Two of the objectives of the Scarlet Alliance of Australia, according to its website, are "to challenge any government at any time when and where it implements legislation, regulations, rules, policies or law enforcement practices which are discriminatory and/or repressive to the rights and autonomy of sex workers; and to actively promote the right of all sex workers to work in whatever area of their chosen occupation, including street, brothel, escort, private and opportunistic work."

Scoffing at "abolitionist" feminists and activists who want to prevent women from "having to do this kind of work," sex-work feminists want the right to work and to be free from all restrictions on that work. Where CATW sees the oppression of prostituted women as inherent, a sex-trade worker looks at the term *prostituted* and objects to their "victimization" of her. "I personally get really uncomfortable when women on this board use the term 'prostituted women.' Many women and children are sexually exploited but other women, like me for example, aren't. So that term is silencing for me. I chose when and where (within limits) and how I do my work; nobody is prostituting me. . . . Unless you are or have been a sex worker, you don't get to have authority over what language is used."[17] To get around the language issue (prostituted women versus sex workers), prostitutes are now referring to themselves as experiential people and their groups as experiential in

> an attempt to underline the fact that those who had lived experiences as sex workers had a particular authority when it came to describing the experience of being a sex worker. In part, it arose because sex worker activists were profoundly frustrated by the fact that everyone, abolitionist feminists included, felt free to label their

experiences and they thought they had the right to name themselves.[18]

Much of the work that sex-worker activists do, in addition to lobbying for better working conditions for prostitutes, involves criticizing abolitionist feminists who, they believe, sensationalize the abuse of women and contribute to the contemporary moral panic about prostitution and trafficking. Jo Doezema, in particular, links the current outrage about sex trafficking to the "white slavery" discourses at the turn of the last century. She argues, in post-colonial fashion, that there is a similar thread of colonialism and "racialized representations" of victimized women in these modern discourses that "serve to further marginalise sex workers and undermine their human rights."[19] Much of her theoretical and practical agenda is to legitimate sex work, so it is not surprising that she particularly criticizes CATW since their agenda is so clearly to eradicate prostitution. She argues that CATW uses the worst examples of prostitution and trafficking to make its case for intervention and that this smacks of repression, racism, and neo-colonialism. She calls for feminists to realize that their interests might not be "those of third world sex workers themselves."[20] As much as we admire some of Doezema's work, we wonder if Doezema has ever been to a third-world casa, since there is a danger both in overstating the harm done to women in prostitution and in understating it.

In any event, the message that sex workers and their advocates have advanced is an important one. Rather than continuing to stigmatize the role of the prostitute and maintaining a gendered Madonna/whore, good girl/bad girl hierarchy, the value of sex work should be recognized. If freely chosen, they argue, there is nothing inherently wrong with sex work, and it should be treated as work like any other. Laurie Shrage, who makes the case for decriminalization of prostitution argues:

> If businesses that provided customers with personal sexual services could operate legally, then they would be subject to the same labor regulations that apply to other businesses. . . . Such businesses would not be allowed to treat workers like slaves, hire underage workers, deprive them of compensation for which they contracted, or expose them to unnecessary risks. The businesses could be required to enforce health and safety codes, provide workers with a minimum income and health insurance, and allow them to form collectives to negotiate for improved working conditions, compensations, and benefits.[21]

There is no better example of sex work being treated as work like any other than the Netherlands. The Dutch tradition of tolerance sees the sex industry as just another social problem, the prohibition of which, like the prohibition of euthanasia and soft drugs, will produce more problems then it solves. Red-light districts are allowed, and sex clubs, private houses, and window brothels are legal. Coming into effect in 2000, "the Dutch Penal Code no longer treats organizing the prostitution of an adult female or male person as a crime when it is done with the consent of the prostitute. If he or she regards prostitution as the best option to earn a living, he or she has the same rights that any worker has"—the prostitute receives health and employment benefits, and pays taxes.[22]

So what is wrong with this scenario? Legalization solves the criminality problem. It prevents the worst aspects of pimping and street prostitution. It allows prostitutes to charge clients with assault and gives some legitimation to the work. All the groups we worked with recognized the harm done to some women in prostitution, but all would have rejected this model. While there is a recognition that something needs to be done about the terrible conditions under which many women work, there is still no agreement on how policy can be devised to satisfy both camps—those who see it as work like any other and those who see it as a violation of human rights. Even the Dutch have recently begun to revise their expectations about the benefits of legalized prostitution. As the mayor of Amsterdam, Job Cohen, said recently, "A move in 2000 to legalize prostitution failed to curb gangsters running Amsterdam's sex trade. Legalization 'didn't bring us what we hoped and expected. . . . We want in part to reverse it, especially with regard to the exploitation of women in the sex industry.'"[23] So what's to be done?

It is hard to describe the emotionally laden language of these two opposing views to people who have never been in the middle of the so-called sex wars. However, it is easy to see why this is such a difficult issue. For people who have been harmed by prostitution, it is unconscionable for feminists to advocate for a continuation of what they see as men's oppression of women. For people who make a living as sex workers, who believe they are not harmed by it, and who have chosen it freely, it is unconscionable that feminists would not support their right to work wherever and at whatever they choose, and who would oppose humane working conditions. Unfortunately, there does not seem to be a middle ground; one group wants to eliminate prostitution, and the other wants to legitimize it. Abolitionist feminists do not just want to reduce harm, they want to eliminate prostitution. Sex-workers' rights groups do not just want to de-criminalize sex work, they want to celebrate it. How do we reconcile these points of view? As Esther Shannon has said about the urgent need for policy action: "the bus to Utopia is running awfully late."[24]

Can These Positions Be Reconciled?

This section is structured around four main questions that have been pivotal in the philosophical debates surrounding sex-trade work and that correspond to the three main perspectives on prostitution noted above. First, does decriminalization of the sex trade constitute a legitimization of the work? And if so, what does this mean ideologically for women? Does this give men rights to unlimited sexual access to women, or does it give financial power and sexual rights to women? Second, should governments follow abolitionist, prohibitionist, or regulationist policies in dealing with prostitution?[25] How do Canada, the United States, and the Philippines adhere or not adhere to these systems? Are there any more appropriate models available? Third, what is the best system for sex-trade workers themselves? What system would make sex work safer for women and enable them to have more control over the working conditions—to control their own money, to be free from police and pimp harassment, to tackle health concerns, like AIDS and STIs. Can prostitutes be self-employed but not regulated by the state? Can prostitutes pay taxes but not be placed in red-light areas or have health checks imposed upon them? Fourth, and most fundamental, is prostitution inherently exploitative? What if anything makes sex-trade work different from other work, and what consequences does this have for government policy and feminist activism?

Using the perspectives of two of our partners (WEDPRO and Stepping Stone) and two NGOs representing the conservative and the sex radical point of view (Third World Movement Against the Exploitation of Women [TWMAEW] and COYOTE, respectively) we can begin to get a practical sense of how divisive the issues are. We examine the conservative's claim of sexual romanticism, the radical feminist's claim of sexual harm, and the libertarian's claim of sexual liberation.[26]

Given the strength of Roman Catholicism in the Philippines, efforts by faith-based groups like TWMAEW (or the Movement), under the leadership of Sister Mary Soledad L. Perpinan, have been particularly important. Sister Soledad's organization was founded in 1980 when it spearheaded protests against Japanese sex tours in the Philippines; her organization was also instrumental in the anti-bases movement, drawing attention to military prostitution in the early 1980s. Seeing the organization not merely as one of advocacy, Sister Soledad has also ensured that it provides services to women in the sex trade. Predicated on what the organization calls "human and Christian development," the Movement has a phased process for getting women out of prostitution: first, it has various drop-in centers (such as Belen sa Angeles); second, it provides alternative livelihoods in its Nazareth Growth home; and finally, it supplies transitional housing through its Bethany Transition Home. This organization also provides economic alternatives to women who have committed themselves to leaving prostitution, including making crafts, doing domestic work, operating BBQ stands, and training as hairdressers. They deal with children as young as eight years old who have lived on the streets of Manila working as prostitutes. The girls usually come from poor rural families and have a history of abuse. This group was in synch with our more conservative partners who felt that prostitution was a moral issue, as well as an economic one, and that it was their religious duty to "save" the young women. Since our project ended in 2004, another group with a similar ideology has begun work in Angeles itself. Called RENEW Foundation (Recovery, Empowering, Networking, and Employment for Prostituted Women), it is also a religious-based organization. Its goals, according to its website, are to rescue women from the sex industry in Angeles, "remove the industry itself and replace it with alternative, sustainable sources of income such as cottage industries." It provides education, outreach, advocacy, and spiritual renewal.

Feminist groups in the Philippines, umbrella organizations like GABRIELA and CATW-AP, differ from faith-based groups in their promotion of women's sexual and reproductive rights. They believe in the use of condoms and other contraceptives as well as the woman's right to choose and control her body. However, they also see prostitution as unacceptable, not on moral terms, but on radical feminist ones. Often citing the work of Kathleen Barry, the founder of CATW, many Filipino feminists agree that "we must separate the individual woman from the institution which controls her, and examine the institution of prostitution not simply as an outcome of poverty circumstances of individual women but as a product of male domination, of sexual violence and enslavement."[27] Sexual oppression is identified as the key reason for the existence of prostitution, while taking into consideration the economic power of American soldiers and foreign sex tourists as well as "racist representations of Filipinas [that] range from the docile and submissive sexual servant slave to the sex-hungry exotic creature," all of which mean that "sex, class, race and nationality all combine in the oppression of women."[28] Implicated in this analysis are foreign men, Filipino men, the U.S. government, the Philippine government, and the conditions created by globalized capitalism. WEDPRO, a member of CATW-AP, is devoted to ending prostitution and sex trafficking in women. WEDPRO's representative prostitute is a poor, uneducated young woman from a rural community who is economically and emotionally coerced into a life of prostitution. This was our main grassroots partner, and its agenda dictated many of our activities.

The third group analyzed was one of our Canadian partners, Stepping Stone, an advocacy group for sex-trade workers based in Halifax. It has outreach programs and street workers who hand out bad trick lists and condoms. It also runs a drop-in center. Stepping Stone offers many services, ranging from housing and welfare referrals to assistance with the legal system and substance-abuse programs. Its work is primarily with street prostitutes who have experienced sexual abuse and are drug and alcohol abusers, but it also works with the city's many escort-service workers, both female and male.

Finally, we look at a U.S.-based sex-worker group called COYOTE to profile the so-called sex-positive position on prostitution. There are no pro-sex-worker groups in the Philippines, so we also look at Empower Foundation, a sex-worker collective run out of Bangkok. Empower, according to its website, works primarily with women who have chosen to work as sex workers. The women run a bar in the red-light district, the Can Do Bar, and they do work with prostitutes to educate them about their rights. Empower also has language- and computer-skills development, counseling, candle-making, and workshops on health and safety issues. Its members participate in comedy shows with skits that parody the idea that they need to be rescued or rehabilitated. A comparable organization is the Global Alliance Against Trafficking in Women (GAATW), also based in Thailand. It deals with issues of migrant women and sex workers, and it sees some of the trafficking discourse as problematic for women who have chosen to be trafficked. It is not clear whether GAATW takes a pro-sex position with regard to workers' rights, though Empower clearly does.

We argue that it is crucial to take into account the context in which commercial sex takes place and that the very different perspectives noted above result from the different economic, social, and political contexts of the various groups and the women they represent. We also look at the question of choice and agency and whether or not choice is reserved only for those working in the sex-trade industry in developed states like Canada and the United States. This idea, of course, is not acceptable to CATW, because it refuses to differentiate between first-world and third-world prostitution, child and adult prostitution, or forced and voluntary prostitution, since CATW considers them all exploitation.

The question of decriminalization is, perhaps not surprisingly, the easiest to answer. All of the groups we worked with and profile here were in favor of decriminalization, at least for the sex-trade workers or prostituted women themselves. The Coalition and the Movement, representing the radical-feminist and conservative positions, respectively, wish to decriminalize the prostitute while penalizing the customer, pimps, and procurers, as in the Swedish model. Decriminalization would prevent the further victimization of the prostituted woman, but because these groups do not want to legitimize sex work as work, they strongly advocate prosecuting the men involved at all levels. Stepping Stone prefers not to take a position on legitimation of sex work, but in a recent survey of its clients, the majority of respondents believed that prostitution should be decriminalized. COYOTE and Empower Foundation, representing the civil libertarian and sex-workers' rights views, take the strongest position on decriminalization. They believe that all laws surrounding prostitution should be repealed, especially for prostitutes and clients, but also those on pimping and procuring. This would allow women to run businesses out of their homes and to have business managers. Other criminal code sections, they believe, would cover child prostitution, assault, coercion, and fraud.

All of these groups acknowledge that women are victimized because of the laws making prostitution illegal. They cite incidents of police harassment and brutality occurring because of the illegal nature of prostitution. They believe that prostitutes lack basic civil rights because of the laws making prostitution a crime, so that prostitutes can rarely accuse clients of rape or abuse because of the nature of their work. If decriminalization is easy, however, issues of legitimacy are not.

The fundamental difference, then, has to do with legitimation of the work itself. COYOTE believes that sex work should be promoted as legitimate service work. The Coalition and the Movement want to get rid of prostitution in the long run and believe that legitimizing sex-trade work normalizes it and makes it an acceptable work choice for women. These differences are based in the fundamentally different view each group has toward sexuality. The sexual libertarian, unproblematically, claims that sexuality equals liberation, and so women's political and social liberation is intimately tied to their sexual liberation. The history of women's sexuality, in this view, has been one of repression, moralism, and sexual double standards, and therefore women must be free to use, exchange, or buy sex just as men do. COYOTE certainly maintains this position by claiming that women will one day take their place as sexual consumers as well. Sexuality is also seen as something that can be separated from one's self as if in a role, with "a clear sense on the performers' part of when they are acting and when they are not."[29] This view of prostitution's "embodied work," therefore, is little different from the "emotional labor" that all women do, and certainly not inherently different from other types of alienated labor.[30] And if the concern is about commodification of women's bodies, what makes embodied work any different from other forms of labor under capitalism?[31]

The sexual conservative tends to believe that all sexual contact outside a heterosexual, legal, and procreative union is immoral, indecent, and anti-family. Sexuality, in this view, is intrinsically something that cannot be bought and sold without profound psychological problems to the seller. Therefore, although focusing on the "sex-ploitation" of Filipinas, the Movement's fundamental position of getting women out of the sex trade is arguably predicated on Catholic Church doctrine, which is against any definition of sexual expression that is not connected to heterosexual marriage and procreation. At the 1995 Fourth World Conference on Women in Beijing, Pope John Paul II made a moral plea against what he saw as the anti-marriage, anti-family, and anti-procreation initiatives of many feminist groups. The Philippines was the only Southeast Asian country to support the Vatican's position at the Beijing conference. The pope constructed feminist initiatives as forces of the West, forces of imperialism, and forces of rampant individualism with no moral base. He saw the promotion of condom use and other contraceptives as the imposition of population control by Western countries on the Third World in exchange for foreign aid. In this view, sex and sexuality belong only in a heterosexual marriage for procreation, and it brings out the extent to which Catholic doctrine rests on the concept of woman as wife and mother. There is no allowance, then, for sex outside of marriage, and prostitution is morally unacceptable.

The radical feminist view of sexuality of WEDPRO and the Coalition is also problematic. Since the 1970s certain elements of the feminist movement have concentrated on sexuality as inherently harmful for women. Debates on pornography have centered on the sexual harm that is done to women by men, and this also informs the debates on prostitution, as evidenced by the Coalition's emphasis on sex trafficking in women and women's victimization at the hands of men. The sex trade, in its view, simply makes women available for men's sexual use. One of the main questions it asks is why *women* are doing this "work." The Coalition believes it is because of men's power over women, rejecting the libertarian claim that sexuality is simply a basic human need that men have in abundance.

Stepping Stone does not take a position on legitimation or sexuality per se. It sees prostitution as an economic necessity for poor women who have problems with drug and alcohol addiction and thus the group is more pragmatically oriented toward service and advocacy. It wants the women it works with to have the rights to live and to be free from violence. Decriminalization, then, may be the only area of commonality for these groups. It is not a total consensus, since there are still some radical anti-prostitution feminist, conservative, and police groups who advocate for continued criminalization, in the belief that nothing else will deter women (and men) from entering prostitution, pimps from pimping, and men from buying. As noted below, however, this is probably the worst model for the women themselves.

Conceptually, we still find Kathleen Barry's framework useful for examining traditional responses to prostitution and ask which, if any, of these models is best for sex-trade workers.[32] For example, the prohibitionist system of the United States, and most other countries, makes prostitution (or solicitation) and pimping illegal. Many studies have shown the problematic aspects of making prostitutes criminals. Women are penalized, while clients and pimps are relatively untouched. Also, it is hard to deter or even determine the victimization of those working in the sex trade because their activities are officially illegal, even if condoned in practice. At the other extreme is the regulationist system of Germany and the Netherlands, which has legalized prostitution and regulates when, where, and how prostitutes can work. There are still many restrictions on women (they are legally required to have permits and health certificates, for example) and the controlling and violent aspect of the trade has not been measurably reduced. Finally, France and parts of Australia have what Barry calls an abolitionist system in which prostitution is decriminalized but pimping is illegal. This is often seen as the ideal for women working in the trade, but Barry herself points out that this has not stopped harassment of prostitutes by members of the legal system or social condemnation.[33] Sweden has taken abolition a step further by decriminalizing prostitution for the women but criminalizing the male customers, pimps, and procurers; recognizing the violence and abuse inherent in prostitution; and legally acknowledging prostitutes to be victims.

Even the abolitionist system is inadequate, COYOTE believes, because though prostitution is technically legal, there is still a social stigma attached to prostitution because it is not seen as legitimate service work and results in social condemnation and police harassment. Finally, the regulationist system is, in the view of all of our partners in the project, very problematic. Many studies indicate the problems with making the state the pimp, and, though well-intentioned, prostitution ends up being run by organized crime or multinational industry and gives the women fewer choices about time, place, and clientele. It is difficult to imagine, even if prostitution is decriminalized, how to avoid these problems. COYOTE, for instance, does not want to be regulated by the government, except as any other small business would be. It does not want prostitutes to be zoned into red-light districts or have health tests imposed upon them, yet the state already imposes zoning restrictions on commercial businesses and health regulations. It is not clear, at this point, how COYOTE thinks it can prevent this and avoid having the state as pimp, which all four groups see as oppressive.

The Philippines has a hybrid model: although the country is officially prohibitionist, prostitution is actually regulated by the municipal government. This makes the system one of the worst for the women because of the double bind involved. Under Article 202 of the Revised Philippine Penal Code, prostitution and any other related activities are illegal. Yet, prostitutes are regulated with weekly health checks in Angeles City and are issued permits that they must carry at all times or face arrest on vagrancy charges. Men are never arrested either as customers or prostitutes since a prostitute is legally defined as female. Canadians and Americans have gotten around this double standard with anti-solicitation laws. This enables police officers to arrest clients as well as prostitutes, but it still criminalizes the prostitute.

In terms of what is the best system for the sex workers themselves, in a study by WEDPRO on entertainers in Angeles City and Olongapo, prostituted women were divided into three groups, based on where they worked. The results are highly illustrative.

The women with the least control over their lives were the regulated casa workers, who work in local brothels patronized by poor Filipino men. They are "maintained, guarded and virtually owned by the casa employers."[34] They have no regular working hours and no regular wages but are used on an on-call basis. Therefore, the biggest problem is having no control over the clientele. They cannot choose customers and have no control over the number of customers. They make the least amount of money, work the most hours, and are the most indebted to the owners. They are the youngest women in the survey, from rural areas, with little or no education. Many were sold to brothel owners by their families or deceived by recruiters.

Bar girls are the second group studied by WEDPRO (and the only registered prostitutes in Angeles City). They fare a bit better than the casa workers but not as well as call girls or streetwalkers. Bar girls work regular ten to fourteen hour shifts and get paid commissions on ladies' drinks and percentages of bar fines. They usually have only one customer a night, who is treated as a boyfriend and who receives other services, such as washing clothes, cleaning rooms, and cooking meals.

The third group surveyed, the call girls or streetwalkers, were better off financially and in terms of job satisfaction, though more vulnerable legally because of their unregistered status. These women worked fewer hours, had fewer customers, and made more money. They had the most control over their time and the type and number of their customers. They were able to keep most of the money they earned, although some might be paid to an intermediary who arranged a contact. Although the authors of the report distinguished between workplaces and levels of oppression, it should be noted that WEDPRO asserted that all the women were exploited.

The WEDPRO study corresponds to the 1998 International Labour Organization (ILO) research study entitled *The Sex Sector: The Economic and Social Bases of Prostitution in Southeast Asia*. Ofreneo and Ofreneo distinguished among four types of women in prostitution in the Philippines: (1) the exported (those who were trafficked abroad or migrated as "entertainers" to countries like Japan—the so-called Japa-yukis); (2) the employed (those who worked in the bars, videokes, massage parlors, cabarets, and other establishments or businesses); (3) the self-employed (those on the street—streetwalkers or freelancers, as they are called in the Philippines); and (4) the enslaved (those in the casas or brothels).[35] According to Lin Lean Lim, editor of the ILO study, although there are cases of exploitation or coercion (as evident in those who are exported and enslaved), and child prostitution is clearly unacceptable, the complexity of sex work needs to be addressed. Some women choose sex work because of poverty, unemployment, and family obligations in countries with virtually no social-welfare programs, and the conditions of their work vary according to their working locations—bar or brothel.[36] Much to the consternation of CATW, the ILO seemingly endorsed sex work as normalized work and recommended that the government do what it could to bring sex-workers' rights in line with other workers. Accordingly, "for those adult individuals who freely choose sex work, the policy concerns should focus on improving their working conditions and social protection, and on ensuring that they are entitled to the same labor rights and benefits as other workers."[37] Prostitution, at least for those who are employed in establishments or self-employed call girls, should be considered a viable employment option for those in poverty—and it is the duty of the state, according to the ILO report, to protect their labor rights.

What these studies indicate are the major factors influencing the lives of sex-trade workers: control over their time and setting their own hours; control over their money; the right to choose customers and to refuse those they dislike; and the right to choose the number of customers. Studies from Stepping Stone indicate the same variables. Escort-service workers or call girls have relatively more control over their time, money, and clientele than do women working for pimps. Brothel workers in the West face some of the same dilemmas as brothel workers in the Philippines—lack of control over the clientele, indebtedness to the owner, and lack of resources generally. These problems indicate to a group like COYOTE that the only system that can work well for the women themselves is one where the sex-trade worker is seen as a service worker, setting up small businesses in partnership with others. But, then, we come full circle, since these questions of legalization and regulation suggest legitimizing the work, and groups like the Coalition and the Movement adamantly oppose anything that will make sex work legitimate. For the Coalition, in particular, making working conditions "bearable" is actually impossible, since in its view prostitution is rape and it is unconscionable to make one group of women responsible for sexually servicing men and enduring rape.

The final question, obviously, is the most difficult to resolve because of its highly contested nature. Like the abortion debates, the pro- and anti-prostitution lobbies take fundamentally different positions on the nature of sexuality and its harm to women. COYOTE, not surprisingly, takes the strongest position on legitimizing sex work as work. Its members equate sex work with service work like massage therapy. They dismiss radical feminist claims of dissociation, claiming that dissociation happens with waitresses and factory workers, for example, as well as with prostitutes. They sometimes use the analogy of marriage as prostitution and consider themselves freer than wives who do the same things in exchange for support from just one man. COYOTE believes that prostitution should be seen as work like any other and that prostitutes should be seen as self-employed workers. If prostitution had a social value, the women involved in prostitution could feel better about themselves and would not have the social stigma that they do today.

In contrast, the Movement actively promotes women leaving sex-trade work, which it believes is degrading and harmful to all women. Sexuality is not a commodity to be bought and sold. Rather, it is part of a loving relationship. The Coalition believes that sexual exploitation is a human rights violation, that men prey on economically vulnerable women and children, that prostitution is a "vehicle for racism and first world domination" and that prostitution "victimizes all women, justifies the sale of any woman and reduces all women to sex."[38] It includes sex tourism, mail-order brides, and casual and military prostitution as trafficking in women. It rejects the idea that prostitution is ever a choice for women. Sexuality, in this view, is harmful or potentially does harm to women, and therefore the men's behavior must be criminalized.

Stepping Stone believes that prostitutes have "rights to safety and access to services regardless of their occupation." It does not "interfere with or attempt to stop their work but rather assist[s] in making street life as safe as possible." Stepping Stone's analysis has a lot to do with the economics of the sex trade, seeing that it is often the only option a woman has to survive. These differences illustrate the three fundamental points of view on prostitution that we were unable to reconcile in our project. We have taken the pragmatic view of Stepping Stone: prostitution is an economic necessity for many women and the worst aspects of sex work must be alleviated. We do not see it as a moral issue, nor do we see it as work like any other. We do see the great harm done to women in prostitution when policies are devised that hurt rather than help them. We believe that all workers need and deserve respect, self-determination, and human dignity.

We also do not believe that sex work is likely to disappear anytime soon. Prostitution has been called the world's oldest profession for a reason: since the earliest recorded human history there have been accounts of prostitution—Greek courtesans (the Hetairae) of 2500 BC, Chinese concubines in the Tang and Sung dynasties, medieval European "harlots," and pre-colonial Asian second wives.[39] Though the common denominator has historically been men's desire for women's bodies, equality in the twentieth and twenty-first centuries has meant that women are paying for sex, too. There will always be men and some women who for a variety of reasons choose to buy sex from others. We do not think this is going to change, but we also do not think that sex work will ever be work like any other. Imagine, for instance, that in order to get unemployment or welfare benefits women or men could be made to work in brothels or escort services. It just will not happen. There is something fundamentally different about sex work compared to factory work in export-processing zones or domestic service under exploitative conditions, for example, or even massage therapy, where parts of the body are used in service to another. What makes prostitution different from other types of paid labor for women is that at this point in history prostitution is inherently gendered. After arguing that sex work is actually not that much different from other work under capitalist conditions, Christine Overall cautions that there is a significant difference between the commodification of sexuality and other forms of work: its profoundly gendered and asymmetrical nature where "women are the workers and men are the bosses." Prostitution, then, is "structured in terms of a power imbalance in which women, the less powerful, sell to men, the more powerful."[40] Maybe someday the gendered nature of prostitution will change (and we see increasing evidence that women are buying sex in West Africa, in the Caribbean, and in escort services in Australia), but as it exists right now prostitution is fundamentally and problematically gendered, which is even more reason to improve the conditions under which women work.

A Middle Way

In our attempts to resolve some of these philosophical issues and hence develop policy as well, we are led in the direction of work by Lenore Kuo, Julia O'Connell Davidson, and Laurie Shrage. All of these authors are attempting to reject absolutes when it comes to prostitution policy and to reconcile opposing viewpoints.[41] They recognize the harm done to women in prostitution, and they advocate safe working conditions and rights for women working in prostitution. But, as Davidson puts it, nothing they (and we) have researched leads them to "want to celebrate the existence of a market for commoditized sex; rather the reverse."[42] Her critique of "sex radical" feminism, as politically dangerous, strikes a chord with us. Equating sexual acts to sexual "needs" as opposed to "socially constructed desires" means that sex-radical feminists can argue that prostitutes are fulfilling a human need or requirement and that their work should therefore have value.

> To attempt to destigmatize prostitution by insisting on its social value also carries risks as a political strategy. There is a danger of simply creating new hierarchies and fresh divisions. If prostitutes are to be respected because they undertake socially valuable work, surely those who specialize in working with severely disabled clients will be deemed somehow more respectable that those who give blow jobs to able-bodied men out on their stag night.[43]

Rather, the human, civil and political rights of prostitutes and their right to dignity should never be in question.

> Those who work in prostitution have rights and deserve respect not because or despite the fact they work as prostitutes, but because they are human beings. Likewise, our claim to legal recognition, rights, dignity and respect lies in the fact that we are human beings not that we are able-bodied or disabled, black or white, straight or gay, shoe fetishist or vanilla sex fetishist.[44]

Conflicting ideas about sexuality underlie our different groups' perspectives, and we agree with Laurie Shrage's analysis that sexuality is a terrain of struggle. Unlike the polarization between civil libertarians and radical feminists, though, we believe that sexuality can be both a major cause of women's oppression *and* a site of resistance. There are no inherently liberatory sexual practices or repressive sexual practices. Sexuality is a discourse that gets its meaning in specific historical, economic, and social contexts. This is shown specifically in Shrage's work on prostitution. She demonstrates how the meaning of sex work is not ahistorical and fixed. Prostitution in the Middle Ages differs from sex work in contemporary America, which differs from prostitution in ancient Babylon and colonial Kenya and contemporary Nepal. So, in this view, it is not surprising that the Coalition, which represents women who have been coerced or trafficked into prostitution, believes that prostitution is male domination of women. It is not surprising that the Movement, which represents child prostitutes, believes that prostitution is a moral evil exploiting small children. It is not surprising that COYOTE, representing Western call girls who choose prostitution as work over being, say, a police officer, believes that sex work is a legitimate choice that needs to be respected. It is not surprising that Stepping Stone, which represents both street, drug-addicted prostitutes and escort service workers and is user directed, refuses to take a position on the legitimation of the work but sees prostitution as an economic choice for women and multifaceted.

We argue that they are all partially right. Prostitution can be male domination; it can be a moral evil; it can be an economic choice; and it can be (potentially) respectable work. It is the context in which prostitution happens, the choices available, the working conditions, and the historic and social specificity that give it meaning. In terms of policy, then, we need to proceed carefully. Shrage's work indicates the dilemmas. Complete deregulation may be as problematic as complete criminalization. Careful consideration must be given to regulation to prevent abuses that now exist with street prostitution, for instance. Would women disappear into brothels and become invisible? How would the problems with brothels be prevented? How could the documented problems of sexual abuse and the entry of young people into prostitution be prevented? Regulated prostitution would, by its nature, not include some women, and what would happen to those women who fall between the cracks, as has happened in Australia? Women still end up in jail for street prostitution because they cannot get work in brothels, get kicked out of brothels for rule violations, or lose their licenses for various reasons.[45]

In Canada and the United States, regulation is needed to protect women from pimps and the hardships of street life. Escort services will continue to flourish, and some regulation is needed to ensure that the workers are protected in terms of working conditions, both financially and with regard to their health and safety. Again, if the legal tensions are not resolved, sex-trade workers will continue to fall outside the boundaries of normal labor practices and have no recourse within the legal system. One model will not fit every situation, but we must at least recognize that prostitution is going on all around us. Even if we could foresee a day when prostitution would no longer exist, working conditions for sex-trade workers must be examined and acted upon. Making conditions even more unbearable in the hope that this will get women out of the life has not worked in the past and, in our view, is ill-conceived and inhumane.

In the Philippines, it is crucial, at the minimum, to resolve the legal contradiction that exists. If prostitution is illegal, then the women should not be regulated with health checks and identification cards. Being illegal and regulated at the same time puts them in a very precarious position. Decriminalization of the women involved in prostitution would be the first move in resolving the contradiction. The Filipino government is attempting to curb sex tourism and child prostitution, but if it makes claims of doing away with prostitution altogether, it risks unearthing the myriad of elite (often male) interests, whether economic, military, or business, that perpetuate the system and practice of prostitution. The Philippines is a poor country, and the women working in the sex-trade industry make more money than the average worker. Without providing economic alternatives, efforts to stop prostitution are doomed to fail. The Philippines is also a predominantly Catholic country, and therefore sex-trade workers are seen as "fallen women." Without cultural changes and attempts to integrate prostitutes back into society, attempts to curb prostitution are again bound to fail. We see here clearly the interconnections among race, sex, and class oppression and the difficulties of trying to change one aspect without another. The next chapter examines the specific context of the Philippines and its historical, economic and cultural realities, and shows how prostitution and sex tourism have flourished in that context.

4

Explanations for Prostitution
in the Philippines

Prostitution and sex tourism are not found only in the Philippines, but the Philippines is unique because of the country's strategic relationship to the United States during the Cold War. Because of the existence of Clark Air Base and Subic Naval Base, two of the United States largest overseas bases, it is not surprising that the Philippines saw a dramatic rise in military prostitution. Cynthia Enloe has argued that it was in the interests of the United States and Philippines to have women available and the globalized political economy allowed such an arrangement to flourish.[1] With the development of the massive bases came the need for rest and recreation for the troops; the result was the area surrounding Clark and Subic. Hundreds, if not thousands, of women worked in the bars and brothels during the bases' hey-day.

When the U.S. military pulled out of Angeles after the eruption of Mt. Pinatubo in 1991, the infrastructure of the base and the hundreds of bars set up for the servicemen remained. Angeles City developed economically because of the Americans, and so it is not surprising that military prostitution was quickly replaced by sex tourism. Australians and other Westerners bought up the bars by marrying Filipino women and putting the bars in their wives' names. Many American veterans chose to retire to Angeles, where they could live handsomely off their military pensions. Along Fields Avenue it is common to encounter aging white men in the company of scantily clad, much younger local women. Sex tourism is lucrative business, both for the city and for individual women. The once bustling landing strips are now used by the Filipino Air Force, and plans exist to develop Clark to ferry Korean, Japanese, Australian, American, German, and Canadian tourists to Angeles City. Angeles is a magnet for sex tourists and the site of a highly developed local prostitution industry of casas, karaoke bars, and freelancers. It is a place where we can easily see how Filipino women are not only exploited by local Filipino men but also marketed to foreigners both in the Philippines and abroad.

77

Looking at the Philippines, Thailand, Malaysia, and Indonesia, an ILO study states that the growth of prostitution in Southeast Asia has been so rapid that

> we can justifiably speak of a commercial sex sector that is integrated into the economic, social and political life of these countries. The sex business has assumed the dimensions of an industry and has directly or indirectly contributed in no small measure to employment, national income and economic growth.[2]

With continued economic restructuring due to global forces (as evident in the Asian economic crisis), the lack of employment opportunities (thus, the emergence of government policies and programs in the Philippines, like the Overseas Filipino Workers [OFW] and the Canadian Live-in Caregiver programs), the pressure to support rural households, the demand created by military prostitution historically and sex tourism more recently, and the prevalence of different types of prostitution activities from bars to brothels to massage parlors, the sex industry is expected to grow. Although it is difficult to determine exact numbers, it is estimated that between 300,000 and 500,000 women and children are in prostitution.[3] How did this come about? How did a country with reportedly no prostitution in pre-colonial times come to be the hub of prostitution and sex tourism in Southeast Asia today?[4]

In this chapter we explain why female prostitution in Angeles City, and the Philippines as a whole, is increasing and why it is so embedded in a local-foreign dimension. We will do this by focusing on three explanations: first, the unique historical and cultural context of the Philippines itself; second, the commodification of women's bodies under globalized capitalism; and third, the access to female prostitution necessary for militarized masculinity. These explanations stem from feminist critiques of the fields of international development studies and of international relations. By positing a gendered view both of development and of security, these critiques implicate both the global capitalist system and the state in the exploitation of women.

Dutiful Daughters and Virginal Wives

The history of the Philippines and the place of women within the Philippines is a fascinating case study of the influences of colonialism, religion, and globalization. Women in the Philippines today are seen as "moral guardians" and "suffering mothers," in large part because of Spanish colonization and the introduction of the Roman Catholic Church in the mid-sixteenth century.[5] Prior to colonization, women were accorded some measure of equality with men, could choose husbands freely, and held important positions within society. This, it is argued, all changed with the Spaniards who imposed their way of life, system of government, and Christianity. The effects were devastating to women. "For the baylan and catalonan—female ritual specialists of animist practice—the introduction of Christianity by male Spanish priests brought a more catastrophic loss of power and status. Such women had earned respect, authority, and their livelihood by conducting public ceremonies . . . treating the sick and dying, and attending women in childbirth. All these activities came under attack by friars."[6]

The friars also imposed their version of female morality on native Filipinos. This included the very important double standard of morality and the Madonna/whore symbolism of the Roman Catholic Church. "The Spanish also established a tradition of subordinating women, which is manifested in women's generally submissive attitudes and in a double standard of sexual conduct."[7] Filipino historians claim that the resulting cult of virginity did not exist before the Spanish. "Women could inherit property, manage farms, enjoy sexual freedom, choose their marriage partners (and) obtain divorce."[8] The rise of prostitution, according to this argument, happened after colonization when women began to be classified as to their prescribed conduct as "dutiful daughters," modest wives, and sacrificing mothers. If a woman did not subscribe to this conduct or if her virginity was lost outside the context of marriage, she became impure, fallen, "lewd or worthless."[9]

By the nineteenth century, prostitution was fully established in the Philippines and the three main types we see today existed in slightly modified forms: indoor or brothel prostitution; what we would now call escort service workers, where women went to men's homes or had them come to theirs; and streetwalkers.[10] The Spanish influence, therefore, in terms of the imposition of the Roman Catholic Church and the institutionalizing of a class-based, feudal, hierarchical, political, and economic system, was deep and long-lasting.[11] Its effects on women's position and status in society were particularly important in establishing that women would be judged according to very rigid standards of morality with clear delineations between "good" and "bad" girls. The effect of being a "bad" or "fallen" woman was *hiya* (shame or disgrace) and a sense of unworthiness that kept women in prostitution, "thinking that this is what they deserve."[12] This double standard of morality continues to this day, as we will see below.

While much of the above is undoubtedly true, the Spanish were neither the first nor the only traders, nor were they the only influence on the Philippines, which, until Spanish rule, existed as autonomous tribal lands and islands.[13] Prior to contact with Europeans, Filipinos had begun to trade and have relations with the Chinese, Indians, and Indonesians;

in fact, many Filipino customs, foods, expressions, superstitions, and myths come from India and China.[14] Helping to build those trading relations was the trading of women as part of treaties or deals, arranged marriages, second wives, and concubines.[15] Other customs derived from the Chinese still affecting Filipinos today include the strong tradition of "filial respect accorded by children to their older brothers and sisters, parents and elders."[16] So, while Spanish influence is crucial in order to understand the status of women in the Philippines, the pre-colonial traditions are important as well. Customs relating to the duty and devotion of daughters and wives do not reflect the influence of the Roman Catholic Church alone. Similar arguments are made about the status of women in Thailand, which has a strong Buddhist legacy. "Many Thai women, including very young women and those still legally girls, construct themselves as good and dutiful daughters, as hard workers whose sacrifice and generosity enable choices and chances for family members, though often in difficult or dreadful circumstances."[17] This has been confirmed through numerous studies in Thailand and the Philippines; there is a strong undercurrent of duty and obligation to family expected of women. "Studies of gender relations in Thai families regularly show that women and girls are expected to be responsible primarily for family rather than their own well-being. . . . Although work obligations can give Thai women a certain financial independence, they often send wages back to their family."[18] This, as we will see, is very common in the Philippines and is a major reason women give for working in the sex trade.

These "Asian" traditions are also thought responsible for the customs of multiple wives and ranking of wives in Thailand and the Philippines. Many men throughout Filipino history, both rich and poor, well known and not, have had so-called minor wives and second families. Though we have not found historical evidence for this as blatantly in the Philippines, in Thailand in the 1800s "the law classified a 'wife' in three categories: (1) a major wife, a woman who becomes the wife of a man through parental agreement; (2) a minor wife, a woman who becomes the wife of a man upon the request of the latter; and (3) a slave wife, a woman who is bought by a man to become his wife."[19] As important, therefore, as the Spanish influence and the Roman Catholic Church were in determining the status of women, there are a number of pre-colonial influences and traditions at play in the Philippines as well.

Accordingly, Mina Roces claims that "politics in the Philippines is not male-dominated but gendered: men exercise official power while women exercise unofficial power through their ties with male politicians—as wives, mothers, sisters, daughters and even mistresses of male politicians."[20] While this might sound like male domination to Western ears, Roces puts her statement in the context of the kinship group politics of the Philippines.

Because Filipino concepts see power as held by the kinship group, women—though marginalized in official political positions—can exercise power as members of the kinship group. Women as the support system in kinship politics (the dominant dynamic in Philippine politics where political power is used to benefit the kinship group) are active political agents. Women as wives and kin of male politicians who exercise power through their male relatives are the political norm.[21]

There have been two female presidents of the Philippines, both with powerful family connections. But while women now can hold power, it seems to remain true that the power wielded by women is still in the context of the family and not in the context of their power as individuals.

In terms of important influences on prostitution in the Philippines today we come back to the Roman Catholic Church. The Philippines remains a Catholic country and is strongly influenced by Catholic teachings. Although the country technically has separation of church and state, the Roman Catholic Church is very influential in determining policy with regard to prostitution. Sex outside of marriage is officially condemned, though many people acknowledge the double standard. Men are relatively free to pursue mistresses, prostitutes, and minor wives. This double standard is not subtle. "While the sale of sex helps to define women, it also condemns her; the purchase of sex also helps to define man but it does not condemn him."[22] She is a whore, with all that that signifies, whereas the man, in buying her sexual services, benefits by becoming a "macho man." In the Philippines the term used is *baptism*—which is the rite of passage for male teenagers, often brought to prostitutes by their fathers for their first sexual experience. He is no longer a virgin but a "real" man.[23]

So, in the Philippines the prostitute can be seen as either the enemy or, perhaps more evidently, the ally of marriage. She is either a sexually active woman who is seen as a threat to male control of women or a whore compared to the wife, who is "Madonna." In the latter case, the husband out of respect for his wife, the mother of his children, must turn to the prostitute for the fulfillment of his perhaps debased sexual needs. The question here, as the argument goes, is that when we think of the different sorts of acts that men desire, can they really do "that" to the mother of their children? Men in the Philippines, therefore, turn to prostitutes out of respect for their wives, as many of our Soroptimist partners informed us. "A lot of Filipino men tend to have two images of women: Madonna and whore, virgin and vamp, "good girl" to marry and "bad girl" to bed. This helps to explain why there is such a strong local demand from men of all social classes for prostitutes."[24] The Roman Catholic Church, of course, officially condemns adultery, but there is also wide acceptance of the adultery of men as opposed to that of women. Again, we wonder if it is the Asian tradition of plural wives being melded with the church's double standard of morality.

> There is also the question of different cultures' constructions of sex and sex work, which requires analysis of indigenous and colonial forms of prostitution and of contemporary local demand for paid sex, too. So some commentators remark on many Thai men's widely accepted use of prostitutes and debates rage over "Buddhalogical" explanations concerning gender roles, women's status, sex and Buddhist culture in Thailand.[25]

In terms of health and safety issues, prostitutes are also at a disadvantage in the Philippines because of its conservatism and moral judgments. Condom use for any purpose is immoral—whether it is being used for disease prevention or birth control—because of the church's position against contraception. Regardless of how helpful condoms are in the prevention of HIV/AIDS, the Catholic Church resists any attempts to link prevention to anything but abstinence. "The secretary of health under former President Fidel Ramos, now Senator Juan Flavier, was denounced as an agent of Satan by the former archbishop of Manila, Jaime Cardinal Sin, for pursuing a bold strategy of condom promotion in the 1990s."[26] This is not just an old-fashioned idea from the 1990s. At the 2002 General Assembly Special Session on HIV/AIDS, "the Holy See joined the United States, Iran, Libya, Pakistan and Sudan in endorsing sexual abstinence 'both before and during marriage' as the only way to prevent HIV."[27] In May 2003 the Catholic Bishops Conference of the Philippines "issued a pastoral letter opposing the enactment of reproductive health legislation to be read at every Sunday mass in the country."[28] It is not difficult, therefore, to see that the Philippines is a highly conservative country in many regards and that its conservatism, particularly in reference to women, is backed up by the ideas of the religious elite.

The impact of religion has also manifested itself politically in the Philippines and was a factor in our project. The fifteen-year battle against Ferdinand Marcos was led to a great extent by the so-called militant nuns. Roces argues that militant nuns of the martial law era (1972–86) were able to challenge the cultural constructions of femininity and kinship politics through their "moral power."[29] The nuns became radicalized because of their work within the national liberation movement and became feminists because of their marginalization within the Catholic Church. The nuns were instrumental in forming many important women's groups, including GABRIELA, PILIPINA, and TWMAEW. They also created the first women's studies courses and programs in the Philippines. These courses examined the "patriarchal elements of Filipino

society, where males are privileged and spoiled and women seek to become self-sacrificing mothers, morally bound to the home."[30]

Politics and religion, therefore, are inextricably bound together in
the Philippines. This is another reason that groups dealing with prostitution in the Philippines tend to be religious based. Roces claims that
the nuns were effective because they acted as a pressure group and exercised power unofficially:

> Though they were inspired by modern ideas and demanded full
> equality and empowerment for women they did so in the tradi-
> tional way women exercised power. . . . [They] . . . were only be-
> ginning to challenge the cultural construction of the feminine,
> particularly the image of Maria Clara (submissive, vapid, demure,
> timid woman made "ideal" through the character of Jose Rizal's
> novel).[31]

Interestingly, this Maria Clara image, which our radical feminist group
was trying consciously to dispel, is still an important image of women's
power and is difficult to dislodge. Roces writes: "Women radicals (apart
from the nuns) shunned kinship politics, closing the door to power behind the scenes. Compelled to compete in a male-dominated environment where male rules prevailed, these women radicals failed to claim
leadership roles and were pushed aside as auxiliaries in the struggle for
national liberation."[32] We also felt this way about the lack of influence of
our radical feminist group within the Angeles community. Its members
were not considered feminine enough or willing to wield power in a
"backdoor," manipulative way, but, in rejecting their power as Filipino
women they had less influence in the community than did our more
traditional partners. "They exuded . . . modern images of women as militant (*mataray*—tough and militant, not sweet and placid) and feminist."[33]
This may have worked for the nuns, but it did not work for our feminist
partners because they did not have legitimacy in the local community.

The second major historical influence on the Philippines after Spanish colonization was, of course, the Americans. After the Spanish-American War and the Treaty of Paris in 1898, the Philippines was ceded to
the United States and a new influence became important to the status of
women. On the one hand, the Americans provided a democratic system
of government, increased standard of living, education, the right to vote
and employment for women. On the other, they began to institutionalize the very centers we know today as social-hygiene clinics for prostitutes so that the American servicemen would not be infected with sexually
transmitted diseases.[34] The Americans ruled the Philippines until after
World War II, but the colonial relationship continued well into the 1990s
because of the Philippines' strategic relationship and importance to the

United States during the Cold War. As we will elaborate below, the most important factor in the development of a prostitution industry was the creation of the two American bases on Filipino soil: the Subic Naval Base in Olongapo, and the Clark Air Base in Angeles. These bases were the largest American bases outside the continental United States, and more than forty thousand servicemen and their families lived at the bases at any given time. As Cynthia Enloe has vividly chronicled, alongside the development of the massive bases came the need for rest and recreation for the troops. The result was the area literally surrounding the bases: around the perimeter fences were located almost fifteen hundred businesses devoted to the sex trade—bars, brothels, strip clubs, and karaokes—all for the foreigners. With thousands of military men stationed at both bases, the areas became magnets for local Filipino women looking for work and/or a foreign husband, and the bases were the impetus for the growth of an entire sex-service industry surrounding both bases.

While the historical, cultural, and religious aspects of the Philippines itself are crucially important to understanding the status of women in prostitution, as is militarized masculinity, which will be explored in the third section, globalization is another macro-level factor influencing the choices of the women who have little options outside factory work or the entertainment industry. Clark Air Base has been converted into a special economic zone where foreign industries and multinationals can set up businesses at good tax rates and ignore the laws against foreign-owned business in the Philippines. Many of the women we met in the entertainment industry were either promised jobs in these factories or see them as their way out of poverty. We explore this connection below.

Globalized Capitalism

The Philippines is a relatively poor country. Often referred to as the "poor man of Asia" due to its economic position relative to the Asian boom of the last decades, the country gained its independence from Spain in 1898 only to be colonized by the United States until it was "granted" its freedom after World War II in 1946. Considered in the tier of countries with "medium human development" according to the United Nations Human Development Index (HDI), poverty remains an overwhelming reality for the vast majority of Filipinos. Reflective of the unequal distribution of wealth, the distorted or uneven development of the Philippines has meant that while a small segment of the society pursues a lifestyle similar to the Western world, large segments of the population are hungry and diseased, live in substandard housing with little or no access to clean water, and have few opportunities to acquire an education or find adequate, if any, employment. Encouraged by their own government to work abroad, overseas Filipino workers are one of the country's primary exports, accounting for a large percentage of the foreign currency coming into the Philippines as workers send money home to their families. Such work is profoundly gendered: men temporarily migrate to become construction workers, and women temporarily migrate to become domestics and "entertainers." For those who stay, their living can easily become dependent on foreigners. For those benefiting from prostitution, the commodification of women's bodies has taken on a global dimension.

Local Filipinas cater to foreign men, selling their bodies in bars along and near Fields Avenue to a male clientele whose economic, cultural, social, and sexual experiences are far removed from theirs. Why does this go on? Why is the prostitution context in Angeles City, and the Philippines as a whole, so embedded in a local-foreign dimension? Joane Nagel uses the term "ethnosexual constructions" to get at "the role of sexuality in the construction of ethnicity" and, in turn, how "race, ethnicity and nationalism shape sexual boundaries and meanings."[35] Nagel compels us to think more systematically about the "sexed" nature of (largely ethnically or racially based) territorial boundaries and the extent to which hierarchies of power are embedded in these ethnosexual constructions. The North is seen to be populated by whites and the South by people of color. The economic dominance of the countries of the North has ensured that its nationals, when traveling abroad in the South, are not merely foreigners, but rich foreigners. This means that the "holy trinity" of feminist thinking—gender, race, and class—is so intertwined in explaining female prostitution in the Philippines that the life stories of the bar girls, who we will meet in Chapter 5, speak for countless others caught up in economic, political, and cultural forces that fundamentally exploit them.

The Philippines is a prime example of inequitable development. It does not face the sorts of developmental challenges evident in so many countries in sub-Saharan Africa, and, as any visitor or tourist to Manila or Cebu can attest, the country has first-class hotels, mega-malls, and areas of affluence that resemble a Western setting. According to the cia.org website, with an estimated population of over ninety-one million, the Philippines ranked 131 in terms of gross national income per capita in 2006, calculated in terms of purchasing power parity in international dollars (the purchasing power parity of the United States is almost nine times larger than that of the Philippines). But this does not capture the differences in income among Filipinos. While a small minority of Filipinos pursue a lifestyle similar to that of the average person in the United States, a vast majority lives in substandard, if not squalid, conditions, both in the cities and in the provincial or outlying areas.

Although impoverished conditions are found in every country, a huge number of people in the Philippines, as in many parts of Africa, Asia, and Latin America, are faced with very little opportunity to escape poverty. On the one hand, the sorts of social-welfare and income-maintenance programs found in Western countries, as well as in newly industrialized countries like Taiwan, South Korea, Singapore, and Malaysia, are virtually nonexistent in the Philippines. On the other hand, the kinds of economic opportunities necessary to build a vibrant and large middle class have not become part of the Filipino landscape. As Benedict Anderson tells us, this can be attributed to the kind of "cacique democracy" that exists in the Philippines, where a national oligarchy of *mestizo* families, descended from Spanish colonial times, has controlled the country, and in post-Marcos times (with former president Ferdinand Marcos being labeled by Anderson as the "supreme cacique") has reasserted its power, thus propagating corrupt practices, institutionalizing nepotism and preventing any real land and corporate reform. Anderson argues that despite the "people power revolution" that ousted Marcos in 1986, the oligarchs were able to reclaim power by winning national and local elections, putting old dominant families back in Congress, provincial governorships, and mayoralties. But the process is important because the veneer of democracy is maintained. As Anderson puts it:

> American electoralism . . . married to Spanish caciquism in a geographically fragmented, ethnolinguistically divided and economically bankrupt polity . . . disperses power horizontally, while concentrating it vertically; and the former draws a partial veil over the latter. "Anyone" can get elected: look at the high, uncoerced turnout; look at the number of competing candidates (you too can run). . . . Precisely because the competition is violently real, it is easy to be persuaded to cheer for, as it were, Arsenal or Chelsea, without reflecting too hard on the fact that both are in the First Division, and that one is watching the match from the outer stands, not playing in it.[36]

With the old dominant families continuing to win office, and therefore controlling the coffers of government, corruption and graft remain. At the same time, corruption was the reason that a second people power revolution ousted former President Joseph Estrada in 2001, and why calls for President Gloria Macapagal-Arroyo to resign are gaining support. This illustrates that, despite an apparent popular will, cacique democracy continues in the Philippines.

According to Anderson, there was a missed opportunity in the 1960s when a large educated class of individuals—who had benefited from the huge expansion of English-language education in the post–World War II

Philippines—stood to challenge the power of the oligarchs. These individuals—doctors, nurses, teachers, civil servants, business people—demanded political and economic reforms, but they were enticed away by immigration policy changes of the United States which eliminated (racial) quotas. Educated in English and skilled in professions deemed desirable by Americans, over a million Filipinos immigrated, eventually bringing their families and permanently settling in the United States.[37] Yet, many of these Filipinos abroad supported extended families at "home" and returned to the Philippines to visit; it was their tourist dollars that sparked the Marcos regime's interest in overseas Filipinos, coining the term *balikbayan*, which joins the Tagalog words *balik* (to return) and *bayan* (home).[38]

By the 1980s, however, permanent emigrants were not the only overseas Filipinos. According to Philip McMichael, the globalization project became ascendant in the 1980s. Coming from the success of export-oriented industrialization undertaken by the newly industrialized countries, the globalization project was predicated on the importance of the market economy as the driver for development and the necessity of each state to find its comparative advantage in the global economy. Economic restructuring took place as governments privatized industries, cut wages, reduced social entitlements, and made concessions to attract foreign investment.[39] According to James Tyner, the Philippine government changed its labor codes in order to make the country's workforce attractive, but by reducing wages and preventing unionization, the government in effect created greater incentives for workers to seek employment abroad.

> The restructuring of the Philippine economy toward commercial agriculture and export-oriented industrialization radically altered domestic labour market conditions and relations. Denied access to traditional economic forms of subsistence production, yet more fully incorporated into the waged labour force, many Filipinos found employment opportunities unavailable, or untenable due to low wages.[40]

In essence, the Philippine comparative advantage became its workforce abroad. Encouraged and sanctioned by the government, overseas contract workers began filling the demands for skilled and semi-skilled labor throughout the Middle East, Asia, and Western Europe. Often underemployed—for example, female teachers becoming domestic help or male engineers becoming construction workers—these overseas Filipinos became the "new heroes" of the Philippine society because their foreign remittances became a major part of the Philippine economy, even cushioning it from the devastating effects of the Asian economic crisis in the 1990s.

The experiences of overseas contract workers have highlighted the costs of globalization. As captured in the 1997 documentary *Modern Heroes, Modern Slaves,* overseas contract workers must deal not simply with the hardships of being separated from their families but also often with exploitative working conditions. Becoming more and more of a female workforce, many overseas contract workers are abused by their foreign employers while receiving little assistance from their government abroad. The film opens with the case of Flor Contemplacion, a Filipina maid who was executed in Singapore in 1995 for confessing to the double murder of another Filipina maid, Delia Maga, and the four-year-old son of Maga's employer. With Filipinos overwhelmingly seeing the case as one of Singapore's injustice and Manila's weakness, Contemplacion has since become a national symbol for the plight of overseas contract workers; the date of her death, March 17, is remembered by Migrante International, a global alliance of overseas Filipino organizations established in 1996. The plight of Filipino migrant workers is part of what Saskia Sassen calls the "excesses of globalisation" and the "feminisation of survival." Sassen asserts that the effects of globalization, such as increasing unemployment, the rise of export-oriented cash crops, and rising government debt in many third-world states, like the Philippines, have led to costly "alternative" strategies for many, primarily women, in the developing world to make a living and support their families:

> Prostitution and labour migration are growing in importance as ways of making a living; illegal trafficking in women and children for the sex industry and in labourers is growing in importance as ways of making a profit; and the remittances sent by emigrants, as well as the organised export of workers are increasingly important sources of revenue for some of these governments. Women are by far the majority group in prostitution and in trafficking for the sex industry, and they are becoming a majority group in migration for labour. These are all economies of excess.[41]

For Sassen, these economies of excess and exploitation are constitutive of globalization. Nancy Wonders and Raymond Michalowski make more specific connections, pointing out that globalization has brought about "the worldwide movement of bodies across borders," most significantly in the form of migration and tourism. Increasing international migration, whether through legal or illegal means, has led to greater mobility of Filipinas, many of whom are in the entertainment or prostitution industries. Found throughout Japan, Western Europe, and some parts of North America, Filipinas (like Thais, Cambodians, Indonesians, and others) have been trafficked primarily for the purpose of sexual exploitation. In many cases transnational criminal organizations, like the Japanese yakuza, play a prominent role in procuring local women and moving them across borders. However, mobility is not confined to the women. Through increasing international tourism, men are also on the move, traveling to various destinations for sex. Why do local Filipinas sell their bodies to foreign men? They do so because they are part of a globalized sex industry that, according to Wonders and Michalowski, has been affected by the contemporary shift from expanding production to expanding consumption to fuel growth. "Globalized capitalism demands the continual development of new commodity forms. The consequence is that many elements of social life that once remained outside the realm of commodity exchange must now be commodified in order to create new markets and to protect or expand profits."[42]

Women's bodies, then, become simply another commodity to be used, bought, and trafficked. Conceptualizing the commodification of young Filipinas helps us to understand not merely the motivations of foreign men who are engaged in sex tourism in the Philippines, but also, and more important, to pinpoint the problem of globalized capitalism encouraging women to sell their bodies in order to make a living. The gendered, racialized nature of sex tourism highlights the (white) male sexual desire for an erotic, exotic other who will embody difference for the men and fulfill their search for adventure. Moreover, many foreign men are able to engage in this type of sexual adventure, once available only to the wealthy, because of their economic privilege relative to local circumstances. With cheaper airfares, low-cost accommodations, and the strength of hard currencies, like the yen, the dollar, and the euro, even working-class or lower-middle-class men are able to afford what so many countries like the Philippines have to sell.

And, like Thailand, Cambodia, Vietnam, Brazil, Colombia, Costa Rica, and Cuba, what the Philippines has to sell are its women. The gendered, racialized nature of sex tourism means that "women themselves are viewed as a tourist destination. Sex and bodies are viewed as commodities that can be packaged, advertised, displayed and sold on a global scale."[43] Aided by the explosion of the Internet, tour operators and bar owners are able to display their "goods" globally. What initially was advertised only in tourism brochures can now be downloaded instantaneously. Whereas tourism material may have been more subtle in the selling of Filipinas, such as one that featured the Filipina Miss Universe with the caption "There's more where she comes from," any web-surfer today can have his pick of explicit sexual material, drawing him to well-known sex tourist destinations, like Angeles City, with pictures of topless or nude Filipina women, likely in a bar setting. The balibago.com website offers this introduction to Balibago, the barangay (or neighborhood) that houses Fields Avenue: "Balibago is a nonstop, drunken revel seven days a week, everyday of the year. Recreational sex is the sport of choice. You can enjoy full privileges with one or more attractive young females regardless of your age, weight, physical appearance, interpersonal skills, wealth or social class."

The packaging of Filipinas as exotic and erotic, submissive and shy, catering and carnal, may draw men's attention, but it is price that allows them to travel and experience their sexual fantasies firsthand. The point is that while selling sex itself may not be inherently problematic, the very conditions of globalized capitalism have left Filipina women with little or no choice but to sell themselves, giving, to put it crudely, "more bang for the buck" to foreign men.

Militarized Masculinity

The ethnosexual liaisons between local women and foreign men in the Philippines, however, have a specific historical context. As recognized widely by scholars, the sex tourism of today is grounded in the military prostitution of yesterday. Once a colony of the United States, the Philippines was, and remains, an American strategic asset. Acquired in 1898 after the Spanish-American War, the Philippines represented a Pacific outpost for U.S. interests that made it imperative to end Japanese occupation during World War II. During the Cold War the Philippines was central to the forward-basing network of the United States to contain Soviet military expansionism. The two largest American overseas military installations were Subic Bay Naval Base and Clark Air Base, both outside of Manila in the province of Luzon. Composed of approximately fifty-eight square miles of land and over forty-two square miles of water area, Subic was the operational home of the U.S. Seventh Fleet, a carrier battle group. Even larger in terms of landmass, Clark was composed of nearly 212 square miles and was the headquarters of the 13th Air Force. In total, the two bases, along with other U.S. military outposts such as the San Miguel Naval Communications Station, Wallace Air Station, and John Hay Rest and Recreation Center, were home to twenty thousand American military and civilian personnel, at least ten thousand Seventh Fleet sailors and marines at any given point, and twenty-five thousand dependents. Encircling the bases was a Filipino infrastructure as well, including not only workers who were employed by the base (at least seventy thousand at any given time), but also retail stores, convenience stores, restaurants, and, of course, bars, massage parlors, and other sorts of entertainment establishments. Olongapo City developed around the Subic Bay Naval Base and Angeles City developed around Clark Air Force Base.

The significant U.S. military presence was precipitated by the first Military Bases Agreement (MBA) between Washington and Manila. Signed within a year after the American Congress granted formal independence to the Philippines on July 4, 1946, the 1947 agreement allowed the United States rent-free use of the bases for a period of ninety-nine years. This was renegotiated in 1966, reducing the period of use to twenty-five years with subsequent rent payments to be made by the Americans. Although the United States and the Philippines have had a unique, historical, "special" relationship, nationalist sentiment has always been evident, with the U.S. bases seen as the most blatant example of foreign intervention in the country, in effect institutionalizing the neo-colonial relationship between the two countries. After all, it was not until 1979 that the bases were finally recognized as Philippine sovereign territory. Particularly after the assassination of former Senator Benigno Aquino in 1983, when the United States continued to face the dilemma of supporting an increasingly unpopular dictator in order to protect American longstanding strategic interests, more moderate nationalists (including, at the time, Corazon Aquino) joined with communists and rebels in demanding the removal of foreign bases.[44] With the bases seen by communists as symbols of American imperialism and perceived by nationalists as compromising Philippine sovereignty, the anti-bases movement gained strength during the latter years of the Marcos regime because it became part of the larger anti-Marcos sentiment.

Moreover, because Philippine feminists had placed prostitution on the agenda of the bases' issue, "militarized prostitution [had become] the most prominent symbol of compromised sovereignty by the male-led nationalist movement."[45] As Philippine feminists continued to document the abuses of women (and children and men) at the hands of U.S. servicemen stationed in the Philippines, the image of the Philippine prostitute in Olongapo or Angeles became part of the rallying cry of nationalists to expel the Americans. Even former President Marcos did not pass up the chance to exploit this kind of growing opposition to the bases: during the 1984 negotiations the former dictator opportunistically "included the social effects of the bases [because he] wanted the U.S. to pay for the 'social costs' of the tens of thousands of prostitutes and the growing number of Filipino drug addicts in the regions around the bases."[46] The social costs of the bases were very real and very visible: bars, discos, and massage parlors with an estimated fifty thousand to fifty-five thousand registered and unregistered "hospitality girls" encircling both Subic and Clark had become part of the Philippine landscape.[47]

At the same time, the presence of U.S. servicemen in the Philippines goes well beyond the issue of national sovereignty. Cynthia Enloe points out that foreign military bases are not uncommon, and the United States is certainly not alone in stationing its troops abroad. She questions, however, why military *prostitution* around U.S. bases has been such a politically charged issue in third-world states, like the Philippines, but largely irrelevant in developed states, like Great Britain, especially since American military *facilities* were objects of controversy in both. Was it because prostitution did not exist around U.S. bases in Great Britain? Or was it because British women had so many economic alternatives that they were not compelled to work in bars or massage parlors? Or was it because, as Enloe states, "Western peace activists have assumed that security and sovereignty are their most serious grounds for anti-bases campaigns and so haven't looked closely to see whether, in reality, sexual politics defines the role that those bases play in their communities as much as weapons politics."[48] In other words, Enloe contends that the framing of the issue of the bases around military prostitution, as in the Philippines, was closer to defining the impact of foreign bases than seeing the issue as merely one of national sovereignty.

Enloe's analysis goes further in making the connection between overseas military bases and the local sex trade industry. Highlighting the links between the personal and the international (by adapting the slogan of radical feminists—The personal is political—to the international context), Enloe asserts that international politics and the conduct of foreign policy have depended on "certain kinds of allegedly private relationships,"[49] such as those between American soldiers serving abroad and local women becoming prostitutes. According to Enloe, military personnel not only have needed affirmation of their manliness so necessary in soldiering, but have also required sexualized "rest and recreation" after having to fight (or preparing to fight) for their country. This is also argued by Spike Peterson and Anne Runyan, Peter Beckman and Francine D'Amico, and Ann Tickner in regard to the linkages among militarism, sexism, and racism. In other words, the sustenance of a state's military force is in part dependent on the availability and convenience of sexual services for its soldiers. Nowhere is this more evident than in the gender relations that underpin a foreign military base.[50]

However, as Enloe also points out: "Militarized, masculinised sexual desire, by itself, isn't sufficient to sustain a full-fledged prostitution industry. It requires (depends on) rural poverty, male entrepreneurship, urban commercialized demand, police protection and overlapping governmental economic interest to ensure its success.[51] The domestic context is therefore central to understanding the sex-trade industry in developing states like the Philippines, just as in developed ones.

Feminist groups in the Philippines understood the connection. When the Legislative-Executive Bases Council, established by the Aquino government in early 1990, was asked to put forward a comprehensive conversion plan for the affected communities after U.S. withdrawal, it asked

WEDPRO to report on the alternative employment, economic livelihood, and development needs of women in the entertainment industry.
WEDPRO's survey of women in Angeles and Olongapo Cities and its
subsequent report, *From Carriers to Communities*, assert that not only
was the issue of the bases a matter that went beyond national sovereignty, but also that the entrance of women into prostitution was not
simply a matter of poverty in the Philippines. WEDPRO asserts: "Prostitution would have remained unknown for thousands of girls and young
women in poverty circumstances in the country had the demands of the
military for their bodies, overlaid by the assumption of many in society
that this is a *legitimate demand*, not brought them to Angeles or
Olongapo."[52]

The sex-trade industry around the bases was essentially condoned by
both Filipino and American authorities. Although prostitution and other
related activities are illegal under Article 202 of the Philippine Penal
Code, prostitutes were (and are) regulated with weekly health checks for
sexually transmitted diseases at government-run social-hygiene clinics
in Olongapo and Angeles City. The U.S. military provided medicine
and medical supplies to the clinics and undertook regular inspections to
ensure that the clinics met American standards. Once the women were
checked, they were issued permits allowing them to work as "entertainers" or "hospitality girls" in bars, discos, massage parlors, and other "entertainment" establishments. The male clientele, however, did not
undergo checkups, although they were often the sources or carriers of
disease.[53] Similarly, freelancers or streetwalkers who did not register with
a clinic faced arrest on vagrancy charges, although the men soliciting
them were never arrested. There was, in essence, a perceived male right
to sexual servicing facilitated, if not encouraged, by the U.S. and Philippine governments.

The anti-bases movement became more formidable after the ousting
of Marcos. With the ascendance of Corazon Aquino as president in 1986
and the passage of a new constitution in 1987, decisions about foreign
(read: U.S.) bases on Filipino soil would no longer be solely under executive control. According to the new Filipino constitution: "Foreign
military bases, troops, or facilities shall not be allowed in the Republic of
the Philippines following the expiry, in 1991, of the Agreement between
the Republic and the USA; except under provisions of a treaty approved
by the Senate, and, when required by Congress, ratified by the voters in
a national referendum." Although the Philippine and American governments had reached tentative agreement on a new military base treaty
that included a new ten-year lease on Subic and a withdrawal from Clark
(the air base was severely damaged by the eruption of Mt. Pinatubo),
with the Aquino government campaigning heavily for support of the
new agreement, the Philippine Senate rejected the agreement by a vote

of twelve to eleven in September 1991. However, by then the dramatic change in the strategic environment caused by the disintegration of the Soviet Union along with the eruption of Mt. Pinatubo had set the stage for American reassessment of its vital interests in the Philippines. By the end of November 1991 the United States had completely withdrawn its forces from the Philippines, leaving behind assets worth more than $1.3 billion, including a ship-repair facility, airport, housing, and other infrastructure. The Philippine government established development authorities to convert the foreign military bases for civilian commercial use, with the latest project being the construction of an expressway between what have become the Clark Special Economic Zone and the Subic Bay Freeport Zone.

By the time the American bases had closed, however, the sex-trade industry had been firmly established. Although there appeared to be a temporary hiatus in the number of bars and other sex establishments, particularly in Angeles in the aftermath of the eruption of Mt. Pinatubo, the *globalized* sex industry, as discussed earlier, continues to flourish. Sex tourism has taken the place of military prostitution in the Philippines— but not completely. In 1999 the Philippine Senate ratified the Visiting Forces Agreement (VFA) between the United States and the Philippines, which, through joint military exercises with the Philippine military, has allowed the American military to resume training in the country. Moreover, since 9/11 the Philippine government has become one of the staunchest allies of the Bush administration in the U.S. war against terrorism, even explicitly targeting Abu Sayyaf rebels in southern Philippines as part of joint military operations. Knowing that the entertainment/ sex industry would be frequented by visiting troops seeking "rest and recreation," many feminist and human rights groups opposed the VFA and continued to protest the American military presence. Why, then, do local Filipinas sell their bodies to foreign (military) men? As Enloe succinctly argues:

> Without a sexualized "rest and recreation" (R&R) period, would the U.S. military command be able to send young men off on long, often tedious sea voyages and ground maneuvers? Without myths of Asian women's compliant sexuality would many American men be able to sustain their own identities of themselves manly enough to act as soldiers? Women ... who work as prostitutes around American bases in Asia tell us how a militarized masculinity is constructed and reconstructed in smoky bars and in sparsely furnished boarding houses.[54]

Complicit in the construction of militarized masculinity is not only the American government but the Philippine government as well. The connection between military prostitution and sex tourism in East Asia is particularly pronounced. Given the prominence of American overseas bases in East Asia historically—Thailand (which closed in 1975 after the Vietnam War), the Philippines (which closed in 1991), South Korea, and Japan—observers are not surprised by the growth of sex tourism in the region. Indeed, despite the closure of bases in the Philippines, many patrons of bars and establishments in Angeles City are former or retired U.S. servicemen who perhaps are not sex tourists per se but are a crucial part of the male clientele. Not only do they help to support the bars, but their foreignness also helps to make those who are coming for a short-term visit—the "real" sex tourists—more comfortable in the area. The point is that they are all foreign men, and what they have in common is the ability (and desire) to buy sex from local women.

Prostitution and sex tourism are big business in the Philippines, and many people benefit: the local and national governments, bar owners, citizens, male customers, and even the bar girls themselves, to some extent. The factors that make the Philippines vulnerable to sex tourism are varied and complex, macro and micro, internal and external to the country itself. The Philippines is a poor country and vulnerable to rich Western countries' capital and rich foreigners, but the indigenous prostitution industry that supports and makes possible the massive sex-tourism industry is problematic as well. Globalization, colonialism, and racism may have been externally imposed, but the internal problems of sexism, classism, lack of separation of church and state, and Filipino cultural traditions also have to be addressed in order to do something about such a gendered and exploitative problem. The next chapter describes the particular situation of the bar girls and their customers in Angeles City using the words of the women and men themselves.

5

Sex Tourism in Angeles City

From the perspective of any conventional map, Angeles City, found in the largest island of Luzon in the Philippines, would be a relatively small place, one easily overshadowed by the metropolitan city of Manila, sixty miles away. Nestled in the province of Pampanga, the city is divided into thirty-three barangays (local districts) and boasts a population of a few hundred thousand. Yet, from the viewpoint of a seasoned surfer of TSM (Travel and the Single Male), an electronic travel agency, or perhaps that of a veteran of the U.S. Air Force who has served his country abroad, particularly in America's largest overseas bases in Asia, Angeles City would be well known. This is the place where male sexual fantasies can come true; where (foreign) men seek out and indulge in (local) women; where prostitution, despite the local Filipino male clientele, is a product of global forces; and where sex tourism and military prostitution have resulted in easily accessible, incredibly cheap bodies of young Filipinas for any man with hard currency.

Sex tourism is nothing new in Angeles City. Stepping into any bar along Fields Avenue, one readily encounters foreign men in the company of scantily clothed, much younger local women. Yet, the prostitution scene in Angeles City is actually a result of the large American military presence historically. The connections to militarism continue, not only because the U.S. military presence is once again becoming more prominent in the post-9/11 context, in which one of the fronts in the war on terrorism is the Philippines, but also because many American veterans have chosen to retire in Angeles City. Military prostitution and sex tourism are inextricably linked with global capitalism and globalization. However, although the exploitative context of prostitution is readily obvious in Angeles City, women in the sex trade are not simply powerless victims of global patriarchy and international capitalism.

The swiftness of the American decision to close its bases in the Philippines with the end of the Cold War, also precipitated by American federal budget concerns, the eruption of Mt. Pinatubo, which devastated both Clark Air Base and Subic Naval Base, and the decision by the

Philippine Senate not to ratify the Military Bases Agreement with the United States was remarkable. "Just like that, the Americans were gone," stated one of our partners. They left behind not only scores of buildings and miles of airfield but also thousand of women in the sex trade. Angeles City has a long history of military prostitution and sex trafficking. However, unlike Olongapo (the site of the former Subic Naval Base), Angeles City has continued to be plagued by the problems of prostitution even after the Americans closed their bases in the Philippines in 1991. Whereas bar owners in Olongapo were given opportunities to buy into the Subic Bay Metropolitan Authority and essentially to get out of the prostitution business, the infrastructure has remained in Angeles City.

Although the American military has gone, nothing has really changed in terms of the sex trade except for the fact that the situation of the women has gotten worse; for example, they no longer have access to health care formerly provided by the Americans. U.S. military prostitution was an extremely complex phenomenon in the Philippines, and like its predecessor, sex tourism is a complex global phenomenon. This chapter looks at the interconnections among race, class, and sex oppression faced by the bar girls; the belief of Western men that Asian women are more compliant and submissive and therefore more desirable than liberated Western women, a (racist) belief that also sustains sex tourism; the economic power of the U.S. service men and foreign sex tourists and the poverty of prostitutes (classism); and the buying of women's bodies for sexual and other, usually domestic, services (sexism). The departure of the Americans was never perceived as a panacea for the ills of prostitution in the Philippines, and, in fact, many in Angeles did not want them to leave. At least, stated a health official in the social-hygiene clinic of Angeles, the American military supplied medicine and medical supplies and undertook regular inspections of the clinic and the bars. At least, stated Perla, one of our partners, the women had options, as it was not uncommon for new American recruits, fresh out of training, to be "snagged" by much older Filipinas who knew that marrying a U.S. serviceman was a way out of both prostitution and the Philippines.

> **Perla** (WEDPRO): [When the Americans ran things] women were already thirty or already forty years old. Now, is different. All young, they need young. So, that's why I a mamasan cause I got too old. It's different than before, even though they have a lot of Americans here. I already old when I start. I was thirty-three years old when I was working. I was already old, not twenty-three years old. . . . So, it's different now.

Because there is no "prostitution" in the Philippines (because of its illegality), there are a number of euphemisms for prostitutes: bar girls, hospitality workers, or guest relations' officers. The girls do not have johns; they have boyfriends. There are no madams but lots of mamasans (female bar managers). The girls do not go on tricks; they are bar fined. Bar fining is the mechanism for prostitution in Angeles. Men pay a bar fine to the mamasan so that they can take the girl out—for fifteen minutes or for the whole night—as a kind of rental to compensate the bar for her time. Many girls get bar fined for weeks at a time, serving as escorts, girlfriends, translators, companions, and sex partners for the men traveling around the Philippines. The bar fines are usually one thousand pesos or twenty U.S. dollars, and the girls get half. The bar owner takes 450 pesos, and the mamasan gets 50. This is a tremendous amount of money in a country where the average wage is 150 pesos a day and unemployment is very high. In relation to prostitutes who cater to local Filipino men, this wage is unimaginable.

As mentioned in Chapter 3, there are basically three types of sex workers in the Philippines. At the top of the hierarchy of prostitution are the self-employed "call girls" or escort workers who cater to upper-class Filipinos and wealthy businessmen in Manila. Unregistered streetwalkers or freelancers are also in this category, but their legal existence is much more precarious than the call girls or registered bar girls. They are usually controlled by pimps (for protection from police and for soliciting of clients) and more vulnerable to arrests on vagrancy charges. The city government is trying to get these women to register and have weekly health checks, as do the registered bar girls, but with no protection from the law, this places the women in a completely untenable position. (The registered bar girls are not arrested because they have registration cards and work out of the bars. Freelancers are not registered and, even if they were, their work is illegal and therefore they could be arrested, either for vagrancy or prostitution).

From what we could determine, the second category of prostitutes, the women in the bars, live in the most favorable conditions (except for the higher-end call girls). They are registered as "entertainers" and have weekly pap smears at the social hygiene clinic—another remnant of the Americans and their attempts to keep their servicemen clean. Hospitality workers are afforded some official protection from the laws against prostitution because of their registered status. But the law itself is highly discriminatory: the crime of prostitution is gendered since only women can be criminalized as prostitutes. The male customers are not registered, regulated, or criminalized in any way.

The third group—the casa workers—are the worst situated of them all. They are kept as virtual prisoners in small rooms in the backs of karaokes, truck stops and patio bars, accessible only by guards and owners. They make 300 pesos (US$6) for two weeks' work servicing 5–15 customers a night. Many of the women we have met in the casas have been trafficked from rural areas, think they are going to factory work in Clark Economic Zone, and then are kept as sex slaves; until they are (sometimes) rescued by the police carrying out periodic raids. To give an indication of the levels or degrees of exploitation, one of the young women rescued from a casa told us her dream was to become a bar girl on Fields. The conditions of the casas are truly shocking.

> **Davida** (PNP): Prostitution in the casas, you know casas are residences in Angeles, these are residence of some people who keep their sex trade within their resident houses, and if you visit this place you can see girls inside their houses and with them are girls, some were forced from other provinces. So, that is illegal, you know that, unlike in the Fields Avenue, those working girls are registered. They have working permits, but in the casa, the owner of the place has no permit because that is residential houses, and the workers are not registered.

> **Maria** (Soroptimists): These casas are houses that are built like, you know, they have cubicles, well, rooms, small rooms that each girl is assigned. Now, these are catering mostly to Filipinos and I would even say that they really cater even to the lowest, you know, to the lowest income Filipino male customers. The reason why I said the lowest was because we were told they are only paying around 50 pesos. And the girls are made to work ten to fifteen times a day, if you can just imagine. You know the last time we were there, I was so depressed because when I saw them eating, I said, my god, you know, looking at them eating that way. How the animals eat, you know, they had no tables and nothing, you could see their plates, you know. That's why I, in fact, in the Lions' meeting the other night I was telling them about our project, you know, and then I was so emotional, that I said "my god, if you could have seen them," and I was talking in front of about 15 gentlemen. I said you should have seen how they're being treated. So, it was terrible, really.

Although we have met groups of casa workers who have been rescued by the police, we have only been able to get to know some of the registered bar girls, because of their greater mobility and because of their access to the social hygiene clinic where our project office was located. We recognize that there are also "higher-class" prostitutes working exclusively for rich Filipinos who experience much more freedom and choice than did the women we dealt with but we had no contact with them, as well as Eastern European women brought into the Philippines for the wealthy. We heard numerous reports of ship prostitution, where women are brought on board ships anchored in Manila Bay but we did not meet any of these women either.[1] We are also not dealing with the "exported," those who are trafficked abroad.

We concentrate here on the stories of a particular sub-group of prostitutes in the Philippines: the registered bar girls working in Angeles. We profile several women below and show how their stories illustrate the different factors involved in sex tourism in the Philippines today: poverty, colonialism, the Roman Catholic Church, sexism, and racism.

We also show how women become bar girls or casa workers. Almost all have been trafficked—transported for the purposes of prostitution—to Angeles, some willingly, some not. There are organized pipe lines of agents and recruiters in the rural and Southern provinces providing access to work in the bars, often voluntarily but in some cases involuntarily. Two of the four women we profile were tricked into coming to Angeles through fraud and deception, and two wanted to come to Angeles to work in the bars. All were brought to the bars by recruiters in the South. Those who were tricked into coming were teenagers. Anna and Liza had very little education and no job skills, and they felt a great deal of shame about losing their virginity in the bars. They were not held against their will per se—some casa workers are literally locked up—but their illiteracy, shame, and "debt of obligation" to the family kept them working. Stories like theirs are commonplace in Angeles. The two women who came to Angeles voluntarily were pursuing their own sense of agency and desire for a better life, Western husbands, and Amerasian children. Josie and Perla decided to take their chances in Angeles. The combination of the "Promised Land" of the West and success stories of women from the provinces who have achieved that dream keep women coming to Angeles.

The Bar Girls

Anna was one of the first bar girls we met. At the time she was a twenty-two year old working in Heaven Bar on E Santos Street in Angeles. The street the bar is on is euphemistically known as Blowjob Alley—because that's what her customers prefer—a "short time" bar fine, as it is called. She could have worked in one of the fancier disco bars on Fields but she was, ironically, too shy to dance and take her clothes off in front of the men. She has worked in the bars for five years now.

Josie works as a cashier at a bar called Niagara. She was twenty years old when we met, and she had been working in the bars since she was seventeen. She has recently stopped going out on bar fines, at the request of her Swedish boyfriend, who sends her money monthly and whom she hopes will marry her.

Both of these young women's stories illustrate some of the reasons Filipinas become bar girls. First, both Anna and Josie are from very poor rural families living in the provinces. Rural communities in the Philippines, as in many places in the Third World, are still basically feudal, agricultural economies, slowly and agonizingly making the transition to a wage economy and capitalism. Families who have been farmers or fishers for generations have few options for retraining, education, or other forms of employment.

Josie comes from the province of Leyte, an island in the middle of the Philippines (south of Manila). She is the youngest of fourteen children, and two of her older sisters have worked in the bars in Angeles. Her parents were poor farmers but are now unemployed; Josie fully supports them.

Anna is from Binmaley in the province of Pangasinan, an old fishing community, about 125 miles north of the capital. She comes from a family of ten children. Her parents are also very poor. Her father was a fisher, before he became a heavy drinker, and her mother is a laundress. They live in a shack by the side of the road, squatting on a piece of land by a barbed wire fence. They have no electricity, no running water, no toilet, and all fourteen of the family members currently residing there sleep out in the elements on a bamboo plank. The poverty is indescribable. One has only to see Anna's hunchbacked little niece (the family had no money to fix her back after an accident), her toothless and skinny mother (the family has little money for food and no money for dentists), her barefoot, drained, exhausted, and pregnant sister-in-law with four children under the age of four, to understand why Anna might choose a form of sexual slavery over domestic drudgery and absolute poverty. Anna and Josie live in tremendous hope that a rich foreigner will transport them out of their poverty. We saw no hope in the eyes of Anna's twenty-two-year-old sister-in-law.

Such factors were confirmed by our partners, who were well aware of the problems faced by the women and the reasons they became prostitutes. While poverty came up as the main reason for women's entry into prostitution, they knew that some women had been tricked into coming to Angeles and others had suffered sexual abuse:

Maria: In the surveys which have been conducted by different organizations it's really poverty. When we have been talking with the girls, especially those at the casa, it's really poverty that brought them here. First, of course, a lot of them didn't realize that they're coming to Angeles to be in this kind of trade. Of course, they were promised to be working in factories because, you know, there are a lot of factories here, but then, they ended up either in the casa or in Fields Avenue.

Davida: For some women, because of poverty, but some because they had prior sexual abuse from their family, and some are being forced or pimped by other people so, those are some reasons why women goes into bars. And although they are educated, they feel discouraged because of non-employment opportunities in our place, so they have to go to bars.

Perla: Oh, cause of the economic situation, you know. The situation is this; it's hard to get a job. Even they already finished go to school but you cannot find a good job cause you don't have somebody [a patron]. You know me so you can tell to the owner I know her, like that. If someone know you, you can easy get this job. But if no one know you, you can never get a job right now. To work in the bar, the requirements only the birth certificate and you can get work. That's the reason why some of the girls would like to get work in the club.

Another explanation for women's work in the bars is the Filipino's strong family-oriented culture, which demands a debt of gratitude (*utang na loob*) from older to younger siblings, and from children to parents. Part of being a dutiful daughter is to sacrifice for the family. This debt of gratitude "requires taking on any type of work for the upkeep of the family, as they have an obligation to their parents who took care of them in the past."[2] Anna and Josie send most of their money to their families in the provinces. Anna has paid for her mother's eye operation; she sends her two little nieces to primary school and pays for the bulk of the food for fourteen people. Her older brothers have families of their own, and they help when they can, but it is really the girl children's responsibility to assist their parents. Sacrifice is expected of them, applauded, and the girls see it as their duty. Anna doesn't think her parents know what she does for a living, but her parents certainly encourage her to keep working and to keep sending money home.

Katerina (WEDPRO): Women get into prostitution because of very basic reasons. Poverty is one real condition which pushes women to sell themselves. It's not something that they really want to happen to themselves, but because of the family situation, women think that it's a noble sacrifice, to do for the family. We also take note that because here in the Philippines, women have the burden of supporting the family, more than the men. So, it's the women who will find every means to help their families. So they go abroad, even if that means being trafficked. They risk and endanger themselves. They would try everything just for the families.

Anna's story is typical of many bar girls in this regard. Anna went to school only until the sixth grade, and then she was sent to work in Manila as a domestic at the age of twelve. The parents could not support all of their children, so she was chosen to work to support the others. She sent most of her money home to support her younger brothers and sisters, even at that young age. When she was seventeen, Anna was recruited (enticed, as they say in Angeles) to work in a factory by a woman who befriended her, took her to Angeles, dropped her off at a bar, and disappeared. Anna had no money and did not speak the local language. She has been working in the bars ever since.

Josie's story is typical of other reasons women become bar girls. Philippine history is a curious mixture of Spanish and American colonialism, and this shows itself in the desire of the women to marry foreigners. Josie's first job was working in a bar owned and operated by a woman from Leyte and all the other bar girls were from Leyte. The owner provides a service, she says, to these young women by bringing them to Angeles to fulfill their dreams of marrying a foreigner. Josie followed her older sisters to Angeles after high school, so she is more educated than Anna and was not tricked into going there. Says Josie: "I've wanted to have a foreigner boyfriend since I was seven years old, and I'd see older girls with their white boyfriends on Leyte." Many of the women we met were from Leyte.

> **Maria:** There's a place here we call Leyte, that's in the south, and when a woman gives birth to a girl, they are very happy about it. They rejoice. I said why is that? Oh because you know, the girls, when they grow up they could go to work in the bar and they could get married to a foreigner. Well, I don't know if that's a joke, but there are a lot of these women coming from this place.

The idea that white men mean money and freedom is not limited to the bar girls. Anna's father, when he talked to us about his Amerasian grandchild, said proudly, "This boy, he will get on a plane." This signified to him an event so big that he could only dream of it, but his half-white, *mestizo* grandchild actually might be able to do it. To Josie, white men represent wealth and power, of course, but also the ability to transmit highly desirable Caucasian physical traits like paler skin, slim noses, and lighter hair to their Amerasian children. It is about money and power, but also significantly about *colonial* notions of white racial "beauty." Josie's desire for foreigners, however, is still about more than poverty or race. White men, oddly enough, also mean acceptance to many of these women. Filipino men want virgin wives, and because of strong Roman Catholic religious traditions, women who are not virgins are deemed unmarriageable in the rural areas. They are not worth anything. They may as well be prostitutes or *pok-pok*, as the Filipinos say. Even women who have been sexually assaulted as children in their own families are considered damaged goods, and many are abandoned by their families. Many North American studies (and more and more Filipino studies) show a connection between childhood sexual abuse and prostitution in later life.[3] Even many of the women we have met from the casas who were tricked by recruiters and kept as sex slaves cannot return to their families because they are no longer virgins.

> **Davida:** But, you know, most of them cannot decide to go home yet because their families are ashamed. They were always to be blamed by their parents because they lose their morals in their place.

> **Katerina:** We have discovered that women's experience of sexual abuse has a lot to do with their entry into prostitution. This is very much our culture, where women are supposed to be virgins, where women are supposed to be, as I said chaste, and once you've been tarnished, so to speak, then your future is gone, and there is no other alternative for you but to go deeper into a situation that further degrades you. So, sexual abuse is a big factor in women's entry into prostitution.

One of our partners from WEDPRO who did not end up in the bars was sexually assaulted by a relative and had his child when she was fifteen. She was rejected by her family because of the shame of losing her virginity and links her work with the prostituted women to her own experiences of childhood sexual abuse:

> **Carmela** (WEDPRO): I ran away from my family because they keep on blaming me for this kind of thing. That's why I was for two years, I'm living alone. That's the lonely part of my life. When I was being abandoned and I was being, you know, ah ... being tortured [abused] like that [they kept] saying [to] me that this is you. They put the blame on me saying that I am the reason why my mother had a stroke, had this kind of illness, you know, that's why I ran away from them.

Regardless of how it happens, women are discriminated against because of sexual activity outside marriage. Roman Catholicism, with its double standard of morality that allows men to go to prostitutes with impunity, that permits them to keep minor wives and mistresses—researchers estimate that 20 percent of men in North America go to prostitutes, compared to a majority of Filipino men[4]—and that causes a

Madonna/whore dichotomy for women wreaks havoc on women's self-esteem and makes them unmarriageable if there is any stain on their reputation.

> **Carmela:** One of my sisters is coming in December. I am so excited to see her, but I don't know if they have forgiven me already. That's the saddest part. I do not know. . . . They doesn't have communication with me because of my situation now. You know, they still remember my past life, they keep on telling [blaming] me [for] this, but it's not really my fault, you know, I am just a victim. I am just a victim of this kind of circumstances. So I do not like this kind of life. And I have also a dream. To marry, you know, but I don't think I can, because of my past life.

The influence of the Roman Catholic Church is profound in the Philippines. Abortion and divorce are illegal, and contraception except natural family planning for any reason (even STIs and AIDS) is condemned by the church. One woman told us that her priest informed her she would go to hell if she didn't have more children. She already had four. Carmela, in dutiful daughter fashion, sees herself as sacrificing a normal family life for working with the women in prostitution.

> **Carmela:** You know these women are my family. These women who I am helping now are my family. They are my rewards. I do hope that this organization can help me also, ah, fulfill my dream, you know, fulfill my impossible dream. This shelter, also for them. So that they will, you know, live together as one happy family.

But Carmela was relatively lucky. After being abused and running away from home, she met a woman who befriended her and gave her a place to live. The woman turned out to be a recruiter.

> **Carmela:** I was maybe twenty years old then, something like that when she, you know, she brought me to a hotel in Quezon City. I forgot the hotel name, but she brought me there and then she had the transaction with this BIR [Bureau of Internal Revenue] examiner and then he paid her you know because this a rich guy. Her intention is for me to have a sexual, you know, contact with these a guys and they keep on paying her big amounts you know, she's a procurer. So I run away from that woman, that night. I have no place to sleep because I sleep in that woman's house. That night I did not sleep because I don't have nowhere to go. So I just stayed the whole [next] day from one place to another looking for a house you know, but I really need to survive. That's why I take a look at

the newspaper to find a job. Then I apply the whole day, you know, looking for a job.

In our experience, the most typical case of trafficking in the Philippines for purposes of prostitution is because of attempted fraud and deception. The girls are promised jobs in factories or restaurants and only later realize where they have ended up. The casa workers who have been rescued from the brothels are tricked and then basically abducted and held against their wills. The process of trafficking varies, but many elements are the same. Local recruiters in the provinces actively look for young women, and sometimes the bars themselves recruit. Josie was voluntarily recruited for a bar where every young woman was from the southern island of Leyte; another bar has women only from Samar; Anna's bar has women mainly from Pangasinan in the north. Bars pay recruiters to bring them women. Sometimes recruiters pay the families in the guise of getting the girls good jobs in Manila, and most families claim they did not know what their daughters were going to be doing. Recruiters hang out at parks in Manila where young people look for work and where runaways congregate. Seventeen women in one casa rescue we witnessed were recruited looking for day work and promised jobs in factories.

Liza's story is interesting in this regard. Liza was almost twenty-five when we met her. She worked with Anna at Heaven Bar. She is from Leyte and comes from a family of fishers, the youngest of eight children. She went to school until grade six and then was sent to work as a housemaid for richer relatives in Manila at twelve to help support her family, just like Anna. At fourteen a "friend" promised her a job in Angeles in a restaurant. She soon found out that she was in fact working at a bar and was expected to go out on bar fines. As she puts it shamefully, she "lost her cherry" in the bars at fourteen and could not go back home. When she was seventeen, she got pregnant by a Filipino boyfriend and sent the child to live with her mother. Her second child is half white. Her family does not know about that child because then "they would know what I do and my mother would get mad at me." She has little contact with her family because of the shame of not being a virgin, and though she says she is mad at her mother and sisters because of the way they treat her, she still sends nearly three thousand pesos home every month. She has been living in the back rooms of the bar for eleven years—since she was fourteen years old. The story of her recruitment is not uncommon. Friends of families and neighbors, mostly older Filipinas, are used as recruiters. The seventeen girls rescued from a casa, mentioned above, were recruited by an older woman working with a young man. They trusted her and did not believe that another woman would harm them. Josie, Anna, Liza, Perla, and Carmela—although Carmela did not end up in the bars—were all recruited and/or deceived by women.

Perla's story illustrates what happens to women after they are considered too old to work in the bars. There was a time when it was acceptable for women to work in the bars even into their early forties, but that time is over. Bar girls do not usually work past twenty-five, and bars are continually looking for younger and younger women.

> **Maria:** I know that if they stay in this kind of trade, what will happen to them when they grow old? As I have been always telling them, "You will never [won't always] be beautiful and you'll never [won't always] be young. There will come a time that, you know there will be no more bars to work or no casas to work." So maybe that's a, you know, probably also giving me inspiration to, you know, to help them more.

Bar girls have few options after working in the bars except working as mamasans—female bar managers. Perla worked as a bar girl for many years, when the Americans ran the bars, and then became a mamasan when they left.

> **Perla:** I started to work in the bars, 1982. I didn't forget it also, that's December 13. I went because of my friend. My first husband left. My second husband uh, messed up. But we have two kids. I have two kids also my first husband. We broke up, so one of my friends told me that we go to Olongapo so we can look for a job there. I said can I get a dollar in that place? Yeah, cause we have a lot of Americans. I said OK. I asked, but can I, even like this? I am a dark color, but she says it's easy to get a dollar. So, I went there to the friend of her cousin and she bring me there in the club, an Australian bar. That's my friend's bar, she said, so you can work there as an entertainer. I don't have a salary in that time. I only have to give a commission if I go out like that.

Perla has been married twice and has four children. She has little education and few job skills. She quickly realized what she would be doing.

> **Perla:** I meet this Charlie guy, and he told me I would like to pay your bar fine. I asked to the lady, what is bar fine? And they say that he pay you and you go with him. And, I asked how much he gonna pay me? The woman said 100 pesos and you get half for that and half for the owner. I said how about the drinks that I had also, and yes, it depend the drinks that you drink. If the mixed drink, you have 15 pesos, if a beer, or juice, you only have 10 pesos, your commission. I said ah, I don't care as long I can get money, that's what I said. So I go.

Although she initially found the idea unpleasant, Perla began to hope that this man would marry her or at least bar fine her for a longer time so that she would not have to go with too many men.

> **Perla:** I went back to the bar. The customer said, don't go home. So I'm scared. Maybe he kill me. But really, he stay in hotel, and he said, I'm going to pay you a long bar fine. That's what it's called, you stay with him until he went back to Australia. And that long bar fine was one thousand pesos. So, half for me and half for the bar, I said OK, that's good cause I can send money to my kids cause it's coming Christmas, like that. So, the customer, he ask me, where am I going to spend my Christmas, here in Angeles or in my brothers. I said, I would like to go home, I would like to see my kids and this is at Christmas time, so my customer also said, OK, you can go home and he give me money to go to my brothers to see my kids. So, I was very happy. But when I get back, I saw him with another girl, so I didn't go back to him. I went back to work again. Of course, if you work in that club you have a lot of customers.

Perla tried to be discerning and particularly tried to avoid younger men who were more demanding and rough. She found the older Australian men to be kinder.

> **Perla:** Then I met another Australian guy, cause I don't like a young boy. I know the young is all American, so I don't like it. I like an old [man]. So, I stay in that place where I worked, cause all the customers in there is old. Cause the older men, they know how to treat you. Or else it is too silly when sometimes the American young, looking for a fight.

Soon after the Americans left Angeles, Perla became a mamasan at her Australian boyfriend's bar. She looked after the girls, handled the bar fines, and worked as a go-between for the owner, customers, and bar girls.

> **Perla:** I always told them that, be careful and select the person that you have as customer. If they treat you bad, easy to call the police. If you see the customer is not good, or else when you get inside a hotel just go to the room boy, not to close right away, the door. I have a lot of girls before, when I was a mamasan. I talk to them. If the customer is bad, not good to treat you inside the room. Don't close the door, first. So that you can easy to run away, like that. So that's what I told them before.

Perla has had bad luck with men in general. After marrying two Filipino men, she was engaged to two Australians, but they both died before she could get to Australia. In the meantime, she helped many of her bar girls marry their Western boyfriends.

> **Perla:** So I have a lot of girls [and] I helping them going to the other country and they all marry. Yeah I only had bad luck; I could not find a boyfriend cause when they would like to marry me, they going to die. The first guy that I meet when he pay me well by bar fine. He would like to marry me. He went to the province with me. And then he went back to Australia, he die. Yeah and then the second time, it happen also. We separate and a few years, I hear that he died also.

Perla finally quit working in the bars after she got a job with WEDPRO as an outreach worker. She had worked in numerous bars as a mamasan but found the owners getting worse and worse, and she thought it unfair that the women, who were the ones using their bodies, were getting less money than the owner.

> **Perla:** I didn't like the owner. He doesn't treat good to the women. They have the bar fine is 1,000—450 to the girls, 500 to the owner. [Perla, as mamasan, received 50.] So I said, the girl, they give you your business, but how come they commission is lower than to the owner, you know? And the girls use their body but they only get small money. So that's why I don't like. I told him treat the girls nice and don't make them beg, you'll look like an asshole. Cause we also human being, you know. And you know we feel, ah, we feel bad if you talk to them nasty, like that. Sometimes if they have a customer, not treated good to my girl, I'm going to fight them. So, in 1994, I quit.

Perla's story also illustrates the many problems faced by bar girls, including unfair treatment, fear of violence, abuse, and more recently, severe health problems. Although the Philippines claims there are very few cases of HIV/AIDS in the country, Human Rights Watch believes that there is a crisis brewing because of the Roman Catholic Church's stand on condom use and the lack of sex education.[5] Of the four women we profile here, two are HIV positive. Liza also had gonorrhea in the throat, and both Liza and Anna have tuberculosis. They have little knowledge about STIs and AIDS, and when they have an infection, they are not told by the social-hygiene clinic what the problem is. Few of the women use condoms because it is considered a sin to use contraception. Even worse, since abortion is illegal and a mortal sin, Josie admitted to having an abortion and worried about the state of her soul. She had had the abortion in order to keep her Swedish boyfriend, who would not marry her if she had a child by someone else. Consequently, there is much depression, self-blame, and drug use.

> **Perla:** I just look after the girl, and everything. I was a bouncer. For example, this time that the girl take drug, I know that this is not good. Don't keep that drug to yourself, so I stopped it, and that's why when I was a bar girl, I said I don't know why I'm doing this. It's better you get drunk than to the drug.

Violence is also a huge problem for the bar girls. All of the women we talked to had been assaulted or roughed up by their customers. Both Anna and Liza have been beaten by their customers, forced to do particular acts they did not want to do, sexually assaulted, forced to work while sick, and burned by cigarettes. Liza has had several abusive boyfriends, including the father of her son, who beat her regularly. She finally broke up with him, and the last time we saw her she was with a sixty-four year old she liked because "he doesn't hit me." She wants to get married and have a regular family, but she doesn't think it is going to happen at this point. After Liza broke up with the father of her son, he became Anna's boyfriend. Though Liza warned her, Anna liked him and hoped he would be different with her. He hit her, too, and Anna has scars on her chest where she was burned with cigarettes. As Anna related to us, he also went with "billy boys" (gay men), wanted to do "everything," whether it hurt her or not, and punched her repeatedly. She took him to the provinces to meet her parents, but he was mean to her mother and beat her again, so they split up. Violence is a common occurrence.

> **Perla:** Not all the time that we are giving sex with the customer. I only give massage, I talk to the customer. But, one time was a bad experience when the customer, he is drunk and he said now take off your clothes, and I said I don't want. I only give you massage, that only we talk? When we are in there, he just grabbed me and he sit down on me, so I think I'm going to die of course, I couldn't breathe anymore, and I think that's close to murder. He thought that I'm going to die cause my eyes going up, like that. So he just got up with me, so that I can breathe. And he said to me, OK, I go; he'll go home. You tried to kill me, I said to him. But he didn't listen to me. You know, that's why, the last (time) I say, I'm quit, I'm really quit, I don't want it anymore.

> **Katerina:** The immediate thing that comes to my head at the moment [in terms of problems faced by bar girls] is violence. Women

get raped, women get harassed, women get sexually abused, women get killed. Women get beaten up and women get intimidated, and that not only limits them, but silences them and prevents them from reaching their potential. I can't speak of development if there are women who continue to be harmed. Physically, sexually, psychologically. We can't say that these are humanity if we treat women that way.

Unfortunately, but not surprisingly, many women in the bars develop a cynical attitude when it comes to men in general, not just their customers, because of all the abuse.

Perla: Even the women [who] has not [been] working in the bar, they still have violence, the way men be in the house, the violence is still there. The verbal abuse, even [if] you are already married. Your husband doesn't treat you good, like that. The nice people, the nice men in the world, you can only count your hand. You can count only in your hand.

Many of the women also mentioned that language problems lead to abuse, both physical and emotional, because the bar girls and customers cannot communicate properly. We saw many Western men and bar girls in restaurants not saying a word to each other or struggling to communicate because of the language barriers.

Perla: [When I started working] I don't know how to speak English. I understand but not for really, it's hard to, it's hard to pronounce the English of Australian then to American, and I could not understand what dialect. They call me "dumb-dumb." I'm just only laughing because I didn't know, I just know what he say is silly, you're dumb-dumb. I just only laugh, but I'm scared, you know, I'm scared. I said, I think I can't work here. I'm going home, back to Manila. Maybe they kill me cause I don't know how to speak English like that.

Maria: You know, hearing some stories from the girls. Sometimes they treat them badly if they cannot be understood, you know, a lot of these girls really didn't even go to school. So, how could they know how to speak or understand the English language? So, sometimes, like one girl, she was telling me and I said, why does he hit you? And then she said, because I cannot understand what he is saying. And I said, why did he get you then? So he will have somebody to, you know, to sleep with.

Another common problem reported by the bar girls is stigmatization and feeling that they are looked down on by the society at large. Josie reports the rough treatment at the social-hygiene clinic when getting her smear. When she complains that it hurts when they do not take care in placing the speculum, she is told by the nurses not to complain and they ask dismissively why it would hurt her since she is so used to it. The social-hygiene clinic itself is in an old, dilapidated building made of crumbling concrete. The women line up to pay their money, to register, and to get their passes stamped; they line up to have their tests done, together, in the same room. The offices are sparse; the lab is inadequate; and the speculums are old, metal, and of doubtful cleanliness. The windows of the building are open (no air conditioning in the 110 degree heat), and in the examination room the stirrups face the open window. The nurse says they have to discourage neighborhood boys from trying to peer inside. There is no privacy because the girls deserve none.

Josie also reported not being allowed into church because of working in the bars and being a "fallen woman." Many of the women, including Liza, felt that they could not tell their family what they did for fear of being rejected. Nonetheless, the family profits from their labor. Several of the rescued casa workers did not want to go home because they worried that their families would not believe that they were tricked or trafficked. Many of the women reported being harassed on the streets and called *pok-pok* by passersby.

> **Perla:** Especially when you are in the place where you work and they know that you been working before. It's called *pok-pok*, like that. *Pok-pok* is called, in English, prostitution like that. So, they haven't let you feel good if they know that you've been working in the bar.

There are also many rules and regulations in the bar system intended to control the women and make them feel bad about themselves. They are fined for every infraction, and this keeps them in a state of indebtedness to the bar owners. In one bar where we met five women, they talked about their working and living conditions and all the fining that takes place. Twenty to thirty women work at the bar and live in the back, most of them from Samar. They get paid to work from 8 p.m. to 5 a.m., but the women arrive at 5 p.m. to "get good seats." They make one hundred pesos a night and a percentage of tips, but this barely covers the fining system in the bar. They can be fined for chewing gum (one thousand pesos), leaving the bar early, being sick, not getting a smear, sitting down, looking in the mirror, or not wearing panty hose (all five hundred pesos). All the women particularly disliked the bar owner and having to line up in front of him every night for inspection, "like we're in the military."

As in most countries with sex tourism, prostitutes are vulnerable to sexually transmitted infections, HIV, violence, the whims of the customers and bar owners, bribery, fraud, and deception. The societal double standard continues to be problematic, with no consequences for male customers, bar owners, or recruiters; women are the "criminals" and men are the "victims." The penalties for prostitution and trafficking in women and children are far less than those for drug smuggling (for which the penalty in the Philippines is death). In many cases, unfortunately, crimes against humans are not taken seriously by the authorities, who consider it the victim's fault that she was "enticed" by the prospects of a better income or a wealthy foreign husband. So the women are considered greedy or just plain naive.

The macro factors influencing sex tourism—globalization, poverty, sexism, and racism—were discussed in Chapter 4. Class, of course, heavily influences the overall sexism that pervades these women's lives. The Philippines, after all, has had two female presidents since the overthrow of Marcos. (The current president is a woman.) But these women are upper class, educated, "good" women who are wives and mothers first, politicians second. Their class and family backgrounds protect them from some of the worst of the sexual double standard and division of labor prevalent in the Philippines. The most vulnerable members of society, on the other hand, find that their exploitation is normalized by and actually benefits the government.

> **Katerina:** I think also the social environment that normalizes prostitution is another big reason why women think that there is no other option than this option, is real for them, and you have officials of the government, you have intellectual people in society who also look at prostitution as the only place that can take in women who have no other choice or no other option. So, we don't think any more of the long term, because we always think of the short term. So, we have government officials who have practically given up on the future for these women.

We met over fifty women during our five-year project, and their stories were similar enough that we can say with some confidence that there were two main stories: some came voluntarily to Angeles and some were tricked, but all came from poor families and wanted a better life; and all were willing to move to an unfamiliar area in the hopes of that better life. Some of the women knew what they were moving to, while others were deceived with job offers in factories and restaurants, but they all had the desire and agency for something more than they had in the provinces.

And, having seen what is in the provinces, that desire for a better life would probably have been our choice as well. Alternative livelihoods, however, are not unproblematic. Work in factories can be dirty, repetitive, and dead end, with no hope of escape. And as we found out, the girls' hope that they will be rescued is profound.

> **Perla:** Like example; you are working as sewer [seamstress] you have a time only to go pee, to go in the comfort room when you have a break time. If you feel bad, you can't get out. You still working there. You must stand up for your work, in the break time only. So not all the factories good or so. There was a lot of regulations, so that's why some of the women get in work in that place but, the regulation they didn't like. You went out, and go back to the bar.

Josie was lucky and had a steady Swedish boyfriend the last time we saw her. He visits once a year and sends her money monthly so she doesn't have to go on bar fines. In fact, he forbids it. His friend owns the Swedish bar Josie lives and works in, and the owner ensures that Josie is loyal to his friend. Josie says she is looking for a factory job while she waits to marry her boyfriend and go with him to Sweden. In our last emails, she had not married her boyfriend, had left the bars, and was indeed working in a factory.

Anna has had the same dream—to marry a foreigner—but has not been so fortunate. She has had several American boyfriends and has recently become pregnant again by one of them. She hopes to give her second Amerasian baby up for adoption and maybe find a new boyfriend to support her. She was not talking about marriage and going to the West the last time we saw her. After five years of trying, she tells us that she is not hoping that anymore. She is HIV positive and has tuberculosis.

Liza was diagnosed with AIDS in early 2004 and died in April 2004. Her Filipino child remains with her family in Leyte, and her Amerasian son was given to the owner of Heaven Bar by Liza's family for a small sum of money. Perla no longer works for WEDPRO because it has discontinued its project in Angeles. She continues to live in the squatter community with her four children, eking out a meager living selling pigs.

The Customers

This chapter also examines some of the characteristics, attitudes, behaviors, and male-bonding rituals of sex tourists in Angeles City. The purpose is to get at the complexity of the issues, not to create the definitive position on sex tourists in the Philippines. Over the five years of the project, we had the opportunity to interview about fifty men who were in Angeles as tourists or residents. The distinction is important, because about half of the Western men we encounter in Angeles are not tourists at all; they are permanent or temporary residents. The men range from many American ex-servicemen who have retired to Angeles, Australians who have married Filipinas and own or manage bars, Irishmen, Germans, Swiss, a retired Canadian auto worker, and a young Dutch man who lives in Angeles six months of the year and works in the fishery industry for the rest of the year. From what we could see, the process of male bonding bridges the gap between these men, regardless of their cultural, linguistic, class, socioeconomic, or age differences; that is, the distance between men is lessened by their experiences of sex tourism. The disparities in race or class are minimized by their shared experiences of prostitution and by their shared contempt for the locals, Filipino culture, and Western women. The tourists included the many stereotypical older, divorced men, and the less frequently seen younger men visiting Angeles who claim that they are on diving holidays, that they heard about Angeles on the Internet and wanted to "check it out," somewhat like tourists in Amsterdam check out the red-light areas. Some tourists are on their first trip. Some are making their twentieth trip. As Ed from Boston told us, "I swore last time I wouldn't come back again, but . . . I always come back." What keeps these men coming back? What are the characteristics of the customers and of the place that make traveling halfway around the world desirable for so many men?

First of all, we asked ourselves why men go to prostitutes. In the past, research on the sex trade has been done mainly on the women and why they sell sex; clients or customers were neglected. It is a shadowy industry, and it was difficult to do research on the customers of prostitutes because of its illegality and men's reluctance to report their use of prostitutes. Only about 20 percent of American men report having gone to prostitutes, whereas the majority of Filipino men are not ashamed to report their use of prostitutes, so normal is the behavior. Recently, more emphasis has been placed on understanding men's motivations, so we can make a few generalizations about why men go to prostitutes. Then we look at why sex tourism might seem to be a better option for some men. Several studies have classified male customers by the reasons they go to prostitutes.[6] These reasons include, according to one summary: "sexual acts they cannot receive from their partners; they are able to have sex with a larger number of sexual partners; they are attracted to specific physical characteristics; they like the limited emotional involvement; and they are excited by the illicit nature of the act."[7] When our partners were asked about men's motivations, one responded that friends had told her it was about wanting sex without commitment or not wanting to get in trouble with their wives by being too demanding.

Maria: You know, I've been asking also, people, you know, men friends, why do men go to this? Well, they said that, you know, when you go out, you do it with them and that's it. No commitment. But when they are serious or get a Filipino woman who is not in the bars, they might be having problems. So, I've noticed that those who goes to this women are probably those who are not committed. Or those who might be committed but you know doesn't like to be in trouble with their wives.

The desire for companionship is also mentioned in studies, as well as lack of experience, shyness, fear of rejection, and "difficulty becoming involved in conventional relationships."[8] Going to prostitutes allows for brief encounters without commitment in order to get particular sex acts with a variety of women. This "commodified approach to sexuality" works for many men because it allows them to control the nature and substance of the acts, particularly because they are paying for them.[9] Many people find the financial exchange part of the deal offensive because of the power it gives the buyer, usually male, and the degradation it causes some sellers, usually female. Does sex tourism cause the same harm? Is sex tourism a form of prostitution, or can it more appropriately be called relationship or "romance" tourism?[10] How, if at all, do sex tourists' motives differ from those of regular "johns"?

Characteristics

Sex tourists come in all shapes and sizes, although as Julia O'Connell Davidson writes, a sizable segment of the sex-tourist population is "disabled, disfigured or 'abnormal' (for instance, men who are mountainously obese)."[11] Jeremy Seabrook argues in his book on Thai sex tourism that the men he meets are mainly pathetic characters: lonely, isolated, unhappy people who use their monetary power in a third-world country to buy themselves tenderness and sex.[12] When we first traveled to the Philippines in the mid 1990s, this did seem to be the norm; the men's average age was past sixty, and for the most part they were not attractive by Western standards. In the past few years we have seen a change in the demographics of sex tourists that illustrates the impact of the Internet and the return of the American Armed Forces for joint exercises with the Filipino Armed Forces. The result is an increase in younger and, from the women's point of view, more desirable men.

Davidson, in her study of the Thai sex industry, divides the sex tourists she has met into three categories: Macho Lad, Mr. Average, and Cosmopolitan Man. Macho Lads are younger men who travel in packs and are interested in bedding as many women as they can and drinking as much as possible over their holiday. Mr. Averages are older, divorced

men who are looking for sex, affection, and may admit to having difficulty in their relationships with Western women. Cosmopolitan Men
are those more experienced travelers, usually on business, who claim not
to go to prostitutes back home and project a worldly air of superiority
about the whole experience.[13] Probably because of the place itself, we
see very few Cosmopolitan Men in Angeles. If they exist in the Philippines, they would be in Manila, in the financial district of Makati. Angeles City is not a resort town, and its only real appeal for tourists is the sex
industry. Men going there are not on business, are not looking for a
beach, and do not care that the place is dirty, rundown, polluted, and
rather tacky. There are literally no other white people in the town, certainly no white women; the only other reason for even passing through
would be to hike Mt. Pinatubo.

In terms of the Macho Lads, as stated above, there are more and more
younger men coming to Angeles, either because of their recent service
with the American Armed Forces or because of curiosity. A young German man told us he was touring Southeast Asia, had heard about Angeles on the Internet, and had planned to pass through after a few days.
He had been there for two months when we interviewed him. Another
young man from Sweden claimed to be on a diving holiday. He too had
heard about Angeles on the Internet and wanted to check it out. He
said he liked playing pool with the girls and hanging out. Interestingly,
these were the only two young men we met who were not in a group at
the time and who were traveling alone. A more stereotypical Macho
Lad was a young Irish man who had heard about the place from a friend
and was on his third visit. He was in a group of older men who gathered daily at a local patio bar, drinking heavily and clearly enjoying his
status as the most desirable man in the group because of his age and
relative good looks. Several women were draped over him as he went
about choosing whom he would spend time with that night; he treated
the women with contempt and rubbed his own desirability in the noses
of the other men. It was clear that the other men recognized his status
with the women and knew that they would be left with his castoffs. By
far, then, the men we interviewed would fit into the Mr. Average category: forty-five to sixty-five years old, retired or semi-retired, divorced,
with problems sustaining relationships, and, on average, on their fifth
trip.

Why Angeles?

The men report many reasons for coming to Angeles: the devalued
peso, which makes for cheap holidays; the warm weather; Filipino hospitality; and friendly women. Many of the men talk about the difference
between bar girls in the Philippines and prostitutes back home. They

say the bar girls are more affectionate and seem to want to be with them, and the men do not think of what they are doing as prostitution. As Davidson writes, it's the non-contractual nature of sex tourism that is so appealing. The women often "perform the kind of acts that in the West are taken to signify genuine affection (kissing, cuddling, sleeping in the bed with clients, providing physical care . . . and so on)."[14] The men can delude themselves that the encounter is more about flirtation and relationship, and less about the economic transaction.

> **Maria:** I think there are customers who comes here for probably a week or two weeks, then they would like to go around the country, so what they do is they bar fine girls for several thousand pesos, then, of course, most of this goes to the bar. What the girl gets is, you know, a few, probably 1,000 pesos plus of course she could go along with the tourist, you know, free food and you get someone to wash your clothes, cook your food and have company, so I guess, well I know these are the packages that the tourists are having here. These men, you know, get a girl, company at night, they get house help, housemaid, somebody to take care of them.

And to be fair, this is what the bar girls want too: a chance to develop a relationship with one man and to travel around as his companion.

> **Perla:** Before, when I was working in bar, I loved, also, I can go anywhere. When I meet a guy, we went to somewhere, the other place. So, I go. I been already around the Philippines, together with a customer. So, I going to the beaches, like that, I called vacation.

When the men do form relationships with the women, they often report that it would have been impossible in their own country because they are too old. They can use their economic power in Angeles to get all the women they want, for as long as they want.

This is a common story. A fifty-five-year-old Australian named Martin went to Thailand "about thirty-five times" before "getting sick of it." He found Angeles "by chance" and has lived there for eight years. He married a Filipina and now manages one of the Australian bars. He has a young child and says he would never have been able to have children at his age with an Australian woman, who would not give him a second glance. The girls working for him think he is OK; relative to other papasans he treats them well. He was very good with the male customers while we were in the bar, ensuring that everyone felt comfortable in a Mafioso kind of way. We felt like we were in a *Sopranos* episode as he bought drinks for regulars and made his rounds.

Another fifty-five year old, Ralph, from Sweden, who now owns one of the bars with his Filipina wife, tells a similar story. He has children and grandchildren in Sweden, and he owned a fish cannery. He got divorced and was "tired of 60 percent taxes." He came to Angeles about ten years ago on vacation and fell in love with the people and their hospitality. He married a Filipina and bought a bar through her; now they have two young children. He claims he "never would be able to in Sweden. Anyone over thirty-five is out of luck." As Davidson writes, this probably is not the case. Though having children requires a relatively young woman, there are many women in the West who are comparable to them. The men just don't want them. They want young and pretty.[15] So it is not the lack of accommodating women in the West that is the problem. It is that these men do not want to have sex with their equals. Quoting Davidson again: "A white British sex tourist in Thailand told me: 'I'm forty-eight, I'm balding, I'm not as trim as I was. Would a charming, beautiful, young woman want me in England? No. I'd have to accept a big, fat, ugly woman. That's all I could get.'"[16]

Berit, who is probably in his late forties, is from the Netherlands. He works half the year in Amsterdam and lives the rest of the time in Angeles. He came to Angeles years ago while he was working as a fisher off Manila Bay. He comes back because he likes the girls' attention and feels he would not have the same chances with Dutch women. He was very "touchy-feely" with the bar girls while we sat and talked to him. He spoke very openly about the progressive Dutch laws on drugs, euthanasia, and prostitution. Berit particularly likes the fact that making prostitution legal cleans up the worst aspects of the trade; that is, getting rid of the illegality eliminates the underworld elements. Prostitution is, in fact, illegal in the Philippines but regulated by the government, making it one of the worst systems for the women themselves. But because he knew that the bar girls go for weekly smears at the local social-hygiene clinic, he assumed it was the same system as in the Netherlands. He was obviously not concerned about being arrested, so common a sight is an older white man bar fining a much younger Filipino bar girl. The authorities do nothing.

Ed, whom we quoted above promising himself he would not come back, has been traveling to Angeles for almost twenty years, first as a navy man, then as a merchant marine, now as a tourist. He stated that he had tried computer dating at home, had no luck with women, and was not meeting people he connected with. He keeps coming back because "it's familiar, it's cheap" and as a pensioner who might be poor in the United States, he can "live really well here." "Add in all the girls . . . that's why I come back."

Hans, a sixty-five-year-old married Swiss citizen, comes every year for two months to visit his Filipina girlfriend (though he sees other bar girls and does not support her, as some men do). He was Liza's boy-friend, and she named her baby after him, but he got angry with her because she got pregnant by another man and is not interested in her anymore. He tells us that his wife thinks he is on his yearly business trip to the Philippines. As Davidson also points out, he seemed to take a particular glee in thinking about this deception.

Allan, the father of Anna's baby, is a fifty-five-year-old American man who has been the customer and boyfriend of both Anna and Liza. He comes yearly to visit, and they think he is nicer than forty-five-year-old British Chris, the father of Liza's son, though he does not support any of his children. One man we spoke to claimed he had ten children in the Philippines by ten different women and he did not support any of them. Chris also likes gay sex and short bar fines, activities he might not feel comfortable indulging at home. Davidson also claims that the exotic nature of the place enables men to do things that they would not do at home.

Pel, Josie's new boyfriend, is a thirty-four-year-old Swede. She met him on his first visit to the Philippines while he was visiting with a friend. He ended up paying her bar fine for four months so she would not have to work. He plans to come back twice a year. Her previous boyfriend, Gustaf, who was also from Sweden, broke up with Josie because she had a fight with her bar owner, one of his friends. Pel is the third Swedish boyfriend Josie has had, and all of them have paid for her to stop work-ing in the bars until they returned. So far, none of them has married her, but their promise of a better life keeps her hooked.

Many studies point out the power these men have because of their relative wealth.[17] Although a woman might not look at them back home, in Angeles their money makes them kings. The local tourism brochure and the balibago.com website sum up the choices these men have with regard to getting sex, regardless of personal attributes, and perhaps gives a more realistic account of why they are there: they can have any woman they want regardless of what they themselves look like, what their social class is, or how personally repugnant they might be. And they can do it without too much cost to themselves economically, and with no need for any cross-cultural sensitivity. "Prices in Balibago are extremely low, which means you can carouse in full throttle without wiping out your life sav-ings. English is widely spoken. You don't have to learn a single word of the native language."

Although some men, then, are in Angeles for the curiosity factor, most are there for sex: cheap, available, and unequal sex with young, pretty, vulnerable, accommodating women. These are men who do not want to deal with Western women's demands for equality, voice, and power; they want their egos stroked by eighteen year olds. How do the men justify what they are doing? Do they think they are doing anything wrong?

How Do They Justify Being There?

Every time we sat down in a bar in Angeles, a white man would immediately approach us and do one of two things: he would ask what on earth we were doing in Angeles, and/or he would tell us why he was there. We didn't have to say a thing. We both found this very interesting because of what we think it means: With very few Western women in Angeles, we were definitely a curiosity, but mostly, we think, we made them embarrassed/judged/accused because we reminded them of who they are and where they come from. Ed literally stopped in his tracks when he saw us, immediately came over to ask what we were doing there, and wanted to know if we were "crusaders for white slavery." His curiosity about why we were there in this "cesspool" and his ambivalence about why he is still coming back are common.

All the men we talked to tried to justify being there in one way or another. Because the place is so sexualized, one man thought we were there for the same reason he was; that is, that we were lesbians getting some sex of our own with the women. Another very creepy American man traveling with his Filipina wife asked us to dance with his wife and said he would pay to watch. Other than those two, who were seeing us as sexualized customers as well, the men would usually justify their behavior in a variety of ways: with racist ideas about the Filipino women and culture; with their own sense of superiority because of their relative wealth; with the belief that they were being victimized by the women and Filipinos in general (rather than vice versa); and with sexist ideas about aggressive, picky Western women. All of the men talked about how different Filipinas are from American or British or Australian women and tended to stereotype all Asian women: "If the Asian woman is constructed in Western culture as super-feminine and hyper-hetero-sensual, then it is not difficult to see why she is desired as a sex provider, and sometimes as a 'mail-order bride.' A relationship with her promises greater sexual, gender and racial complementarity and thus it almost guarantees romance."[18] It seemed clear that the men we talked to had all bought into this stereotype. And though several men said, defensively, that they were not ashamed of being there and that they were "not doing anything wrong," it is very interesting that none of the men we talked to was willing to be interviewed on camera for the film. They were happy to talk about their disdain for the locals, the city, the women, and their own justifications for being there, but refused, to a man, to admit publicly what they were doing or to be identified as a sex tourist. Most men, then, must have a sense that what they are doing is morally ambiguous (at the very least), if not exploitative, even if they say they think they are not doing anything wrong.

Some of the men, however, claim that they are helping the women by giving them money to live and supporting their families. Ed, in particular, told us that he can rationalize what he does because he knows that the girls do it because they are poor and support their families in the provinces and he feels he is helping them out. We think he was being genuine in his intentions to help, but also that he was deluding himself to a certain degree because he benefits tremendously from the relationships. This is not an act of charity with nothing back but a tax receipt—the men are exploiting very young girls for very little money. He had no sense of exploiting their bad circumstances, just that he was, in some ways, acting charitably. He got defensive about the Americans being blamed for the situation in the Philippines and instead blamed the Filipinos for the prostitution situation in Angeles. It is part of their culture, he thinks. The local men are used to using women, and he specifically mentioned ex-President Estrada to illustrate how all Filipino men have mistresses, minor wives, and go to prostitutes (Estrada is reported to have kept at least three households before and during his time in office). "It has been around for a long time; it will continue and can't be stopped." He is also of the popular opinion that it was better when the Americans were in Angeles: "more business for the locals, more customers for the girls, and better medical care." When he was a medic and docked at Subic, for instance, he estimates that 20 percent of the returning sailors had STIs from visiting the women of Olongapo. The men and the infected women would get treated and the offending bar would be closed down until the infection was under control. Nothing like that is done now in Angeles and he knew that, in many ways, he was taking his chances with the bar girls of today.

Given all the differences among the men we met in terms of age, nationality, language, class, status, and even physical appearance, there is a commonality that happens once the tourists get to Angeles. Whether they travel in groups or alone, the men invariably bond over the experiences of Angeles and their negative assessments of the locals; it is the male bonding that bridges the gap between very disparate men.

Male Bonding

A common pastime of ours, when we are in Angeles, is to check out the alleys surrounding Fields Avenue at about 6 p.m. to watch this male-bonding ritual at work. At all the patio bars, and even *sari-sari* stores, men gather in groups of five to ten to talk and drink beer. They do this from about 6 p.m. to 8 p.m. ordering round after round of San Miguel beer, and then stumble up the street for some barbecue before heading out to the disco bars on Fields. There they sit in smaller groups with young bar girls and flirt, buy more drinks, and eventually negotiate a bar fine. It never ceased to amaze us how consistent the men were in their gathering times and places, how drunk they got, and what they talked about. They clearly spent more time with each other than with the bar girls. This is also confirmed by Davidson's study. She thinks this is mainly because of the language barriers with the women and Macho Lad behavior generally.[19]

Through a process of overhearing their conversations, observing their behavior, and on occasion being invited to partake in their groups (again, as soon as we sat down, the questions begin), we were able to establish that the men talk about four main topics: disdain for the locals and Angeles itself, including how tacky and dirty Angeles is getting and how corrupt the mayor, city officials, and police are for "letting this go on" (without a word of reflection on their own behavior); how many women they have "had" and why they like Filipino women; how they cannot wait to get back to Ireland, Sweden, Australia, Canada, America, or Germany because everything is so much better there, except, of course, the women, weather, and devalued peso; and the biggest male-bonding commonality, the feeling of being cheated, of being victimized, by someone, either a local Filipino man or more commonly, a Filipino girlfriend.

As Seabrook states, "They are working women with families to support. When Westerners . . . discover this, they frequently become angry and claim they have been cheated. It is then that overtly racist responses . . . become explicit."[20] The men's comments are also common on websites, and the World Sex Guide in particular warns neophytes not to be suckered by the local women and buy into their claims of love and attention. The following quotation is reproduced from the Angeles City Message and Question Board. A man is posting on the angelescity.com website a "warning" to other foreigners. It indicates his disrespect for the women and anyone dumb enough to be fooled by them:

> Most foreigners are surprised on how quickly their beautiful young Filipina flower turns into an overweight pig oinking on the couch sucking down chips all day. Then the foreigner bitches about how they can't get rid of her because the house is in her name, but she turned fat and he can't fuck her no more and now he has to go short time all the time. Avoid the above scenario!!! Don't get a live-in, just have a girlfriend at a distance. In the beginning they're great: sweet and nice. But, eventually they change into money-grubbing monsters.

Male bonding, then—before, during, and after their trip to Angeles—seems to be a unifying process for male sex tourists. It gives them a sense of inclusion and belonging, and it enables them to justify what they are doing. This creation of a subculture of like-minded men allows them to put the blame for the terrible conditions in Angeles (which even they cannot miss or deny) on the bar girls or the local Filipinos who either ignore the problem or are too corrupt to do anything about it. As Ed said, it is part of their culture, since the local men are used to using women. There is a disdain for the poor and disadvantaged, for the Filipino culture that "degrades women," and no self-awareness that they might, in fact, be contributing to the problem.

So what's to be done about all this? The past three chapters have given a theoretical and practical overview of the problems of prostitution and a sense of how many and how diverse the explanations are for the very complex sex-tourism phenomenon in the Philippines. These chapters, we hope, set the stage for the next chapter, which outlines the small aspect of the problem we decided to tackle. We didn't try to eliminate prostitution; we didn't try to get men not to come to the Philippines; we didn't even try to get the women out of prostitution. We tried to educate the citizens of Angeles about the lives of the young women in their midst and show how badly they were treated by everyone in the hopes that the citizens would then try to change the laws, stop the double standard, criminalize the traffickers, and help the women get into alternative livelihoods if that is what they wanted to do.

6

Making a Difference

The Project

The goal of the official project was to strengthen civil society in the Philippines, with an emphasis on the role of women, by specifically increasing the country's capacity to deal more effectively and more sensitively with the most marginalized of its citizens, namely, young women in the sex-trade industry. It was mainly a gender-sensitivity training program focusing on prostitution, with four groups as the targets: the judiciary, the police, members of the community, and bar girls. The project tried to give tools and training to members of the larger Angeles community to help them sympathize with and understand the desperate situation faced by those in the sex trade and to judges and the police to help them be more sensitive and knowledgeable about working in a criminal court system that punishes sex workers unduly. The project emerged from the desires of women community leaders in Angeles to educate and reach out to their community about the continuing sex trade in their city. More fundamentally, they wanted to alleviate the economical, social, and legal hardships of prostitutes. The project was never intended to stamp out prostitution in Angeles City. Rather, project partners hoped to reduce the harm to women in prostitution and to give them choices in the matter of livelihoods.

We took our lead from the Philippine Plan for Gender-Responsive Development, 1995–2025, which outlines ways in which prostitution is discriminatory and suggests what needs to be done to alleviate the hardships of women in prostitution. The following four points were incorporated into our training plans:

1. Expose the racism and sexism of tourism, militarism, and sex trafficking.
2. Design and initiate feminist consciousness-raising programs for law enforcers and members of the judiciary.

127

3. Intensify public information, education, and communication campaigns with a focus on the double standard of morality, the premium placed on virginity, and the images of women in the media.
4. Educate women in the hospitality industry in respect to their right to file charges for rape, physical injuries, and sexual abuse and inform them of the protection and assertion of the rights of workers in the hospitality industry.

As stated in Chapter 1, we worked with five Filipino partners, two NGOs (WEDPRO and the Soroptimists), two government organizations (the police and the judges), and the university. We chose two NGOs that had links with women in prostitution or links to the broader community. Both groups agreed that the education of the larger community was a necessity and that such education could come about only with the cooperation of the local citizenry. Members of the Soroptimists, as recognized community leaders, had both the credibility and long-term interests in the community to undertake such a sensitive community-education initiative. In terms of capacity building, the Soroptimists needed information about prostitution, public-speaking skills, adult education, literacy training, micro-enterprises, and gender-sensitivity training. WEDPRO, the grassroots partner, had three community organizers in Angeles when we started the project and had articulated the need to increase its capacities to educate the bar girls through peer education. WEDPRO also wanted training in program evaluation, counseling skills, and organizational and resources development. It had the knowledge about the bar girls' situations, but it lacked a public forum to deliver its message. In addition, Angeles University had worked in many community-based projects and was interested in working with us on adult-education programs for the partners and the larger community. The university articulated a need for more information on the prostitution problem.

Our expected results were fourfold:

1. Partner institutions in Angeles would be able to carry out appropriate training programs for judges, police, the general public, and prostitutes.
2. Partner institutions would have increased capacity to conduct social research.
3. Links between governmental and nongovernmental organizations in the Philippines and those between the Philippines and Canada would be strengthened.
4. The Canadian public would be informed of development issues related to the international sex trade.

Our first and most important component consisted of developing the training programs for judges, police, and Soroptimists. In our first year we were able to do a needs assessment of all the groups and introduced the partners to gender-sensitivity training. All groups, except WEDPRO, which already had the necessary training, received basic gender-sensitivity training and then train-the-trainers sessions. Maria puts it this way:

Maria: I know that this project will benefit, not only the local partners for the training that they're going to get, but ultimately the women in prostitution. I usually tell people that it's something like trainers' training, wherein each partners are trained on gender sensitivity, toward the women, and this training that we are having since we started, I think has made a lot of difference already.

All of the Filipino groups had a Canadian counterpart in either the judiciary, police, university, or community group, and at each session they would devise together "best practices" based on the current training programs in both Canada and the Philippines and an assessment by the Filipinos about which aspects of which programs would be culturally appropriate in the Philippines. The judicial training was conducted by a Canadian judge and law professor in conjunction with the Philippine Judicial Academy and Filipino judges and law professors. The police training was conducted by current and former members of the Halifax City Police and the Royal Canadian Mounted Police, as well as an adult-education facilitator. They worked with a core group of PNP officers, male and female, and gradually expanded their training to over seventy-five police. For the most part, the training was conducted separately according to groups, but approximately every six months all the partners would get together to make sure the training was consistent and on schedule.

Davida: With the Canadian partners, we plan a training for the trainers, the PNP trainers. We develop modules for the PNP trainers, and recently we undergone the advance gender-sensitivity training for the PNP trainers that is called the "Filipino approach towards prostituted women." So, before this [advanced] training, we had already undergone the basic gender-sensitivity training when the two Canadian counterparts visited Angeles.

Much of the capacity development for the partners took place through informal channels and "learning by doing" rather than through formal training programs. As Appendix 1 shows, in addition to the training delivered by Canadians in Canada and in the Philippines, Filipino partners carried out a number of other activities (with and without Canadian participation). Specific examples include the gender-sensitivity training programs developed by the PNP, the social-context training program developed by the judiciary, the community-outreach program developed by the Soroptimists, and the research projects carried out by AUF. Both the PNP and the judges of Angeles City delivered the gender-sensitivity and social-context training modules that they developed to other police and judges. The police and Soroptimists also delivered gender-sensitivity training to barangay officials involved in law enforcement at the local level. (See Table 6–2.)

The second component of the project consisted of social-research skills, requested by the partners, to allow them to evaluate the effects of the project and their own work. We did methodology and statistical workshops with the different groups and focused on interviewing, needs assessments, and alternative forms of research such as video and theater of the oppressed. In the early years of the project, several partners carried out very preliminary needs assessments and information gathering about the women in prostitution. The AUF is now conducting research on a more systematic basis. It completed a community survey on attitudes toward prostitution and other related social issues. The results of this survey were shared with other partners and with the community during a 2003 mini-conference. (See Table 6–1.)

The third component of the project turned out to be one of the most important: strengthening the links among the Filipino organizations and providing a forum for dialogue between the Philippine and Canadian partners. In our first planning mission in 1999, we reported to the Association

Table 6–1

Expected results	Actual results
Staff from all partners trained in social-research methodologies	All partners conducted community consultations and research projects. The AUF carried out a research project in Angeles City measuring community attitudes toward prostitution and other social issues.
Improved information/research on prostitution in Angeles City	Project partners collaborated to share knowledge both among themselves and with other government, nongovernment and community-based organizations.

Table 6–2

Expected results	Actual results
Training program curricula for PNP (male and female)	Gender-sensitivity training programs delivered by the identified PNP trainers to the Angeles City PNP and to barangay officials
Training program curricula for judges	Two social-context training programs delivered by judges in Angeles City to other judges
Training program curricula for female prostitutes, including basic human rights and economic alternatives	Production of a draft handbook on legal rights for prostitutes Livelihood and literacy training programs delivered at the Women Helping Women Center (WHWC), primarily by Soroptimists
Public education capacity of Soroptimists enhanced	Soroptimist-created materials distributed to the public and public-education programs related to prostitution in the barangays of Angeles City delivered, in collaboration with the PNP and AUF; Soroptimists working on an educational video for the public.
International project management capacity enhanced	Filipino partners learned about project design, proposal writing, project management, and monitoring and evaluation. They have begun to produce funding proposals related to the WHWC and the shelter. Project management skills are also being used on other projects carried out by individual partners.
Counseling skills improved for AUF, Soroptimists, and PNP Women's Desk	A counseling manual was developed by AUF for use in the WHWC.

of Universities and Colleges of Canada (AUCC) that the results were "electrifying" because, for the first time, members of governmental organizations like the judges and police realized what an asset an organization like WEDPRO could be because of its research on prostitution. WEDPRO realized how valuable it would be to work with the Soroptimists and develop a broader public-education campaign, because WEDPRO had the information but it needed the Soroptimists in order to get its message heard in the community. This collaboration was to continue throughout the life of the project and beyond. It enabled all the partners to expand their activities, through collaboration with other local organizations, coordinate their activities and in the end come together to build a shelter for the women. To further illustrate, Maria tells us a story about how three of the groups (Soroptimists, WEDPRO, and the PNP) worked together to help a bar girl after the project was over:

> **Maria:** Like one girl who tried to get out of that business, and the bar owner confiscated her things, you know, so what we did was, when Carmela [WEDPRO] called me up, I called up Davida [PNP], so Davida did some persuasion, you know, until finally we were able to get her things, plus the things of the other girls that were confiscated. She got her stuff back and now she's out of Angeles. Davida was able to talk to the bar owner, and the bar owner agreed to give her stuff back. Because, at first, the bar owner was asking for ten thousand pesos, to pay, well of course, you know, they said they owe the owners for food, and blah, blah, blah. . . . But actually, she has worked so hard for it, and she just want her stuff back, so, she was able to get it back. And now she's out of Angeles. I could say that that's a success story. And this makes me happy, if I hear stories like that.

There was history of collaboration between the Soroptimists and the PNP Women's Desk going back some five years before the start of the project, but the other partners had little or no history of working together. Within a year of the start of the project, partners began working together on developing and staffing the WHWC. The center, which is located next to the clinic that the women visit for their weekly health checks, opened in June 2000. It is used as a drop-in center for the women, houses a "children's corner," and provides a space for the women to interact with some of the Filipino project partners. Further, as can be seen under the list of activities, a number of social and training activities had taken place at the WHWC. These activities have provided the women with some practical skills training and, perhaps more important, tried to raise feelings of self-esteem and self-worth among the women.

The project, then, gave its widely disparate partners the opportunity to interact and share information in a way that was not previously possible. Now that strong relations have been established among the partners, they have turned their attention to exploring possibilities for collaboration with other organizations such as the Department of Social Welfare and Development and the Angeles City municipal government. An important indication of the strength of the partnership is the fact that the partners turn to one another first for assistance in carrying out further projects. For example, when the PNP Women's Desk identified a need for a women's shelter, it immediately involved the Soroptimists and the AUF in raising funds and developing plans for the shelter. The judges and the PNP have been collaborating on a plan to reduce the number of customers going to brothels in the casa area by increasing police presence at the entrance points to the area. AUF and the Soroptimists have also been involved in these plans through assisting in the building of kiosks or outposts for the PNP at strategic points near the area.

Table 6–3

Expected results	Actual results
A network is now in place through which Filipino partners can communicate.	Project partners meet on a regular basis to review progress and plan future project activities.
Filipino partners collaborate with one another in a variety of areas.	Project partners are collaborating with one another and with a variety of other groups—including the municipal government, prosecutors, the Department of Social Welfare and Development, and an organization of bar owners—to work on the problems relating to prostitution.

The final component of the project was public engagement and internationalization, and for this we produced a film called *Selling Sex in Heaven* for a North American audience, helped create a training video for the Soroptimists, and did a participatory video and theater-of-the-oppressed project with WEDPRO. Though its main function was to work with the other groups and give them the necessary information about prostitution in Angeles so they could do their educational work, WEDPRO was committed to producing a video for the bar girls.

Katerina: Under the project, WEDPRO is doing a participatory video project. It started as a small project that we wanted to do with the women, with the assistance from our Canadian partners, but it's turning out to be a video project that incorporates our dreams and our visions and we're getting excited about that. We see the women on the video, and we also see them in a different perspective, and that's new to us. We see them all the time, but when they start talking about themselves, about their own dreams, about their plans and what they have gone through in their life that also inspires us. And I think if they also see themselves on the video, and other people, other women see these survivors, talking about their struggles and how they've managed to make something of their lives, even as they continue to be in difficult circumstances, I think it's going to do a lot for the women who continue to remain in prostitution. For WEDPRO, I think we have not expressed that as we have been doing the video, maybe because we are immersed in the production of the video, but at the end of the process I think it is also changing us in a way. In a way it's true that it is participatory. Participatory in that it is also for us, for WEDPRO, as much as it is for the women.

The overall impact we wanted to have through the project was to create fundamental changes in attitudes toward prostitutes in Filipino society and to strengthen the capacity of the Filipino partners to educate and train all those involved in or affected by the sex trade. Over the five years of the project, we did training programs for eleven municipal and trial court judges, fourteen appeal court judges, sixty-five male police officers, ten women police officers, countless community members through the Soroptimists' outreach in the barangays, and several dozen bar girls through WEDPRO's workshops (see Appendix 1). We evaluate the changes we made in "So, What Did We Accomplish" later in this chapter.

The Partners

Our main Filipino partner was the women's group Soroptimist International; a longstanding member and past president was the Philippines' project director. Using the Soroptimists as our main project partner was controversial at first because in these university partnership programs the main partner in the South is usually a university. We believed that, given the parameters of the project, community leaders were needed more than academic researchers. WEDPRO, which expressed interest in being the lead partner, also did not have the community buy-in required to meet the needs of the project. One of the other justifications for working with the Soroptimists, though this was not explicit at the time, was the intuitive belief that "it is the elite women in any society who are likely to be the fundamental change agents because they are most likely to be admitted to the halls of education or the realms of power."[1] In the Philippines we found this to be true, and the support of these more privileged women was crucial to the success of our project.

Soroptimist International is a very active, voluntary organization making a difference in its community; the "clout" of its members translates ideas into action. We witnessed many times not only how its members can move and influence the community to care about social issues, but also how successfully they can raise money and solicit governmental support. As mentioned above, one of the first activities of the Soroptimists was setting up the WHWC at the social-hygiene clinic where we had our office. The Soroptimists themselves were astonished by the extent of the problem in Angeles, felt that many people had no idea this was going on around them, and therefore believed that something had to be done.

> **Maria:** As I have said, maybe God is leading us to this way to tell us really, so we will know what's going on. You know, when I talk to friends, even in Manila, I tell them, you always say that Angeles is an entertainment city. So, I said why? Because it's just here in Fields Avenue, and we never knew what was going on there. I live how many blocks only from Fields? And I'm sure it's not only me. Most of the people here don't know.

The Soroptimists have tried in the past to do alternative livelihood training for the bar girls, but they were not able to keep it up because the bar girls could not commit to particular days and times due to their erratic schedules and demanding bar owners and customers.

> **Maria:** Well, actually what's disturbing really is, like the Soroptimists, we try our best to give them an alternative livelihood. We started training them. Teach them how to do manicure, pedicure, or haircutting, but they cannot finish the course, even just for a short time. We tried to adjust to their schedules, to what they want, but still, you know that, according to them, that when there is a customer who comes and they are bar fined for a week or two weeks, so, we can never have them on those days so it's just frustrating, really. But, of course, you know, as I have been telling my fellow Soroptimists, let's not give up.

The Soroptimists also worked closely with the PNP Women's Desk and helped to sponsor the pilot project. They had a respectful, class-based relationship, and at first the members of the PNP were very deferential to the other partners, particularly the judges and Soroptimists. But the policewomen became some of our strongest trainers and allies, and they regularly had contact with the bar girls.

> **Davida:** Our role in this project, because as a police officer, we are one of those who the abused women, particularly the prostituted women comes into contact, like ah, there are women who are involved in some bars, entertainment establishments, like casas, so we are there, the officers that are responsible to look after their welfare, and likewise, of course, we have clues pertaining to prostitution that's why as a police officer, we do investigations regarding this case.

The PNP in particular knew that because prostitution is illegal, the women were reluctant to report injuries or offenses against them, and that the girls did not trust the police to protect them. This was something that the Women's Desk wanted to change by becoming more involved in community outreach.

> **Davida:** I think some problems we encounter in this with regards to this prostituted women is that some are not, especially when they come to our office and they were reportedly victimized by their customer. Some are not willing to file charges against their abuser, maybe some are afraid they might be laid off by the owners or by their mamasan. And when the case was filed in the prosecutor's office, they come to amicable settlement, that is, they were paid by the suspect not to prosecute the case.

The PNP's relationship with WEDPRO, however, was not good. There was historic animosity between the two groups because some members of the PNP were involved in protecting the prostitution industry and because WEDPRO saw the police only in their role as law enforcers—those who criminalized the women and enforced an unfair law.

> **Davida:** Actually, all the partners know that the WEDPRO and the PNP were not in same perception, because the WEDPRO, I think you know that also, that they always blame the PNP of what is going on, or because they don't understand our situation. Now that we have closer relationships with them, so now they understand that we just do our jobs, same as them. Their ideologies is

different in us, so, but now, because of the project we have one goal. That is for the benefits of the prostituted women, so, we came to understanding what is our part and their part.

The very fact that Davida and the PNP referred to the bar girls as *prostituted women* was a huge victory for WEDPRO, because it was committed to the use of that term, not *prostitute* or *sex worker*. WEDPRO, as mentioned, was our main grassroots partner, and the directors in Manila and the outreach workers in Angeles were dedicated to the prostituted women. They saw their work as a calling—something they had to do.

Katerina: My personal motivation, I think, comes from my activism. I have no word for it at the moment, no other word for it, but one thing, to change certain conditions in society. I cannot change the world, but, if I can do my bit, then, that's . . . that's what I have to do. It is very important for me personally to change conditions in society. Education is one, but beyond that, short of saying we want a revolution. I want that, that by education, by engaging with other sectors in society we can change the conditions for women and children and for everybody else.

WEDPRO had been working in Angeles since the American bases closed, and WEDPRO members were researchers, lobbyists, and activists not only for the prostituted women but also for the larger Filipino community. They saw themselves as advocates for the most disadvantaged. They had been instrumental in getting sexual-assault and domestic-violence legislation changed and were key organizers for the women's movement in the Philippines.

Katerina: WEDPRO works mainly with women in prostitution and women in situations of sexual exploitation. We do training with them, education work with them, on their rights and what alternatives are out there for them and they can think about, once they've decided to leave prostitution. Apart from that, we also do preventative education work with the communities, because we see prostitution as existing in societies that allow such exploitation to happen and that is the precondition for the exploitation of women, so we need to educate also the public, that this should not happen to our fellow women, and to our children, to our neighbors, to our own relatives. We try to do advocacy with the different sectors in Philippine society. We have worked with legislators; we've lobbied, for example, for the passage of an anti-rape law in the country. That changes the nature of the crime of rape. It used to be a crime against chastity, and under that law, prostituted women cannot be raped because, after all, they are not chaste any more. But, because we have changed that law and we've redefined it as a crime against persons, regardless of where you come from, and that's a triumph for women in general. We also work with people in academia, trying to do research with them and getting also their expertise in trying to understand more the situation of women, and we do networking, we exist within the women's movement. We see ourselves as part of a broader movement of women trying to create the conditions within which women's rights can be fully exercised.

WEDPRO saw its role in the project as particularly important because it had access to the "beneficiaries" of the project and believed that it had the prostituted women's best interests in mind at all times.

Katerina: WEDPRO's role in the project is to bring the women in prostitution's perspective into the discussions, into the activities, and make everything that they do within this project, work for the women. That means, getting the women's sentiment across to the police, across to the judges, across to the people working in the universities and to other NGOs within the project. It's basically trying to make our partners understand the women better because WEDPRO has a direct link with the women in the bars, the streetwalkers, women working in the karaoke bars, and the casas.

The other two partners, the judges and the university members, were less involved with the bar girls themselves but crucial to the overall success of the project. Their evolving understanding of the problem came about largely in their interactions with the other partners. For example, the social-context training of the judges, or the social-research training of university faculty needed community voices, often supplied by members of WEDPRO or of the Soroptimists. In many ways those in the university became resource people for the police, the Soroptimists, and WEDPRO, and they in turn were resource people for the judges.

The Problem of Social Change

Just as we could not have picked a more divisive issue than prostitution, we may also have underestimated the problems working with such a diverse coalition. The problems of coalition-building have been well documented.[2] Women's groups are particularly fraught with conflict because of different ideologies, different goals, and different strategies. Our project was no different. There was passion from every person involved and a real commitment to making a difference in Angeles, even though the end goals (clearly spelled out in the beginning of the project) might have been quite different. For instance, we attempted to incorporate the feminist message of WEDPRO, the grassroots advocacy group, into the discourse of the community of Angeles without alienating the rest of the community. WEDPRO did not see its approach as alienating and wanted to be the lead trainer. We trained the Soroptimists, who have status and legitimacy within the community, to be the messengers, because they could deliver the message in a way that would be heard. WEDPRO felt it should be the messenger because it knew the bar girls best and had the best political message. We conducted gender-sensitivity training for the police and judges to raise their level of awareness about the problems of gender, generally, and to the plight of prostituted women, specifically. WEDPRO felt that the police and judges were, in many ways, irredeemable. These conflicts made for interesting conversations and debates. We still believe it is only by cooperating in this and similar projects that the situation of prostituted women will be improved, but it is long, tough work.

WEDPRO had been working in Angeles since the bases closed with mixed results. It did excellent research and had contact with the bar girls, but its relations with the rest of the community were not good. Coming from a Marxist, revolutionary perspective, the directors from Manila operated in an adversarial way that upset many of the partners. They saw themselves as being at the forefront in trying to create radical change and resisted working with governmental organizations and privileged upper-class women. Consequently, WEDPRO had the research and the passion, but its delivery was dogmatic and antagonistic, and therefore not conducive to or effective in making change because the other partners found it very difficult to work with its members. For WEDPRO, there was a constant tension (rage even) that the other partners were not doing enough and did not have the "right" political perspective.

Katerina: Another friend once asked me, how come Filipinos are always smiling in the face of this injustice? At the time I could not express to him that there is rage inside, but it's a rage, that if it just let out, it will drive us mad. How come we are not acting like the Arabs? It's what the Arabs are doing, it's a kind of insanity, and it's the anger that's driving them insane, and I think, my personal thoughts about this is, if . . .

My personal feeling is that, if I let this anger overcome me, it will kill me, and I think Filipinos have, in many ways, turned that anger inside and have tried to cope with it by our own laughter, by our own, you know, in a way our perverted sense of humor. We have a, you know, a perverted sense of humor. We think we are funny, and we like ourselves that way, but never mistake that there is no anger. There is, there is rage inside.

There is no question that the directors from Manila were very committed to WEDPRO and the prostituted women. They were devoted to their cause to the point that it was the focus of their lives, almost to the exclusion of all else.

Katerina: I can't think of a single event or single incident that is most satisfying in my work, in WEDPRO, because I see my work in WEDPRO as always taking so much from me and it also makes me, wait, I can't express myself . . . [starts to cry]. . . . OK, it's every time I have to push myself and I have to find, search a certain part of myself that will make me able to respond to the situation or to an issue. So, satisfaction is not something I can derive literally, but it's always a searching for something that's inside you that you have to find. No, I don't think so, it's not a job, it's more of a commitment and more of a responsibility. Sometimes, you want to get out of it, but you feel you are responsible also.

One of the problems we encountered, then, is the dilemma for a project when one group holds so strongly to an ideology and particular prescription that it is not willing to compromise and do the necessary community building required to make change. In this case, WEDPRO's desire to eliminate prostitution undermined the practical issues of how to do this. It was so used to "preaching to the converted" (other radical abolitionist feminists) that it was unable or unwilling to change the message so it would be more palatable to the community. The other problem for the partnership from the beginning was the lack of agreement on goals and strategies. Four of the five Filipino partners were interested in changing people's behavior and attitudes toward the bar girls, changing the laws on prostitution, and setting up a shelter—clearly reform-oriented goals. WEDPRO was peripherally interested in those goals, but saw itself primarily working toward the radical social, economic, and political transformation of society. This was difficult for government employees, like the judges and police, as well as the "pillars of the community," the Soroptimists. WEDPRO was not interested in making the women's lives better within prostitution, only in getting them out of prostitution. But with no alternatives for them, the women would have had no livelihood and would be worse off then they were before. Our non-feminist community partners wanted concrete ways to help the women: a shelter for when they left the bars, not charging the women with vagrancy, and alternative livelihoods. The radical feminist group wanted too big a change, too quickly (even though all groups agreed that in a perfect world, there would be no prostitution) and came across as berating the other partners when they would not use the same strategies.

Group dynamics being what they are, we did not presume that all would go smoothly all the time. But we were hampered by the ideology of one group that did not want to compromise. As Piotr Sztompka argues, "Too strong an emphasis on the articulation of the ideal structure produces utopianism and various brands of dogmatism."[3] This kind of dogma, he argues, can cripple an organization and weaken its ability to make change. WEDPRO had a very rigid view of the world, and it could never accept the role we (the Canadian and Filipino project directors) gave it. Its attitude was: give us the money, let us do the training, and get out. Unfortunately, though it may have had wonderful theoretical knowledge, it lacked the contacts with and confidence of the bar girls, and it had a very adversarial relationship with the other Filipino partners. WEDPRO was antagonistic with anyone in authority, whether the governmental authority of the police and judges, the class-based authority of the Soroptimists, or the knowledge-based (neo-colonial) authority of the Canadians.

> **Katerina:** It is difficult because in the project I was confronted with a bigger context and it's rooted in our history. Working on the project and seeing the Canadians speaking and dealing and relating to all the Filipino partners and telling them, talking to them about human rights and how to treat women in prostitution, while the Filipino partners do not talk to each other and have not learned to listen to each other, that disturbs me, because again, we are listening to foreigners more than the Filipinos. We are identifying with foreigners more than ourselves. I see what's happening in the project as not totally unrelated to what's happening in Fields Avenue between the bar women and the white men who come here to buy sex. It's a continuum, I think, of a relationship that has to be critically challenged within the project. It's a history of looking after the foreigners and not seeing ourselves as the source of our own power, or the source of our own enlightenment.

Unfortunately, while this might be theoretically true and very familiar to the post-colonial critique, Canadians did some of the training because all of the partners had issues with WEDPRO; some of these issues came down to its ideology, and some to its lack of interpersonal skills and, ironically, a lack of appreciation of its own cultural norms. When WEDPRO members berated someone publicly, they didn't seem to realize how they alienated WEDPRO's Filipino partners. WEDPRO members, because they saw themselves as on the side of "Truth" (and therefore of the women), felt justified in telling the partners exactly what they thought of their liberal or conservative ideas and how misguided they were. There was no sense of how the delivery of the message might be taken by the other partners, and no sense that people might not like to be berated and judged, or that sometimes *how* we say something is as important as *what* we say. In this we were reminded of an anecdote told by Trina Grillo in her article on anti-essentialism: A colleague goes to a Thanksgiving dinner party and proceeds to correct his host when she tells him she made vegetarian dressing for him, and regular dressing for everyone else. Says he: "No, there is vegetarian dressing and there is meat-eater's dressing, but neither one of them is regular dressing." . . . The lesson [he] taught his host was that of anti-essentialism.[4] Maybe, but at what cost, we wonder, to his relations with the host? His desire to make a political point, it seems, was more important than his gratitude to the host for remembering and accommodating his "difference." The lesson for us all, perhaps, is not to take ourselves or our ideologies quite so seriously.

WEDPRO had a particularly tough time with the police, which was not surprising given the police's historic role in arresting the women and criminalizing them. Some police were also implicated in extortion and kickbacks related to the casas, so WEDPRO was right to be suspicious. But we also worked with wonderful police officers who became champions of the project and of the bar girls. The other partners understood that there are good and bad people in any organization and that we should not write off an entire group. Refusing to work with a group is especially counterproductive when we need to change the attitudes and behaviors of individuals in that group. We made a strategic decision to work with the police, believing that changing even one individual will have a ripple effect and that people will see how they themselves can make a difference. Rather than closing a door and making more enemies, we chose to work from within the system and, in the end, WEDPRO could not do it and left the project.

This frustrating experience made us very curious about the process of social change. Can change actually happen as quickly and in the revolutionary way desired by WEDPRO? Why were we not able to convince WEDPRO that incremental change leads to more fundamental change? Why were they not able to convince us that revolution was the way to go? These questions led us to reflect on the nature of change.

Change, growth, and *development* are all words that mean some form of evolution, transformation, difference from one time to another, or changes in beliefs, ideas, and behaviors. The words have very different meanings depending on one's ideology and world view. Is growth merely organic and effortless? Are we indeed progressing in a linear fashion from one stage of development to another? Does development of thought and idea happen naturally? Or does change require human commitment and human sweat, struggle, and exertion? Is change merely imposed on societies externally, or does change not occur within societies? Is the idea of change all of the above?

There are many theories of social change, and sociologists have claimed that the desire to understand a rapidly changing society is what prompted early social scientists to develop the study of sociology in the first place—to understand, predict, and ultimately control the chaos that they saw around them. Although there is no one singular theory of change, change is seen to be ubiquitous, normal, and usually non-violent.[5] Theories of change range from the cyclic theories of Toynbee to the evolutionary and dialectical development theories of Comte and Marx, the structural-functionalist theories of Parsons, and the social-psychological theories of McClelland. Whether the theories are dealing with linear or nonlinear change, with a predestined end point or not, these theories help us to understand how change occurs—the mechanisms, agents, targets, and strategies of change. They show how ideologies affect change, both positively and negatively, and attempt to explain which has more influence—action or ideas. They have shown how revolutions like those in France and America produced political changes but little change in people's economic, social, and cultural life, while the Chinese revolution transformed the overall culture. Theorists have shown how social reform takes place through intensive, long-term activism and how it is usually "the achievement of active minorities which, while sometimes militant and always persistent, were also patient and non-violent."[6]

Traditional theories of change, such as evolutionary, cyclical, and historical progress, have given way to the importance of process and dynamic cause and effect; the idea of inherent or inevitable change has fallen by the wayside. The notion of social progress has been with humanity in one form or another for at least three thousand years,[7] but it has only been recently that disillusionment with progress has been theorized about and hotly debated. Some progress has been unquestionably "good," things like medical advances and cures for contagious diseases. Others have been "bad," such as the pollution arising from unfettered development and the poverty and inequalities of the Third World. The terms *development* and *modernization* have become value laden, but *development* can mean simply the "improvement in the health, wealth and wisdom of everyone."[8] Most theorists recognize that improvement in people's well-being is not guaranteed by taking a singular, inevitable path but must be advanced, politically and ideologically. The notion of progress and the postmodern disillusionment with progress and modernity that started with Marx continue with the post-colonialists and post-structuralists of today. The effects of industrialization and urbanization on developing nations have been decidedly mixed. Global inequalities seem worse, pollution seems worse, as do wars, but at the same time, we are now at a moment in history where we search for solutions for problems rather than thinking of them as inevitable, and where we take personal responsibility for the wrongs we see around us. Only a century and a half ago, these "bad" things were seen as fated, inevitable, or God's will.[9]

The targets of change are many—individuals, groups, and societies—depending on the goal of the change and the extent of the desired behavior or attitude modification. Structural change can be brought about by the state, mass movements, revolutions, or social movements exerting pressure on those in power.[10] The methods of change are also very important and were crucial in our project. Robert Lauer distinguishes between power strategies and attitude strategies and argues that both strategies are needed at different times and in different contexts. For instance, he uses the example of Saul Alinsky to show the effective power tactics he used—demonstrations, confrontations, and active resistance—but how antagonistic he was and how he alienated more people than he converted. Attitude strategies, on the other hand, are more subtle and used to influence people behind the scenes; they involve more use of media and education. This difference was evident in our groups. WEDPRO believed in using power tactics and was active in many demonstrations against the government. It believed that the four other Filipino partners should join it in protesting and embarrassing the local government for its hypocrisy about the sex trade. In the Philippines, in particular, there is a clear cultural context for the effectiveness of protest. The country has a history of mass movements leading to a change of government. In the past twenty years, two presidents have been removed from office and, in one case, a democratically elected president was brought down by mass action. However, the other groups were very uncomfortable with these strategies and did not want to participate. The judges and police obviously had a conflict of interest because they worked for the government, but the Soroptimists and professors were also reluctant to undermine the influence they felt they could exert by working behind the scenes and interacting with the mayor and council through more informal networks. WEDPRO believed that this tactic was coopting and made it clear, as did Saul Alinsky, that it had little use for attitude strategy.[11]

> **Katerina:** I have thought and thought about how WEDPRO can affect the project in a constructive way without offending, without attacking people, but [we need to] make people see how they ought to see things. I do not expect people to see the project the way I see it, immediately, but at the moment I just want the space to be able to express that and to be heard.

This perfectly illustrates the dilemma with the critical left's view of change. Marxist and post-colonialist arguments tend to take the "all or nothing" approach because small changes translate to no change to some. Incremental change is suspect because, they would argue, small change merely allows the existing system to continue. For years, some Marxists objected to the welfare state because it would delay the revolution; that is, if the working class is kept from complete ruin and the workers have access to a basic standard of living, then they would not feel as motivated to overthrow capitalism and the ruling class. Some feminists hold a similar outlook on prostitution. Anything but eradication means that women are victimized and their exploitation legitimized and normalized—regardless of whether or not they choose to work as prostitutes, or whether or not they themselves feel victimized, or whether or not decriminalization would protect them from violence. Anything that legitimizes the work, even if it benefits the individual woman working in the sex trade, is a slippery slope to sex work as work like any other. As we point out, a more nuanced, contextual viewpoint is necessary if any change is to occur, and that means recognizing that the circumstances of a call girl in Los Angeles or Toronto is very different from that of a trafficked Nepali or Filipino child.

Post-colonialists also tend to have a very ahistorical, static account of cultural change, seeing the changes as one-way and detrimental. Sociologists have long differentiated between the notion of diffusion, that is, the spread of elements from one country or culture to another, an example being the spread of tea from Asia to Europe, with the notion of acculturation, a much greater "influence exercised by one culture on another, or the mutual influence of two cultures, that results in cultural change."[12] Maybe the problem is also one of concern for complexity. Left-wing academics do not want to condemn a culture they do not know much about and are anxious about being seen as racist or colonialist. They are worried about the real problems with doing development and "interfering" in another's culture. Who are *we* to say something is wrong? As we discussed in Chapter 2, academic ambivalence about action seems rooted in a reluctance to offer seemingly simplistic solutions to complex problems. Unfortunately, this leads to the paralysis dilemma. As Jay Weinstein argues, the huge costs of development and the Gordian knot—"a problem so complex that no ordinary mortal can solve it"—means that post-colonialist and post-structuralist theorists give up on solutions.[13]

Sometimes the problem is genuinely so big that people can be overwhelmed by its magnitude, and this can cause paralysis as well. Noam Chomsky, the activist-academic, often ends his lectures with a question-and-answer period and inevitably receives the same sort of question: "You've told us the problems, now what can we do about it?" His answer is vague. "'You've got to organize,' is Chomsky's perennial response."[14] What does that mean concretely? What will it do to solve the world's problems, especially when the culprits, according to Chomsky, are global capitalism, militarism, and American imperialism? How does one eliminate something as amorphous as imperialism or something as widespread as global capitalism or something as longstanding as the deadly rivalries in Rwanda? It seems to us that taking on anything that big will inevitably bring on political paralysis. Chomsky himself recognizes the problem, and Baumgardner and Richards believe he tells them to organize "to comfort people from his depressing predictions about the state of the world."[15] The problem is how to get to the next step—from awareness and critique to action—without creating paralysis and indifference or apathy. Perhaps a more realistic understanding of how change occurs will help.

Many scholars argue that for social change to occur a critical mass or a tipping point is required—that increased numbers of people thinking, believing and/or doing something will gradually lead to change in that behavior or attitude.[16] As issues become more commonplace, and therefore more acceptable, more people will adopt the same behavior or think of it as normalized. Some compelling examples of these types of changes can be drawn from issues of morality. Whereas in the 1960s it was still shameful for women to have children "out of wedlock," this is a far more common and acceptable act today, especially for Western professional women. The same can be said for other so-called moral issues such as the use of contraceptives, abortion, premarital sex, and living in a common-law relationship. It seems quaint today to tell students of a time when only married women could get a prescription for birth-control pills or when couples had to show marriage licenses to rent a hotel room together. These changes in morality seem unlikely to be reversed in the Western world, despite the efforts of some conservative and religious groups. More recent examples include the notion of same-sex marriage. Unheard of thirty years ago (when homosexuality itself was illegal in many states), this is also becoming more widespread and familiar. Four countries, including Canada, have now legalized same-sex marriage, and many other states are moving in that direction. Years ago, single or gay people could not adopt children; it is now becoming a much more normalized practice. Other examples include the widespread use of seatbelts and helmets compared to even ten years ago, the decline in the numbers of people who drink and drive, the increasing numbers of people who claim that the environment and recycling are concerns for them, and the increased visibility of, and action against, violence against women. All of these activities are relatively recent, and most people over thirty can probably remember a time when there were no such things as car restraints for children, and helmets or seatbelts were for the timid or elderly.

The reason for these sea changes in attitudes and behaviors can partly be explained by the concept of critical mass or the more recent notion of a tipping point. This idea has been used for some time to explain the dearth of women in politics. As the argument goes, until the numbers of women in politics—or any other male-dominated institution—equal a certain percentage, usually over 30 percent, women will have to adapt themselves to the attitudes and behaviors of men. When a critical mass has been reached, the theory claims, women will be able to act as women, and there will be a normalization of women's place in politics, thereby encouraging even more women to see themselves as politicians. This was the argument of Rosabeth Moss Kanter and Barry Stein in their book on critical mass in organizations.[17] Kanter looked at the rates of minority group members in organizations, and her work has been extrapolated for use by political scientists interested in why there are so few women in politics in some nations and why so many in others, such as Norway and Sweden, where women are close to 50 percent of the politicians. Kanter argued that in a group with less than 20 percent of any minority group, whether divided by sex, race, or any other difference, the majority members of the group will overcompensate for their recognition of the women (or minority) in the group. For example, a male group will exaggerate masculinity when a woman is put in its midst, and that woman must adapt herself and her style to the men. A woman or minority is highly visible because of physical differences, and the men or dominant racial group become threatened by the presence of the difference, or, in postmodern language, the "other." This threat creates a hyper-masculine environment in the case of a male-dominated workplace, making it an even more difficult place for women. Women attempt to fit in by becoming more like men, trying to minimize their differences. Former British Prime Minister Margaret Thatcher is often held up as the perfect example of a woman in a male-dominated arena who became more masculine than the men—thus earning her the title Iron Lady. This has been confirmed by numerous studies in the 1980s that documented the difficulties faced by pioneering women in police forces, the military, and many blue-collar occupations where men were the majority. The 1997 movie *G.I. Jane* perfectly illustrates the problem of critical mass by depicting what happens when the first woman is admitted for training with the all-male Navy Seals. The men are hostile, threatened, and critical. She has to perform better than the men, and she has to do it by leaving any trace of her femininity behind: she shaves her head, lives with the men, and behaves as crudely and brutally as they do. Even more telling is the scene marking her acceptance as "one of the boys." She viciously fights their sadistic instructor and proves her worthiness (and his submission) by yelling at him, "Suck my dick!" to the roars of approval from the men. She has become one of them, symbolically. Of course, as Kanter points out, she can never be one of them literally, and therefore she will never fit in.

But how do changes in critical mass occur? In recent years the media have been huge purveyors of changes in attitudes and behavior. Another influence is education; awareness of a problem leads to feelings of shame, guilt, or anger about the problem, and these emotions eventually lead someone or a group of people to take action. In 2005 a right-wing weekly, *Human Events*, listed the ten most harmful books of the nineteenth and twentieth centuries. Along with the not surprising inclusion of works by Marx, Lenin, and Mao were Ralph Nader's *Unsafe at any Speed*, Rachel Carson's *Silent Spring*, and Betty Friedan's *Feminine Mystique*.[18] What we find interesting is what these books have in common, and why they are named by the conservatives as dangerous. All of these books are said to have had a major impact on changing social policy in the United States and elsewhere by laying the groundwork for changing behaviors and attitudes with regard to wearing seatbelts, caring about the environment, and believing that discrimination against women is wrong. The conservatives are right in their worry about these and many other books because they know that books, and other idea-generating media, can change people's ideas, beliefs, and eventually social and political legislation.

Examples of other agents of change are films and novels. John Tomlinson discusses how important mediated experience is in changing people's attitudes and beliefs (in lieu of direct experience).[19] Films like *The Killing Fields*, *Magdalene Sisters*, and *Shake Hands with the Devil* bring home the horror of what people can do to other people when their humanity is disregarded. "Harriet Beecher Stowe's *Uncle Tom's Cabin* made Blacks—the weight, solidity, injurability of their personhood—imaginable to the White population in pre–Civil War United States. E. M. Forster's *Passage to India* . . . enabled the British population to begin to reimagine India's population as independent."[20] Martin Luther King Jr.'s "Free at Last" speech in 1963 is said to have galvanized the remaining states to pass the twenty-fourth amendment, so that it was ratified in January 1964. All of these mediated experiences led to concrete changes in policy or constitutions. People became aware of a problem that triggered emotion for those affected, and, consequently, people (including many privileged people) were moved to action.

In the broader sense, then, how are emotion and empathy for others created? How do we get people to care about others who are not family, friends, or neighbors? How do we help people respect differences and see through the stereotypes of AIDS victims, gang-bangers, prostitutes, or drug addicts in ways that will make them care? How do we humanize the poor and disadvantaged in ways that will empower them and motivate others to try to do something? How do we open people's eyes about problems? In *Changing Minds* Howard Gardner says: "It is more difficult to change the mind when perspectives are held strongly, and publicly and by individuals of rigid temperament. It is easier to change minds when individuals find themselves in a new environment, surrounded by peers of a different persuasion."[21] This is what we consciously set out to do with training in Canada and the Philippines (and getting people out of their comfort zones)—training with similar groups and heterogeneous groups—and on the whole it worked. We did change minds. We began with the notion that, for the most part, as Gardner states, "minds change as the result of efforts by external agents" and that after starting with the original idea, we gave contrasting perspectives that could either be accepted or rejected until a tipping point was reached. A problem has to be recognized, and consciousness has to be raised about the problem. Then, with an awareness of the options—costs, benefits, and motivations—we often get a change in behavior. Most change, however, occurs gradually, often unnoticed and largely beneath the surface. "Moreover, when one's changes of mind co-occur with changes that have simultaneously occurred in the minds of millions of one's fellow citizens, they are unlikely to be noticed at all—they blend into the gradually evolving 'conventional wisdom' or Zeitgeist."[22]

Although at the time we would not have used these terms, this is what we attempted to do in our participatory video and theater-of-the-oppressed workshops, which were key parts of our educational and consciousness-raising work.[23] Feminists have not embraced either participatory video or theater of the oppressed wholeheartedly because critics claim that they are too individualized and put the emphasis on transforming the actions of the oppressed person rather than the actions of the oppressor. In practice, there is an acceptance that more privileged persons do not want to change the status quo, so it is incumbent on the less privileged persons to look at what they can do to restore their own power. What we have observed in practicing theater of the oppressed is the transformation of both oppressor and oppressed because of their mutual participation and dialogue. Everyone engages with the material, and the oppressor sees how he or she appears to the oppressed and vice versa. So, in practice, it is a consciousness-raising experience for all.

Gardner also believes that to change minds we need to reconcile stories that clash and look for similarities. He gives the examples of Bill Clinton and Newt Gingrich and their respective abilities to create change. Clinton looks for ways to paper over differences and find commonalities; Gingrich underscores differences and alienates "even some who might have been converted to his causes."[24] In doing so, Clinton was the better change agent. This very much resonates with our experiences with WEDPRO. We were not able to persuade WEDPRO that our similarities were more important than our differences, and our great failure was not convincing WEDPRO that it would benefit more from being in the

coalition than working alone outside it. This is the similarity we unfortunately see with post-colonialism, as discussed in Chapter 2. There is a
dogmatic quality to the beliefs that will not allow for reform-oriented
change and a reluctance to look for similarities rather than differences.

Ironically, we found that the more traditional liberal and conservative
women of Angeles had a far better sense of their community and could
effect change more easily from within than WEDPRO could from without. Amy Lind writes:

> Feminists from Third World countries are perhaps more aware of
> how local communities must negotiate male-based power embed-
> ded in local social relations and cultural practices, on the one hand,
> and the "Western gaze," which involves a universal agenda influ-
> enced by Western ideas promoted particularly by international
> development and human rights organizations on the other.[25]

Though Lind is referring to groups like WEDPRO, it was definitely the
privileged women of the Soroptimists—at most, liberal feminists—who
knew how to negotiate power both with the men in Angeles and with the
Canadians on the project.

What Did We Accomplish?

The project made many changes in the Philippines through several
different channels and strategies. We made changes on the individual,
community, and societal levels, and these changes were both subtle and
concrete. On a personal level, we think everyone who was involved in
the project changed to some degree. Some of us found the project life
changing; others were not so deeply influenced. Several participants specifically mentioned the policewomen as "blossoming" as the project un-
folded. They went from being timid, passive, rigid, and lacking confidence
to being active players in the project, speaking up at meetings, able to
take action, gaining confidence in their abilities, and seeing themselves
as having a "right to be there." Three of the policewomen were promoted during the project, and we surmise that this had to do with their
increased confidence and ability to speak up for themselves.

> **Davida:** In this project, the Canadian partners, I mean, you know,
> we learned very much from them. It helped the PNP a lot, the
> PNP in particular. Like myself, you know, before I can't even talk
> to a person who I think that she is more educated or higher posi-
> tion than mine. So, now, I can talk to them. That's one thing. But,
> ah, also in our internal organization the PNP, before the female

officers were not recognized or were dominated by male PNP officers. So now they also understand and so they now recognize us as their counterpart in the organization.

And we do not discount the influence of one person or the tremendous value of changing one person's mind or developing the confidence of one person. "Frequently, an unintended by-product of such [economic development] work is a change in attitude among those involved in the work, and the changes for women are often enormous. Because many women in developing areas have never left their village . . . what appear to be small changes to an outsider can have enormous consequences."[26] The consequences for our project alone were enormous because of Davida's influence on our training programs.

We saw real movement in the social consciousness of the Soroptimist and PNP participants, and a real change in how they perceived the bar girls. Within the casas the police started to treat the girls as victims of violence rather than criminals, and in several cases the casa owners were arrested rather than the women working in the casas. Through their involvement in the project, many individuals from the police to the Soroptimists started to see their role in the women's victimization. They came to recognize that by taking advantage of them or by ignoring them or by saying derogatory things about them, they had played a role in victimizing them. As a result of the training programs and other project activities, changes have been made to procedures and practices within the PNP in Angeles. Formerly, only male police officers were involved in the raids on the casas, and any women arrested were brought back to the Women's Desk at the police station. Now, female police officers accompany male officers on the raids.

Maria: I really saw a lot of difference in the way the PNP react now to the women in prostitution. Especially when we started involving fifteen PNP policemen and women. Well, one thing is, you know when we started this project, when they referred to the women, they just say "oh, those prostitutes," but now you don't hear them talking that way. And, one thing good also, there was something like a ruling that whenever they make raids in bars, it is now understood that there should always be a policewoman with them. And I believe that this has been done because of the project also, because of our persistence in talking to the directors, the city directors that have been taking over the PNP in Angeles.

Also, on the individual level, women working in the casas who used to be arrested are now offered the opportunity to leave the casa and either return home or pursue another line of work. The number of women taking advantage of this opportunity grew over the course of the project. In a recent raid, thirty-nine women expressed a desire to leave the sex trade, and several girls did go back to their families in the provinces to start new lives with the help of the partners. Before the project, only three or four women would agree to leave with the police. From the project perspective, this change in the number of women being "rescued" reflects the growing willingness of the women to trust the PNP Women's Desk and to accept its help.

> **Davida:** One experience is that we had survivor. We help her to go back to her family, and that she changed her life. She has now a new life. She has a family of her own. Happily married, so, that one thing I think we did our best. So that is one consolation that we get from them.

At the community level, we were able to get very diverse groups to come together to talk about the problems in Angeles. The groups learned from one another about what they do in the community and began to see the challenges that the others faced. Getting groups together face to face enabled some of the stereotypes that existed to be overcome and the diverse groups to gain respect for the contributions of the others. We built a strong alliance across socioeconomic levels, professions, and gender with groups that had never worked together before. There was an increase in awareness and social consciousness about the status of women in Angeles, not just about prostitution, but about women generally. Partners also collaborated on community-outreach programs in the barangays to raise awareness of the issues around prostitution and to help change attitudes within the community toward women in prostitution. In this way, prostituted women are less shunned by the community and thus have more opportunities to find alternative employment, should they decide to do so. Also, a more informed community, the partners believed, would act as advocates for the prostituted women and would then put pressure on policymakers within government to make changes to the laws governing prostitution. A major factor in the success of the WHWC and the hoped-for success of the women's shelter was the support of such groups as the Mayor's Office, the Department of Social Welfare and Development, and other women's groups and NGOs in Angeles City.

In terms of prostitution, specifically, the groups came to understand that the women were not always there because they wanted to be, but because they had little choice or were victims of violence; they came to be seen less as "others" and more like somebody's daughter, sister, or mother. The groups went from wanting, perhaps paternalistically, to save the women to seeing them as human beings. And it wasn't just the individual Soroptimist or police officer who was affected. Those trainers went back to their groups and influenced more people within the broader community as well. It was a forum for the issue to be recognized and talked about.

> **Davida:** Before this project, we always go to those casas and raid them and then prostituted women are always to be blamed and filed vagrancy for them, if we cannot find evidence for prostitution, we will prosecute. Up to vagrancy charges. Now that the project comes in and we understand the situation, we go to the casas, not for them to arrest. We go there and get them from the casa and bring them to our office, not to detain them, but to tell them their rights, to counsel them and if they wanted to go home actually we give them some financial [help].

In terms of the bar girls, our female PNP officers were able to make a connection with them through the WHWC—we always had an officer stationed there in case the women had problems—and through their regular trips into the bar area.

> **Davida:** Yeah, we are very happy that the results of our program, we win back the trust and confidence of this not only the women, as a whole, you know these prostituted women before, they are afraid of the police, but now they treat us as an older sister or friends, so, now that they are willing to confide their problems, they go to us and ask some help, that's it. And, for these minors, they treated us as their second mothers.

The number of casas also decreased during the project because the police were raiding and shutting them down, not just taking the women away to jail.

> **Maria:** When we started this project, and we went first to the area, there were more than twenty casas there, but now I heard there are only fourteen or fifteen casas, so, you know, I'm happy about that. And at the Christmas party yesterday at the center, there were two girls there who were brought by the PNP [rescued from a casa], I think their ages were around thirteen and fourteen, and I think these girls were being used by their parents to look for customers, you know, and bring them to the casa. So, probably to be used, and now these girls were rescued and I think that PNP are watching them.

Davida: Before this project, there are more than about twenty casas. But when we go there and talk to the owners as well as the maintainers, the pimps, the managers, they reduced to thirteen casas. When we go there and talk to them, we emphasize to these managers that, they know that their activities is illegal. We go there and have a dialogue to them that they are liable if they have minors, they keep them in the casa, they lock them. We advise them to let them go out, even out in the place to undergo medical examination, when the social hygiene come in, and not to hire minors. But, you know, they are hard-headed. They still hire minors. That's why we conducted some raids. Hopefully, we have cases filed in court and the same person, the same casa owner, she's facing now charges. I think there are four charges against her, of hiring minors.

This change in police procedures led to a need for a women's shelter at the head office of the PNP Women's Desk. Women "rescued" from the casas, as well as other women trying to escape domestic violence, need a place to stay for a few days while their cases are being prepared or while they decide what they want to do next. The project partners raised funds; obtained donations of equipment, furnishings, and supplies; and gathered community and local government support for the shelter. Several of the activities toward the end of the project focused on preparing business plans and procedures manuals for the shelter. The collaboration of all the partners in creating the shelter, which extends well beyond the life of the CIDA funding, is a good indicator of the sustainability of the project goals and the project partnership.

Davida: I think, if from this project, may I tell that if only we have a temporary shelter for them, for these women, because you know that when we do our rescue operations, we don't know where to bring them instead of sending them again, sending them out and they go back to their, to the casa. I think if we have just a, not a so sophisticated one, just a, for them to stay while waiting for their decision to go back or to find another job. I think that is where we fulfill, or where we can truly help these women in our, as for our part. So, because when they signify that they don't want to go back to the place, but, nowhere to go. Of course, they are not prepared to go back to their families, but instead of going back to the casa, if they had a place to stay for short term, while preparing themselves, looking for another job, so, I think that is the best we can give them.

Because of the project, the partners could see what was needed in the community, and they forcefully went after it. How and what they changed on the personal level became institutionalized. Fundamentally, the project demonstrates the success of investment in what Robert Putnam calls social capital. He differentiates among three types of capital: physical, human, and social.[27] Physical capital refers to tangible objects or structures, such as drop-in centers and shelters, that can aid in reducing harm to prostituted women. Human capital refers to the training and education of governmental and nongovernmental organizations in order to aid them (in this case, in our efforts to reduce the harm to prostituted women). Social capital refers to community networks, trust, and reciprocity between individuals and organizations that allow collective action (in this case, to address and redress the level of exploitation of prostituted women).

Above all, we created champions in making change by mobilizing people in Angeles to want to do something about the problems of the bar girls. We created champions by building personal relationships and by removing people from their own environments and contexts—both Filipino and Canadian. The partners were able to humanize and give voice to marginalized women, and in doing so they were able to create networks of like-minded people who were able to work together to make change.

> **Davida:** The Soroptimist International is our adoptive organization, so they were the ones who adopted the women's desk. So no problem about that there. We had this link with them ever since the women's desk was established. But, as to working relationship with this judges, of course we regard the judges as high. So we cannot talk to them, to come close to them and share what is our problem in a certain case, so, we just meet when we sit down in the court, for to testify for our case filed before them. But, now we can talk to them, we can visit them to their office and share what is our problem and ask them their opinion and assistance regarding our problem. So, that's one best result. Another one is that when we conduct seminars and we need an expert, we go to Angeles University as resources speaker so they provide us one resource speaker, like when we took our basic counseling skills.

All of the partners (except perhaps WEDPRO) realized the slow nature of change; they all acknowledged that it would take time to change the attitudes of the people of Angeles and would involve a lot of repetitive, focused work over a long period of time. The results, however, would come relatively quickly once the groundwork was laid.

> **Maria:** Well, I think it will take time. It's not an overnight, you know, we cannot expect people to change overnight. Actually, it

took us more than a year, no? I think the PNP trainers that are chosen, it took them also several months, you know, before they really would like, you know, to change their attitude towards these women. So, I guess, I think, maybe, the five year project is good timing for us to maybe say that ok, now we are well trained already. We know what we want. We know what to do already, so I guess, you know, when you know already what to do, it will be very easy already to influence other people.

We also had influence by being outsiders who brought a different perspective to the community, just as the Filipinos were when they had reactions about things they saw in Canada, whether it was our nursing homes—appalled—or the large numbers of cemeteries—astonished and amused. Even WEDPRO, which was not very happy with our involvement generally in the Philippines, recognized the value of the Canadians as outsiders in showing community members what they had become so accustomed to, and that mobilized them to further action.

Katerina: When I was talking with our Canadian friends, they would always express their shock at what they've seen in Angeles, particularly the exploitation that they see in the casas or the hunger and deprivation that we see on the faces of the streetwalkers and I wonder why I don't react that way, and I realized that I don't get shocked as easily anymore. We've become desensitized, a lot of us here in WEDPRO.

Davida also mentioned many times that it was the Canadians' reactions to the casas and particularly seeing them on a television screen through the film that changed her mind dramatically about what was going on in the casas. This insider-outsider dynamic is an important catalyst in making change, because when we can see a situation from the perspective of another person, we can begin to see how something about our situation might be improved or changed. It can open our eyes.

Maria: I think one reason why we had this project, maybe you and Edna and Mrs. Suarez really saw the need for training. I know we cannot do it on our own. It's not just the funding, you know, it's not just, of course the funding helps a lot, but I know that sometimes, as they say, it takes someone to tell you, you know, to tell you . . . to open your eyes. If we had never started this project, do you think that the Soroptimists will be openly talking about prostitution? Will the police be sensitive about the women, when they go to their raids? Do you think the judges will be sensitive about women in prostitution? Or a university being involved in this? They will never know and they will never understand. That's how I see it, you know. It opened our eyes, and as I have said, if not with you guys, you know, I don't think we will ever know what's really going on here.

The biggest impact we had, then, was opening one another's eyes; by seeing through the eyes of another, we created champions. Does the fact that WEDPRO left the project mean that we can only work in coalitions with like-minded groups? We don't think so. WEDPRO was crucial in keeping the lives of the bar women in our minds at all times, and WEDPRO's theoretical perspectives were an important reminder to us always to reflect on our own attitudes, beliefs, and behaviors. The group's "radicalness" may have been too much for the project and Angeles, but perhaps that happens in any movement when some members are ahead of their time. Even though we had problems maintaining the coalition, the project was worth doing because of the change created and the personal relationships built.

In the end, nothing we have read, seen, or heard, no theory or experience, has led us to believe that we can eradicate prostitution in our lifetimes or even that eradication has to be our goal in order to begin the process of eliminating or reducing harm to women in the sex trade. In fact, it seems clearer to us now that for the most part change happens incrementally and through the efforts of individuals and groups of like-minded and unlike-minded people, debating issues, moving each other forward, taking action, and making a difference. The project showed the importance of individual champions. Despite seeming to be composed of institutions and organizations, in the end it was individuals within the institutions and organizations who acted to make a difference. Moreover, individual champions, both Filipino and Canadian, not only worked in concert, but also served as role models to others, which was particularly evident in the case of the Filipino partners. Solutions may be seen to be reformist, but nothing that we have experienced leads us to believe that there is a better way to deal with a global phenomenon like the global sex trade and sex tourism. Action will be localized, specific, and contextualized, as it was on our project and as we argued in Chapter 2.

The next and final chapter goes back to what our project taught us: that the elimination of prostitution, although perhaps laudable, is an unrealistic goal at this point in history; that we can, and sometimes should, speak for others if we are mindful of our own prejudices and understandings; and that state donor agencies can be useful partners in the creation of change. We also outline the need to refocus on our similarities instead of our differences and to develop empathetic understandings that propel us as individuals, particularly in the privileged West, to continue to "do something."

PART III

THEORETICAL
AND PRACTICAL
PRESCRIPTIONS

7

No Conclusions,
Just "Continued Somethings"

Change Happens Incrementally

Prostitution is embattled territory, let alone in another place, and we stepped into the theoretical and practical debates with some trepidation. From the outset the goals of our five-year development project were modest, limited to the capacity building of Filipino groups in Angeles who worked directly with the bar girls and casa workers, but the impacts on individuals, and *by* individuals, were significant. Although the focus of the funding program was to build up the capacity of organizations or groups, it was the actions of specific individuals that made, and will continue to make, a difference in the lives of the women in Angeles. Problems identified by Canadian and Filipino partners included community ignorance and hostility to the bar girls. By grasping the opportunity to change minds, the project succeeded in addressing a small part of an enormous problem in a specific context.

Whether we are attempting large-scale changes in the nation-state or institution; changes through art, science, or scholarship; or changes in a small-group setting, Gardner argues that a change of mind "involves a change of mental representations."[1] This is what we attempted to do in our project—change people's minds about the prostitutes living in their midst. It is what the "john" schools do when they bring in prostitutes to tell their life story to the customers so that they will create empathy for the women, recognize the part they played in harming the women, and in the end, not offend again. Gardner argues that our "mental representations are not immutable . . . and, while altering mental representations may not be easy, changes can be effected."[2]

Arguably, to start with the goal of eliminating prostitution in such an exploitative context as Angeles would have prevented the germination of a project like ours, where the process of harm reduction to women in the sex trade began. That did not mean that our partners, particularly .

161

WEDPRO, did not continuously express their desire or hope that prostitution should be eradicated.

> **Perla:** I would like if the president could do it for the women so that you didn't have prostitution; the first one they make a big factory and all the women in the bar can go to that place and to work there so that no more club. That's the one thing that, no more prostitution.

> **Katerina:** I see a future where there is no sexual exploitation, and I hope to see women, myself included, I hope to see women who are able to determine their own lives. Women who are able to take hold of their dreams, and women who will just be allowed to reach their full potential.

At the same time, the Filipino partners understood, as we did, that wanting to eliminate prostitution and working to improve the lives of women in the sex trade were not mutually exclusive. Indeed, the Soroptimists in the material that they developed for community outreach contained the slogan: *Ang mga kababaihan ay dapat mahalin. Galit tayo sa prostitusyon pero mahal natin ang kababaihan* (We hate prostitution, but we love the women). This differentiation of the women from the system of prostitution was crucial because it allowed the Filipino partners to be empathetic to the women and to move beyond seeing the women as immoral, criminal, or simply wanting a foreign husband. These attitudinal changes came about because of workshops and training sessions undertaken with Canadian partners.

Thus we disagree with feminists who dismiss the importance of the individual and of individual change. For example, Chandra Mohanty critiques "prejudice reduction workshops" and other psychological "fixes" as too individualized and organized around the discourse of civility and harmony. These maintain the status quo, she believes, by neglecting the social and structural inequality causing the prejudice.[3] But this becomes a bit of a chicken-and-egg dilemma: what can we do about structural inequality that is not about changing legal and attitudinal prejudices? We recognize that structural inequalities remain, but it was heartening to witness, for example, the Filipino partners delivering workshops and outreach sessions to change the minds of people within their communities, or undertaking initiatives for prevention, focusing on the responsibilities of the family and the rights of children because they understood that many women are drawn to the sex trade because of abuse.

> **Davida:** For those who are runaways, and they go to bars, we set programs for this family. So, I think what we now doing, is to go to

the community and educate the parents about their responsibilities, their liabilities to their children. So, and for the school, we go to school and conduct dialogues to the pupils, telling their rights as a child and what abuses that might happen to them and what to do if there is a case like abuse by their relatives or within the family, so, we put out, when we go out and have dialogue with the students we put up a complaint box. If they can't report personally, they can write it and put it in the complaint box. Those boxes are left in the school and we check them at least once a week.

The partners also understood that the project had gaps not only in our access to the bar girls, but also in our understanding of the criminal justice system. We should have involved the mamasans (who have direct control over the women) and prosecutors (who decide if charges are to be laid), and not only the bar girls, the police, and the judges.

Davida: The mamasans are in between the owners and the workers. I think they must be involved in this project. We must sensitize these mamasans. Why they are doing this to the women for the benefit of their managers. I think, for my own opinion, I think it's good to involve these mamasans, so I think if we can involve one or two or three from them then their mamasans, and sensitize them, so, I think this is the one best way of helping these women. And one more is why not the prosecutors are not included in our project. As the PNP we cannot do the preliminary investigation, until the prosecutors, before the judges have the case, it will pass to the prosecutors. If we have working relations to this prosecutor (they) will think before dismissing it.

In addition, focusing on community outreach and education did not mean that the partners did not see the importance of providing alternative livelihoods and microfinancing or ensuring that women had support in finding a place to live as ways to deal with the situation of the bar girls and casa workers.

Perla: Number one is the microfinance. Cause they need help and they would like to start a small business that they can sort of buy, but WEDPRO, they have a small capital only, but there have a lot of girls need that, but the money is not afford to the women that would like to be out in the bar.

Maria: We are looking into the possibility of training for basic computer, so I guess we could do that, even just for a few girls, and then maybe, again, we'll have the manicure, pedicure, because you know the manicure, pedicure, you know here in the Philippines, if you go to the barangay, even you know the housewives there, they all have nice manicures and pedicures, even the men. How much is manicure/pedicure, you know? Seventy pesos? That's what my workers pay for it, you know, so I said, you know, if you know how to do manicure/pedicure, and how many can you make in a day? So I said, at least you can make four, seventy times four, that's 280. That's already something, you know. So I think we will have that kind of training again. And, maybe also the sewing, high-speed sewing.

The partners also understood the dilemma of providing alternative livelihoods that were just as exploitative as the bars.

Katerina: The bar women have come to us in the past and even in the casas they have connected with us and they've asked us to find them jobs. We don't know where to refer them, sometimes, or if it's the kind of job that will suit them, or if referring them to a factory will not only place them also in exploitative situation. It's a dilemma. We take them out from the casas and then we refer them to a sweat shop, and that poses a real dilemma for me. Is that a real option for the women? We say to them, OK, can you do domestic work? Is that something that is different then what they are doing inside the casas or inside the bars? So, there is a total lack of options, sometimes you feel that helplessness, but what you try to do is talk to them, find out what their skills are, help them to think through their options and not just as thinking for them.

Many women lived in the bars and casas, so the partners understood that in order to get the women out of the sex trade, it was as important to find alternative housing as to offer alternative livelihoods.

Katerina: Another real problem, they just want their own houses. Once they leave the bars, they will not have anywhere to stay. We've had a woman, who stopped working in the bars, and later we found out that she had been on the street for some time, begging, and we thought that maybe she had gone crazy, and we hope through this project a level of coordination among the partners will be done. A referral system will be done, so that the women will have something to go to, if they do decide to leave. Their problems inside the bars are not simple, but they don't want to be battered by the customers. They don't want the bar owners to confiscate their things when they've decided to leave. If they don't want to get bar fined then they shouldn't be penalized or they shouldn't be fined. These are reasonable demands from the women, but they are not being addressed at the moment, and we are working toward that.

In the end, the Filipino partners understood that the goal was helping the women, not making judgments, and within their particular context, continuing to make a difference in the lives of the women living in their midst. This development project, as they said, opened their eyes in terms of the challenges within their own community and emboldened them to continue their work.

Davida: The political will, I think, that this is a very, very big problem. But in our part, as the PNP, I think, if we continue our programs, that is continue reaching them, talking to them, and with the help of the other partners, I think we can fulfill our goal. And aside from that, what we have started, is because, I said that the family is one reason, so we continue our program of educating the parents and also continue our linkages to our partners, even this project will end 2004, I think. We have started and we must go on until, really it's our goal.

Maria: You know what I'm praying always? How to reach out, really, to the women. How to make them understand that we really care. That we are really doing something. We would like to make a difference, you know. That's just what I really would like. Every time I go to the Center, you know, and when I see these women, I said, oh my God, how I wish one day that they would come to us and say that, "I'm fed up with this work. I don't like to work in the bars anymore, I'm tired. I'd like to go home," and at least you know when they go home that they have something to do there. That's what I wish, really.

Outsiders Can Contribute

The excesses of globalization and the ill effects of military prostitution are readily evident to both residents of and visitors to the Philippines. Our project brought out the complexities surrounding the idea of insiders, and the role that outsiders can play. Members of WEDPRO understood the extent to which bar girls and casa workers were exploited in Angeles. Its members had researched the problem; they had worked with and reached out to the women, some being survivors of the sex trade themselves; and they were advocating changes in the treatment of the women. Our other four partners initially approached the problem as that of the bar girls and casa workers themselves. Through the course of the project they came to understand the degree of exploitation and victimization the women faced, and this changed their attitudes and propelled them to institute changes, whether in terms of no longer arresting them, in the case of the police, or of educating the community that it was prostitution that was the problem, not the women. The point is that it was the involvement of the four partners with Canadians—with outsiders—that propelled these attitudinal changes. In essence, WEDPRO's message was best delivered through, and by, outsiders who understood the degree of exploitation from the outset. As an organization, WEDPRO was treated as an "outsider" by fellow Filipinos in Angeles because of the group's radical feminist views; these views undermined WEDPRO's credibility in the eyes of the other groups.

The important role played by Canadians tells us something about the role of insiders and outsiders and about the necessity of placing identity politics and post-colonial thinking in context. As we have seen in Chapter 3, feminists have been divided philosophically on whether female prostitution is an expression of men's violence against women, and thus inherently exploitative, or if prostitution is a testimony to women's sexual liberation from male-dominant understandings of female sexuality, and thus fundamentally empowering. However, with the emergence of critical works coming largely from women of color, either as citizens of the Third World or as immigrants to the First World, the study of prostitution has taken on a familiar post-colonial critique that pins the problem on primarily Western, Euro-centric, white feminist understandings of prostituted women in the Third World. On the issue of whether prostitution is inherently exploitative, the critique highlights the extent to which Western scholars turn prostituted women into mere "subjects" of study and effectively remove any sense of agency on the part of third-world women. This places Western women in a privileged position and they are, thus, implicated in propagating colonial or neo-colonial understandings. On the issue of whether prostitution is fundamentally liberating, the critique points out that choice or consent are Western concepts, derived from Euro-centric liberal understandings of the world that exposes, too, colonial or neo-colonial assumptions of Western scholars. Essentially, if a feminist perspective demonstrates how problematic it is for men to study female prostitution, a post-colonial feminist perspective highlights how problematic it is for Western women to study female prostitution in the Third World. Gender may not figure in the latter case, but race and class obviously do.

This does not mean that Western, white women (and men) have not studied female prostitution in the Third World. They have. And they have produced works that help us to explain why local, poor, usually dark women sell their bodies to foreign, rich, primarily white men. Along with contributions from women and men of color, these works have focused on issues of sex tourism and military prostitution to high-light the problems of globalized capitalism and militarized masculinity, and these global problems are clearly evident in the Philippine context. However, it does mean that works by Western feminists on Third World women are often called into question, precisely because of the privileged positions that Western women hold. The problem, then, becomes the nature of feminism or feminist inquiry itself—who can study whom?—as opposed to the practice of female prostitution as it is occurring, for example, in the Philippines.

Accordingly, there seems to be an inherent legitimacy by having wom-en of color study women of color, or in this case, a Filipina studying female prostitution in the Philippines. Given the sense of marginalization articulated by women of color who have immigrated to the First World, it does not seem to matter if the scholar is a Filipina-Canadian, because the fact that a woman is one of color is primary. Race, then, is at the foreground of gender and class, and although many women of color re-flect their own privileged position in terms of class, that privilege, argu-ably, is characteristic of all academics. In our case, a collaborative project becomes crucial, not simply or even primarily because of mutual aca-demic interests, but because the "Filipino-ness/brownness" of Edna ap-pears to mitigate the "whiteness" of Meredith. As we have argued, we think this is politically problematic, and we come back to this point in the final section of this chapter. The fundamental problem with post-colonial critique, then, is that it forces us to focus on the nature of femi-nist inquiry as opposed to the nature of the problem. And when we focus on the problem, many feminists take an anti-capitalist, anti-state stance that in the end further paralyzes movement toward a program for ac-tion.

We Can Work Together Globally

How do we reconcile the issues from Chapter 2 and bring praxis back to theory? Chandra Mohanty and Nancy Fraser provide some answers to this question, thus providing insights into the justifications of North-erners doing development work. Mohanty is a self-identified post-colo-nial feminist and is very influential in these circles. In her latest work, however, she attempts to look for solutions and how to build bridges between first-world and third-world women and feminists. She outlines a vision of the world and a strategy: "This vision entails putting in place anti-racist feminist and democratic principles of participation and relationality, and it means working on many fronts, in many different kinds of collectivities in order to organize against repressive systems of rule." Her prescriptions for the "politics of solidarity" between peoples include "mutuality, accountability and recognition of common interests,"[4] and she is specific about what represents a good research study in a cross-cultural context. For example, Mohanty singles out Maria "Mies's study [on lacemakers as] a good example of what careful, politically focused, local analyses can accomplish" and gives criteria for what that looks like.[5] She revisits her famous article "Under Western Eyes" in an attempt to more carefully elaborate, not only her critique of Western feminism, but how we might go about working together to make change.[6] While much of her book is still about decolonizing and reorienting feminism, Mohanty gives us hope that a progressive feminism can be derived by looking for common interests and working together to build diverse coalitions.

Nancy Fraser is even more definitive about the need to act and to move beyond identity politics. She has been working for years to produce "a model for politically engaged scholarship" that "critically interprets the world in an effort to change it," a "critical social theory with a practical intent."[7] Her most recent books, *Redistribution or Recognition*, and *Justice Interruptus* are part of a model for radical democracy, which means she wants to combine the "struggle for an antiessentialist multiculturalism with the struggle for social equality."[8] This has put her into a debate with post-structuralists. Butler, in particular, thinks that Fraser downgrades sexual and cultural studies and struggles.

Fraser's historical analysis sees the developments within feminist theory "in terms of the life cycle of social movements"—not to be condemned moralistically but to be understood. As the world moved toward neoliberalism in the 1980s, the feminist movement was also transformed as it could no longer depend upon the welfare state. "With social democracy on the defensive, efforts to broaden and deepen its promise naturally fell by the wayside. . . . Enter the politics of recognition." As part of this historical legacy, Fraser states that the "struggle for recognition so thoroughly captured the feminist imagination that it has served more to displace than to deepen the socialist imaginary. The effect, I fear, has been to subordinate social struggles to cultural struggles."[9] The timing, Fraser argues, could not have been worse:

> The shift to a culturalized politics of recognition occurred at precisely the moment when neoliberalism was staging its spectacular comeback. Throughout this period, unfortunately, academic feminist theory was largely preoccupied with debates about difference. Pitting essentialist against antiessentialists these disputes usefully served to reveal hidden exclusionary premises of early theories and they opened women's studies to many new voices. Even at their best, however, they tended to remain on the terrain of recognition where subordination was construed as a problem of culture and dissociated from political economy. The effect was

to leave us defenseless against free market fundamentalism, which had meanwhile become hegemonic. Effectively mesmerized by the politics of recognition, we unwittingly diverted feminist theory into culturalist channels at precisely the moment when circumstances required redoubled attention to the politics of redistribution. Thus, we inadvertently helped to consolidate a tragic historical disjuncture between theory and practice.[10]

She recounts a story from a class she taught on globalization in which the majority of her students were women, not identified as feminists but avidly anti-globalization activists. She writes:

I found much to admire in these students. They were bold enough to think that they could remake the whole world. It was as if they were saying, "Look, it's our world. The whole of the world is our world. We don't have to limit ourselves to matters that mainly concern women." To me this is a hopeful sign. It made me dare to hope that perhaps we are finally coming out of the identity politics phase.[11]

In the end, Fraser always ends with the slogan, "No recognition without redistribution" because it "insists that struggles for recognition, however progressive, can only be distorted and deformed in the absence of political economic transformation."[12]

Lisa McLaughlin makes a similar argument in terms of what to do about representational politics. She argues that with greater numbers of Western feminists pursuing cultural studies, feminism is "implicated" in an approach that often "overcompensates for Marxist determinism by ignoring structural constraints imposed by political and economic realities." She, like Fraser, asserts the need for a feminist political economy that reconciles the insights of "the politics of representing the other" with the much-needed material dimension that only a political economy approach can provide. She criticizes post-structuralists for being so rooted to the discursive that they suggest equality might be realized if we would only "speak" differently of our subjects. She criticizes Spivak and post-colonialists for being politically irresponsible in failing to locate where the problem really lies. As she states, they must be aware "it is not First World feminism but the transnational corporation that is the primary agent of globalization and colonization today." Therefore, feminists should reconcile "the insights of cultural studies and political economy at the site of the politics of representation."[13]

So what insights can we glean from the writings of post-structuralists and post-colonialists? Kapoor culls from Spivak's work several suggestions about how to work with the subaltern. These suggestions are very useful: learning from below, unlearning one's privilege, acknowledging complicity, and being hyper-self-reflexive.[14] Butler's work forces us to look more critically at the concept of gender and, in that way, as Webster points out, enriches "our understanding of the process through which 'women' and 'men' are constructed in particular ways."[15] Mohanty's work tells us that we should not generalize about third-world women's experiences and that women's lives must be put in historical, local contexts. We cannot assume that all third-world women are victims or that they have limited agency. We cannot assume patriarchy means the "same thing for all women."[16] We cannot assume on the basis of being women that we automatically have knowledge of other women's lives.[17]

We can agree with all that. We are not trying to construct categories that will fit all three billion women on the planet. We are not arguing that development has never been ethnocentric or imperialist—it certainly has been—but what we do want to say is that it is not by definition or necessarily ethnocentric, which is what some development and feminist scholars argue, particularly post-colonialist theorists. We also see how little post-structuralism and post-colonialism have done to alleviate people's real suffering. "Moves against 'hegemony' . . . most likely do little to feed, clothe, or make literate any number of persons."[18] These theories have wonderfully illuminated the problems, but now we need solutions.

Privilege Should Not Preclude Action

Change does happen globally because ethical individuals, including those living in the privileged North, know that global injustices and inequalities must be addressed. Janet Billson and Carolyn Fluehr-Lobban argue that they want to go beyond feminism to a global humanism, and in a sense that is our goal as well. We see the need for a feminist analysis in terms of the effects of development on women, but in the end we see progress as a human endeavor that must take place for all. Billson and Fluehr-Lobban devise a template for the dimensions of female well-being through their empirical studies of eleven countries and utilize the World Values Survey, Nussbaum's capabilities approach, and Narayan's well-being and ill-being survey to come up with common themes of material, bodily, social, community, and spiritual well-being, as well as security and freedom of choice and action. Development is defined as "programmes, policies and activities that expand capabilities and positive freedoms" and for women, therefore, "positive development that fosters enhanced capabilities should lead ultimately to greater female well-being; failed development leaves women and girls with restricted life chances."[19] Through the Convention on the Elimination of All Forms

of Discrimination against Women (CEDAW) and the Millennium Development Goals, signatory countries are supposed to ensure that women's
needs are taken into consideration in planning and development goals
and to recognize the gender differential in social change, highlighting
"the fact that the entire experience of social change is often fundamentally different in its source, nature and consequences for females compared to males."[20]

Billson and Fluehr-Lobban also argue that social change for women
means

> moving through three stages: (1) penetrating the historical barri-
> ers that have kept women out of power through changing minds;
> (2) normalizing women's participation in the public sphere to reach
> the tipping point of acceptance; and (3) consolidating gains through
> legislation, court cases to test the legislation . . . and writing fur-
> ther law or policy.[21]

Beyond analysis, then, there must be action. This is where our engaged
scholarship takes us. As academics, we need to be as concerned about
moving people to action: to seeing the value of incremental, small-scale
change; and to celebrate individual efforts and successes. We need to
understand that we, too, have responsibilities, and by perpetuating ways
of thinking that paralyze others, particularly students, and prevent them
from making a difference in the world in which we live, we end up perpetuating the very systems, whether capitalism or patriarchy or another,
that are the culprits of injustice and inequality. After all, this is the twenty-
first century. Far from being a type of noblesse oblige or the "white
man's burden" to "do something" is to recognize that societies have
changed and the sense of economic, cultural, or racial superiority that
existed in years past has been replaced by a belief in justice and equality
that *transcends* borders and, indeed, identities.

The notion of transcendence is a contested concept in feminist theory,
as we saw in Chapter 2. Although Butler and Alcoff have made many
valuable contributions to feminist theory, they believe that transcendence
is either impossible (Butler) or extremely difficult (Alcoff). And even when
these theorists give us some hope for relations among differently located
people, it is done so grudgingly, as though to reinforce its seeming im-
possibility. Alcoff writes:

> Although it is important—and often easy—to expose the persis-
> tent racism in avowedly antiracist efforts, we need also to affirm
> that *some* of the time, in *some* respects even when not in *all*, whites
> empathize and identify with nonwhites, abhor how white su-
> premacy has distorted their social interactions, and are willing to

make significant sacrifices toward the eradication of white privilege.[22]

We think anti-racist activism is actually a very common occurrence today, but in advocating this so reluctantly and tentatively, we believe they do a great disservice to the possibilities of feminist and humanitarian actions. And if anyone thinks this is an attitude from years ago, we should point out that a fairly prominent British feminist, Sara Ahmed, uses the term "fantasy of transcendence" at least five times in her article "Declarations of Whiteness" to argue that anti-racism is basically impossible for whites because any attempts at anti-racism just act to confirm white superiority. Her article, which is problematic in many ways—she sees white bodies "as white, not human" (imagine substituting black for white), also illustrates the disregard for solutions in some critical left writings. She feels no obligation to offer "suggestions about 'what white people can do'"—her job is to "expose racism," not do anything about it.[23] Her "fantasy of transcendence" is in fact a huge failure of imagination about the possibilities of change through compassion, friendship, and dialogue between peoples.

Transcendence means to rise above or go beyond the limits of . . . to surpass . . . and it is often linked to transformation of perspective or even a change in one's character, not in erasing or leaving behind identity markers such as race, class, or gender. We consciously tried to change people's views, to get them to identify with the bar girls, through self-reflection, mind-opening new experiences, and making a personal connection with them. We tried to create empathy for the bar girls by taking the participants out of their comfort zones and giving them new information. We recognized that we would never know what it is like to be a bar girl, or for that matter a transgendered person, or any number of other identities that we don't have, but we can know certain things about them—that it is wrong for them to be discriminated against, for instance.

We have struggled with the question of how experiential knowledge, so important to identity feminists, can help us in ways other than understanding and empathy. Information from people "not like us" can, for example, create new knowledge, allow us to ask different questions, or correct old knowledge. When anti-racist feminists pointed out in the 1980s that reproductive rights should include the right to *have* children, not just the right not to have children, other feminists understood that and consequently our view of the world expanded. When black feminists argued that intersectionality was a better description of the oppression of black women than descriptions that had come before—criticizing the idea that "all women are White and all Blacks are men," it transformed feminism.[24] When second-wave feminists pointed out that marital rape was wrong even though in law it wasn't, men eventually understood that men could not have a legal right to their wives' bodies. When we read Sojourner Truth's speech, we get that white women were put on pedestals but she wasn't and ain't she a woman? We get that. Do we have to be a black woman to understand that exclusion, or be a woman who has been raped to understand why that change in marital law should have occurred? This is how change happens.

So when we hear feminists say that they are tired of educating everybody else about what it's like to be female or a person of color or transgendered, we see once again the lack of awareness of how change occurs. It is part of our responsibility to pass on this knowledge when we have it, no matter how many times we have to repeat it. It took feminists years of lobbying to get politicians to repeal vagrancy laws, and other discriminatory prostitution laws and we are still struggling with how best to change laws to better the lives of women working in the sex trade. Throwing our hands up in the air and saying we are tired of explaining ourselves is understandable but bad strategy. It is counterproductive and, in some cases, just plain silly. In her well-known article on the problems of speaking for others, Alcoff quotes Joyce Trebilcot, who states that she "will not try to get other wimmin to accept my beliefs in place of their own on the grounds that to do so would be to practice a kind of discursive coercion and even a violence."[25] Has Trebilcot never changed her mind about something? What is consciousness-raising if not changing one's mind and the minds of others? Rather than getting angry at others for not knowing something, would it not be more productive to educate them? Can we not communicate information to others?

People can and do change their viewpoints, behaviors, and actions. We believe we are educable, and so are most others we know. Why assume the worst of people? Why judge others based only on their presumed privilege? Are we not just reversing the prejudice? Rather than assume potential allies are guilty until they somehow prove otherwise, why not assume their innocence until proven guilty? There will always be some people who are incapable of seeing the world through the eyes of another, but we still need to try to communicate that knowledge to those who might be open to it. As Harvey Cormier states so eloquently in "Ever Not Quite," "Getting things wrong, being ignorant, is not a matter of betraying logical, material, or racial reality; getting things wrong on the way to getting things right is just what we do as we try to make things better, we makers and remakers of ourselves and the world."[26] We can rise above ourselves, and in the process of expecting more of people, they often deliver.

Given the complexity of forces in the world, it is tempting to throw up one's hands and to declare that the possibilities for positive, deliberate changes of mind are modest. That may be true. But unless one is willing to become a full determinist—and no one ever leads his or her own life that way—we must continue to believe that the will is free and that individuals can make a difference. . . . We can change our minds and the minds of others around us.[27]

Uma Narayan, in a wonderful article about feminist epistemology from a non-Western feminist point of view, makes some very moving points about the double bind of being a woman in the North, from the South, that we think are illustrative of the problem. "As an Indian feminist currently living in the United States, I often find myself torn between the desire to communicate with honesty the miseries and oppression that I think my own culture confers on its women and the fear that this communication is going to reinforce, however unconsciously, western prejudices about the 'superiority' of western culture."[28] We find this very troubling. Can we not separate out the two ideas—that many cultures oppress women, including our own, and that there are wonderful aspects of all cultures that we want to celebrate? Narayan writes specifically about "knowledge based on sympathy or solidarity," of the kind that we think is so important. She also gives us hope about the "possibility of understanding and political cooperation between oppressed groups and sympathetic members of a dominant group."[29] However, in a very telling passage that to us gets at the heart of the problem, she writes about criticizing the dominant group for lack of attention to a problem,

> as well as for our frequent hostility toward those who express interest, even sympathetic interest, in issues that concern groups of which they are not a part. . . . [We are] suspicious of expressions of concern and support from those who do not live these oppressions. We are suspicious of the motives of our sympathizers or the extent of their sincerity, and we worry, often with good reason, that they may claim that their interest provides a warrant for them to speak for us, as dominant groups throughout history have spoken for the dominated.[30]

Although this is understandable emotionally, hostility, resentment, and suspicions are problematic strategically. She knows this because in the end she agrees that people who are "differently located socially" can "attain *some* understanding of our experience or *some* sympathy with our cause." But she believes these questions still have to be asked: "Should we try to share our perspectives and insights with those who have not lived our oppression and accept that they may fully come to share them? Or should we seek only the affirmation of those like ourselves who share common features of oppression and rule out the possibility of those who have not lived these oppressions ever acquiring a genuine understanding of them?"[31] In other words, should we continue to preach to the already converted and accept there will be no change, as WEDPRO did, or should we actively try to get others to see the world from a different point of view? We understand her point about why some feminists are hostile to sympathizers, but we respectfully wonder if she understands that this hostility will be a warning to sympathetic individuals not to participate and to abdicate their responsibilities. It divides those who could be allies; it makes differences into "unbridgeable barriers," gives victims a "badge of honor," and is a form of "apolitical narcissism."[32]

We reiterate that no one will ever know what it truly is like to be another individual or have that individual's problems, but we can have empathy for that person's pain or suffering or joy. We may never have had a broken leg, but we can imagine the pain. We can use the facts and circumstances of our own life to identify with the pain of a burned hand, for example, or a sprained ankle or childbirth. We recognize the humanity of another when we share human emotions, feelings and put ourselves in the shoes of another. In some of these theorists' writings there is a sense that "we" can understand and perceive a bias but "they" can't, as WEDPRO thought the police were irredeemable. But the police are no more monolithic than, say, white feminists or feminists of color. Change is not easy. It takes time, but we can help people identify with others and see their humanity whether through one-to-one interaction, media, education, or social movements of like-minded and unlike-minded people.

We are also advocating an end to the negative labeling of others. Spivak deals with this issue when she says that to her "great desolation," she was called a racist by a woman from Africa. Perhaps we shouldn't be so quick to label people or accept the label. As she writes, "I'm of course, with every bit of my conscious thinking, every bit of my work, in all of my interventions, strongly, fundamentally and in every way anti-racist."[33] Not knowing her personally, but being aware of her anti-racist writings, we believe that to be true. But rather than reject the label of racist she writes, "But history is larger that good-will. Therefore I think we must confront the possibility that in what we produce there may be residual elements that can give fuel to the other side."[34] While that may be a sensitive and sensible thing to do in this case, we are also in danger of doing more harm than good when we accept what might be malicious and uninformed opinions that have more to do with the speaker than with the recipient. We are a society that uses the words *racism* and *sexism* entirely too quickly, without looking at the negative consequences of labeling someone racist or sexist. It immediately silences the one being labeled and makes dialogue impossible. And in order to change minds, whether male minds or white minds, we need to be able to speak freely and be able to dialogue with each other. We need to be able to exchange information and ideas, and feel relatively safe doing so.

In terms of the importance of dialogue and learning from and about the "other," we can learn much from theorists like Maria Lugones, Nira Yuval-Davis, and Kathy Davis. Lugones, in her now-classic article about the possibilities and necessity of transcending our locations, argues that we must be able to identify with other women in order to be able to connect across differences and that we must be able to see others through their eyes. To do this she uses the term "world traveling" to indicate the "experience of being different in different 'worlds' and of having the capacity to remember other 'worlds' and ourselves in them." As she states: "The reason why I think that travelling to someone's 'world' is a way of identifying with them is because by travelling to their 'world' we can understand *what it is to be them and what it is to be our selves in their eyes.* Only when we have travelled to each other's 'worlds' are we fully subjects to each other."[35] We need to reject "arrogant perception" and get to know other women through friendship and dialogue. Alison Bailey writes: "Lugones believes that women's failure to love one another stems from a failure to identify with women who inhabit worlds they do not share; it is a failure to see oneself in other women who are different. . . . Because arrogance blocks coalition building, world traveling must be done with loving perception."[36] Using Lugones's concept of traveling, Bailey differentiates between "privilege-evasive" and "privilege-cognizant scripts" to show how differently located people can shift from one perspective to the other, again indicating how attitudes and behaviors can change. "A key feature of privilege-cognizant standpoints is the choice to develop a critically reflective consciousness. . . . Traitors choose to try to understand the price at which privileges are gained; they are critical of the unearned privileges granted to them by white patriarchal cultures, and they take responsibility for them."[37] Although we are not sure how helpful the word *traitor* is in the above statement, we completely agree with the sentiment behind it.

Nira Yuval-Davis's concept of "transversal politics" is also helpful, and hopeful, in establishing contact and connections among peoples. As Charlotte Krolokke and Ann Scott Sorensen write:

> What defines transversal politics is not only the fact that differences . . . are recognized but also that a commitment to listen and participate in a dialogue is required. . . . Participants are encouraged to position themselves as women with particular national, ethnic, or religious roots, while also shifting to other ways of thinking, being, and practicing in order to realize the partiality of their own position and to identify possible common stands and interests."[38]

In this strategy, therefore, particular identity standpoints do not get in the way of alliances and coalition-building. In attempting to build alliances in the Philippines, for instance, much of our time was spent in dialogue with other women, trying to find the commonalities and relevant differences in order to offer training programs that would be appropriate in the Philippines. Our dialogues became friendships in many cases, based on respect for our differences in beliefs, customs, and circumstances, and on our personal connections. Transversal politics

> assumes that although knowledge and imagination are situated, there is a possibility of transcending the limitations of the specific situatedness of the subject in the shifting. Such transcendence is assumed possible first as a result of a combination of listening to the situated knowledge and fantasy of the other participants in the dialogue and second, via empathetic imaginings in which the subject attempts to position herself in the standpoint of the other participants.[39]

In another important work about the possibilities of a truly transnational feminism, Kathy Davis examines how *Our Bodies, Ourselves* traveled across borders and how it was transformed in the process. She shows how the information in and the inherent consciousness-raising of the book was challenged, embraced, and transformed according to particular cultures and women's perceived needs. Though dismissed by post-structuralists like Donna Haraway as merely "feminist self-help," Davis argues that this misrepresents the impact of the book, its transformations in content, and underplays how the book helped to transform women's health advocacy in the United States and abroad. She argues that feminist political alliances need to be made across lines of similarities and differences, not shared identities or the radically anti-essentialist "discursive agency" of Butler. Discrediting women's experience altogether, she writes, may risk throwing the baby out with the bath water.[40] She also criticizes post-colonial feminists for critiquing Western feminist assumptions rather than exploring what happens when feminism crosses borders.[41] Davis argues that the "imagined communities" of *Our Bodies, Ourselves* are communities of engagement, not shared identities, and in this way feminism can encompass all women who are linked by alliances, globally. For her, "good" transnational practice will include the "acknowledgment of differences among women, an awareness of privilege and complicity . . . and an attempt to discover common concerns and struggles."[42] She recognizes the need for allies, dialogue, and empathy in order for change to occur: to end sexism, we need to engage men; to end racism we need to engage whites.

We end with the very important work of Sonia Kruks on the politics of privilege. Kruks doesn't just argue that privilege shouldn't *preclude* action; rather, she says, let's use our privilege strategically to make change.

In discussing the case of Josephine Butler and contemporary historians' criticisms of her as condescending and as merely reinscribing middle-class privilege, Kruks argues:

> We should not automatically assume that oppressed groups are always able to speak or act for themselves better than others can do it for them. In the case of the Contagious Diseases Acts, prostitutes could endeavor individually to evade regulation, but as marginal women—impoverished, uneducated and socially stig-matized—in a society where all women still lacked the vote and were marginal to national political processes, the possibility that they themselves could have mounted the campaign that was to lead to the actual repeal of the Acts was about zero. Educated and "re-spectable" women, who could write, speak in public, had the re-sources to travel around the country and organize, and had personal contacts with men of the political classes, were much better posi-tioned to be effective agents of change.[43]

Similarly, using the example of Simone de Beauvoir's "discovery" of her complicity with the French colonizers in Algeria, Kruks shows how Beauvoir changed public opinion in France about the war and about the use of torture by *using* her status as an upper-class privileged woman, not by becoming less French or rejecting her own culture.[44] Although Kruks recognizes that we first need to acknowledge our privilege through the transformational strategies we mention above, she argues that those same strategies, as we examined in detail in Chapter 2, often lead to paralysis and guilt. She writes: "Since the attempt to expunge one's own last ves-tiges of obliviousness to race, or insensitivity, can never be brought to an adequate closure, 'working on oneself' may heighten one's feelings of guilt in ways that only lead toward despair, self-hatred, and demobiliza-tion." Although guilt is important when we first "become aware of our privilege . . . it may become quite crippling as a basis for effective long-term political action." Therefore, using her Beauvoir case study, she ar-gues that "rather than investing oneself in the more self-referential task of disclosing the subtle benefits that accrue from one's personal privi-leges and struggling to renounce them, it may be preferable to acknowl-edge them but then to act *from* one's privileged location, to deploy one's privileges as effectively as possible, to endeavor to use it well."[45] This seems to us to be the only sensible solution to the problem of analysis paralysis, and we wish we had had the benefits of her insights during our project.

In many ways this is the strategy we used on the project from start to finish, but it also brought us into conflict with our post-colonial group. We strategically decided to use the privileged women of the Soroptimists to deliver the message to the community and to do the training, knowing that the message would be delivered in a far more palatable manner, and with a better chance of being heard. We used male trainers with the police and judges, knowing that the gender-equality message they were delivering would be heard better coming from a privileged white male judge. We used our Western privilege to gain access to the bars, because Filipinos were discouraged, if not barred, from entering them, in order to meet with the bar girls, customers, and owners so that we could expose the sexism and racism of the industry through the film. This privileged access, and strategy generally, was a constant source of tension with WEDPRO—understandably, because it exposes the structural racism of the bar system—but it enabled us and our interns to know the problem better and use that access to further the cause of the project. At the same time, we should add, the Soroptimists worked behind the scenes with the mayor's office to discourage (and to eventually make illegal) the foreign owners' ban on Filipinos entering Western bars.

We know how controversial using one's privilege can be and we understand that to many post-colonial theorists it simply reinscribes the privilege. But again what is the alternative? In the face of global problems that require global solutions, we need to use all the strategies at our disposal to help make change. Rather than simply renouncing our privileges, then, we need to "learn to use them responsibly."[46] In the end, we can only echo Kruks's important insights and Kathy Davis's suggestions for a "truly transnational feminism—that is, a feminism that joins a respect for difference with critical reflexivity and mutual empowerment."[47] We tentatively explore the theoretical basis for such a transnational feminism in the final section.

All Humans Are Human

Although we hesitate to use the term *cosmopolitanism*, given its divisive nature and negative political connotations, we have come to believe that a *feminist cosmopolitanism* or *global humanist feminism* might best address theoretically the problems of identity politics and be a more realistic, pragmatic form of transnational feminism. Being a "citizen of the world" allows us to explore how all people can come to see themselves as connected and important to one another. We recognize the political problems of a world state, or a lack of a world state, and the colloquial and elitist connotations of the word *cosmopolitan*—the globe-trotting white male tourist—but we are referring more to the attitude of cosmopolitanism, that is, that we have responsibilities to others not in our own circles by virtue of their humanity and that we respect the diversity of all peoples. According to Kwame Anthony Appiah:

There are two strands that intertwine in the notion of cosmopolitanism. One is the idea that we have obligations to others, obligations that stretch beyond those to whom we are related by the ties of kith and kind, or even the more formal ties of a shared citizenship. The other is that we take seriously the value not just of human life but of particular human lives, which means taking an interest in the practices and beliefs that lend them significance. People are different, the cosmopolitan knows, and there is much to learn from our differences.[48]

Cosmopolitanism is not relativist—human rights violations are unacceptable—but it is not "homogenizing" either—cultures in all their varieties are respected. It encourages cultures themselves to pick and choose which aspects they want to keep and which ones they want to discard. It acknowledges the strong globalizing nature of the economy on local cultures, with both positive and negative effects. It allows for individual and collective action, for small-scale and large-scale change, and insists on the fundamental premise that all humans are human.[49]

But this notion that all humans are human is unfortunately controversial. It is perhaps one of those debates with no resolution: to be or not to be colorblind or gender blind or "other" blind. While some activists think of eventual colorblindness as the goal of an anti-racist movement (that we need to move beyond race and gender and focus on what unites us), others believe it is a fundamentally racist strategy. "For example, most liberal discourse on racism illustrates a form of linguistic privilege-evasiveness characteristic of the whitely scripts. Phrases such as 'I don't see color, I just see people,' or 'We all belong to the same race—the human race' erase color, which also amounts to a failure to recognize whiteness."[50] We mean "all humans are human" in the way Roméo Dallaire means it. At all his public talks, retired General Roméo Dallaire, UN commander in Rwanda during the genocide, asks, "Are all humans human?" He does so in order to point out how the West abandoned the people of Rwanda and his belief that it did so because they were Africans.

> 'Are we all human, or are some more human than others?' Certainly we in the developed world act in a way that suggests we believe that our lives are worth more than the lives of other citizens of the planet. An American officer felt no shame as he informed me that the lives of 800,000 Rwandans were only worth risking the lives of ten America troops; the Belgians, after losing ten soldiers, insisted that the lives of Rwandans were not worth risking another single Belgian soldier. The only conclusion I can reach is that we are in desperate need of a transfusion of humanity. If we believe

that all humans are human, then how are we going to prove it? It can only be proven though our actions. Through the dollars we are prepared to expend to improve conditions in the Third World, through the time and energy we devote to solving devastating problems like AIDS, through the lives of our soldiers, which we are prepared to sacrifice for the sake of humanity.[51]

Humanity, however, is an unpopular term with both conservatives and the critical left—conservatives because they believe it gets in the way of nationalism, patriotism, and the self-interest of nation states; critical theorists because it supposedly masks all our important differences and because of the "'post-colonial suspicion' of the idea: the suspicion that western cosmopolitanism is tied deeply into western 'cosmology.'"[52] Cosmopolitanism has been called moralistic, abstract, and superior, and most critics believe that it is naive about the aggressive nature of human beings.[53] According to Hilary Putnam, cruelty and aggression are ignored by cosmopolitanism, and there is "not the slightest reason to believe" that human nature is going to change.[54] Imagination takes a kicking as well in the critics' view—there is apparently not enough creativity and imagination in the world to overcome human nature. "The human capacity to injure other people has always been much greater than its ability to imagine other people. Or perhaps we should say, the human capacity to injure other people is very great precisely because our capacity to imagine other people is very small."[55] What we have here is a failure to imagine other possibilities, and a fatalism about human potentiality.

Cosmopolitanism obscures all such unwelcome facts—obscures, indeed, the reality of the world in which a good many human beings actually reside. It is utopian, not only in its unrealistic assumption of a commonality of 'aims, aspirations, and values,' but also in its unwarranted optimism. . . . Cosmopolitanism has a nice, high-minded ring to it, but it is an illusion, and, like all illusions, perilous.[56]

But again we ask, what is the alternative? How do we overcome such pessimism and fatalism? If we can't transform human nature and we can't transform global capitalism, what are we to do about the problems in the world? Do we not need a little vision of utopia for the planet to survive, as well as movements of deeply committed, hopeful individuals with a good sense of their own efficacy?

Being a "citizen of the world" means "having a cultural disposition which is not limited to the concerns of the immediate locality, but which recognizes global belonging, involvement and responsibility and can integrate these broader concerns into everyday life practices."[57] It means recognizing that while people can be very different, their problems generally are not. So, rather than be overwhelmed by the difficulty of imagining other people, perhaps we should spend some time changing the way people think about their world—getting them to see that we are "interdependent parts of a single natural system."[58] Most important, we should encourage people to see that "the globally transformative action of individuals within their situated localities is dependent on the cultivation of a specific cultural disposition—a 'set towards the world.' . . . The most important change that people can make is to change their way of looking at the world"[59] because global problems require global solutions. We live in a time of great change and possibilities. As problematic as some aspects of globalization undoubtedly are, the technology, communications, and medical advances give us the chance for a truly global morality, not just the "morality of proximity."[60] Clive Kessler writes:

> Globalization processes are arguably now creating, for the first time in human history, the detailed social infrastructure of a single unified humanity, a universal human community: a network of mutual human interdependence and of worldwide involvement in one another's fate. . . . Such a development creates the possibility for something dramatic, novel and significant in the moral progress of humankind to occur; it represents a transformative moment in the history of the human moral imagination. For the first time, a sense of the unity and moral equality of humankind will no longer be a difficult matter of abstract moral intuition. Instead, as a result of advancing globalization processes, it will have a socially objective and material, an experiential and existential, foundation.[61]

This notion of the existential foundation of human life resonated with us as we explored our shared humanity with the bar girls of Angeles. And it was not just us—two privileged Western feminist academics. It also resonated with our conservative, relatively affluent Filipino partners in the judiciary, the university and, of course, with the Soroptimists. It also resonated with our Filipino police partners who in many ways "saw" the girls for the first time not as criminals but as victims. Our differences were evident, but our shared humanity was obvious as well, and it was our recognition of shared humanity that propelled the action and change in Angeles. We recognized that, but for the luck of birthplace, family, race, gender, or class, we could be those girls. "We are all born naked and poor; we are all subject to disease and misery of all kinds; finally we are all condemned to death," writes Martha Nussbaum. "The sight of these common miseries can, therefore, carry our hearts to humanity—if we live in a society that encourages us to make the imaginative leap into the life of the other."[62] And as Nussbaum and others have said, imagination is not enough. It takes action. "World citizenship, then, places exacting demands on the imaginations of each of us. To be sure, the imagination is not enough. . . . If we left our world citizenship to the vagaries of our own daily reflections, we would act less well than if we were to institutionalize our best ideas. . . . We must, therefore, cultivate world citizenship in our hearts and minds as well as our codes of law."[63]

Appiah poignantly reminds us why we should all choose to act when he writes of his Ghanaian father and the note he left his children when he died. "After a few paragraphs reminding us of our double ancestry, in Ghana and in England, he wrote: 'Remember that you are citizens of the world.' And he went on to tell us that this meant that wherever we chose to live . . . we should make sure we left that place better than we found it."[64] And surely that should be the goal of all acts of imagination and resistance—to leave our world better than it was.

We end with a little story and a cautionary tale. In June 2005, in Mississippi, the former leader of a local chapter of the Ku Klux Klan was convicted, forty-one years after the fact, of orchestrating the killings of three civil rights workers who were trying to register black voters in 1964. They are memorialized as "young activists willing to put their lives on the line for a principle and for 'folks they didn't even know.'"[65] The three had been investigating a fire that had destroyed a black church and were arrested for speeding. When they were released they were followed by Klansmen, beaten and shot, and their bodies bulldozed into a pit. They were found forty-four days later. Their deaths were an important part of the civil rights movement that led to the significant changes we see today in black rights in the United States. Two of these young men were white, one was black. We wonder if that could happen today, with the emphasis on identity politics. According to much academic theorizing, we shouldn't work in the Philippines because we are contributing to neo-colonialism, we shouldn't do research in communities other than our own because we have to avoid paternalism, we shouldn't work toward eliminating female genital mutilation in the Gambia because to do so as Western women is ethnocentric. But what if we felt that way about slavery in the nineteenth century or the civil rights movement in the twentieth or about any other human rights issue? How would those three men have come together if the young white men felt they were being paternalistic, or if they felt it had nothing to do with them, or if they had been told to stay out and let the African Americans do it themselves? Would the white men have been accused of "othering" the African Americans, of making them into objects of study by those "more fortunate" in the North? Luckily for us, these men believed in the equal civil and moral rights of all people and thought that they could make a difference by working together with other cultures and peoples to achieve change.

In the end, then, our project has led us in the same direction. We have come to believe that the "Filipino-ness/brownness" of Edna and the "whiteness" of Meredith do not seem to matter much. Not only do we find the often-implied prescriptions stemming from anti-capitalist and anti-state critiques wanting, but our own self-reflections highlight that we—Edna and Meredith—are not so different after all. One does not have to be a Filipino to see and understand the exploited lives of women in the sex trade in the Philippines any more than one has to have been a prostitute *truly* to understand their lives. The divide is less about race and post-colonial understandings and more about empathetic knowledge. Edna *knows* the women are exploited in Angeles. Meredith *knows* the women are exploited in Angeles. Edna's knowing this stems not from her "Filipino-ness/brownness" but from observing and feeling, just like Meredith. We do not have to have been poor to know that it is right to have social programs in the United States. We do not have to have been born female to know that it is right to have gender equality and that "culture" does not trump women's rights. We do not have to have been born a person of color to know that it is right to eradicate racism in all forms. And we do not have to have been born in the Third World, like the Philippines, to know that it is right to help and care for those outside of one's national borders. Twenty-five years after the publication of Maria Lugones and Elizabeth Spelman's famous article "Have We Got a Theory for You!" in which they argue that they couldn't write in one voice because Spelman is white and Lugones is brown,[66] our hope is that we have moved forward in transcending our "whiteness" and "brownness" and that someday we will come full circle to a place of recognizing our differences *and* our similarities. Why? Because we are human—and only then will we be free at last from racial, gender, class, and all other prejudices.

Appendix

Project-related Training Programs

In Angeles with Canadian Partners

Date	Partner	Topic
Dec. 1999	AUF Judges PNP SI WEDPRO Municipal	Training needs assessment (1 day)
Dec. 2000	SI/AUF	Public speaking (½ day)
	SI, AUF, WEDPRO	Questionnaire development (½ day) Gender-sensitivity training (½ day)
	PNP	Gender-sensitivity training (4 days)
Jan. 2001		Data analysis (½ day) Community outreach (1 day)
Apr. 2001	PNP SI AUF WEDPRO Judges	Project M&E (½ day)
	AUF	Lifelong learning (½ day) Ethnographic research (1 day)
	Judges	Prostitution and violence against women (½ day)
	Judges	Social context workshop (2½ days)
Jun. 2001	SI	Community outreach
Dec. 2001	WEDPRO	Video skills

Date	Partner	Topic
	PNP	Advanced gender-sensitivity and human rights training (3 days)
Mar. 2002	PNP	Facilitation training (3 days)
	PNP, WEDPRO	Counseling skills (1 day)
	SI, AUF	Counseling skills (1 day)
	AUF	Project monitoring and evaluation (1 day)
	WEDPRO	Project monitoring and evaluation (1 day)
	PNP	Evaluating training programs (1 day)
	SI	Project monitoring and evaluation (1 day)
	Judges	Project monitoring and evaluation (½ day)
May 2002	Judges	Social context training (2 days)
	Court of Appeals	Preliminary social context training (½ day)
	Judges	Decriminalizing prostitution (½ day)
	SI	Community outreach (3 days)
Feb. 2003	SI, AUF, PNP	Proposal writing (1 day)
	SI	Video techniques (1 day)
	SI	Community outreach (1 day)
	SI, PNP	Practice community outreach (1 day)
May 2003	SI	Making partners in the community (2 days)
	PNP	Abnormal Psych for police officers (1 day)
	Judges	Social Context Education (½ day)
	All	Building partnerships in Angeles City—Partners
	All	Building partnerships in Angeles City—Community
	All	Sustaining partnerships in Angeles City—Partners
	PNP	Suicide intervention (1 day)
Nov. 2003	PNP, SI, Other	Transformational theater training (6 days)
	Other	Theater performance

Date	Partner	Topic
Feb. 2004	AUF, SI, PNP	Social mobilization
	SI	"Primer to manual": Sharing experiences with SI throughout the Philippines
	Ventures	Involving Ventures in SI project activities
Apr. 2004	SI, AUF, PNP	Project design Project communications
Aug. 2004	All	Project wrap-up meetings

Filipino Partners in Canada

Date	Partner	Topic
May 2000	SI Judges PNP AUF WEDPRO Other	Canadian best practices
Jun. 2001	PNP	Gender-sensitivity training curriculum development
Sep. 2001	Judges	Social-context training
Apr. 2002	SI	Community outreach
	AUF	Research skills and community outreach
	SI/AUF	Entrepreneurship training
Sep. 2002	Judges	Social-context training
	PNP	Gender-sensitivity training curriculum development
	WEDPRO	Video techniques
Apr. 2003	AUF	Community outreach/ community mobilization skills, Counseling and sexual-harassment policies
Apr. 2004		Documentary presented to graduate IDS students in Halifax
Jun. 2004	SI	Canadian best practices—women's shelters
	PNP AUF	
	Judges	Domestic violence

Filipino Partners in Angeles

Date	Partner	Topic
Dec. 4, 2000	All (led by WEDPRO)	Community dialogue on women in prostitution
Jan. 2001	AUF/WEDPRO	Video camera skills
Feb. 1, 2001	WEDPRO, Nagka	Discussion of participatory video
Feb. 16, 2001	PNP/SI	Consultation dialogue with barangays and casa owners
Feb. 20, 2001	SI, WEDPRO, PNP	Orientation at WHWC for prostituted women
Feb.–Mar. 2001	SI	Information gathering in thirty-three barangays of Angeles City
Apr. 4, 2001	SI, PNP, WEDPRO	Community dialogue in Barangay Sta Teresita
Jun. 2001	PNP	Investigative skills training
Aug. 7, 2001	PNP	PNP gender-sensitivity planning program for fifteen trainers
Sept. 12, 2001	SI, PNP	Community dialogue in Holy Rosary Parish
Jan. 12, 2002	All	Consultation of judges and community for social-context training
Jan. 15, 2002	SI, PNP, WEDPRO, AUF	Meeting with Department of Social Welfare and Development
Jan. 16, 2002	SI, PNP	Dialogue with bar women at WHWC
Feb. 18, 2002	PNP	Seminar on coping with family violence
Mar. 14–15, 2002	PNP, SI	2nd National Summit for PNP Women's Desk
May 2002–Feb. 2003	AUF	Community research project
Jul. 16, 2002	SIL, PNP	Radio panel with Feliz Medina
Aug. 28, 2002	WEDPRO, SI, PNP	Stop Rape Forum
Oct. 2002	SI, Ventures	Play center set up at WHWC for children of prostituted women visiting social hygiene clinic
Oct. 11, 2002	SI, PNP	Bar women assisted with health check
Jan. 3, 2003	PNP	Gender-sensitivity training program delivered to Santo Domingo and Balibago barangay officials

Date	Partner	Topic
Jan. 15, 2003	SI, PNP	SI Quezon City visit WHWC to learn about project
Jan. 25, 2003	PNP	GST program delivered to Pulung Bulo barangay officials
Jan. 29, 2003	SI, PNP	PNP presented award to SI for activities relating to PNP Women's Desk
Feb. 1, 2003	PNP, SI	Open forum on empowerment of women in Barangay Sapang Bato
Feb.–Mar. 2003	AUF	AUF students offer English language tutorials to women at WHWC
Feb. 6, 2003	SI	Livelihood skills training for prostituted women at WHWC
Feb. 8, 2003	PNP	GST program delivered to Pampang barangay officials
Feb. 19, 2003	PNP, SI	Community outreach in Barangay Lourdes Sur Est
Mar. 7, 2003	SI	Presentation on women in prostitution to Rotary Club of Angeles City
Mar. 12, 2003	SI, PNP	Community outreach in Barangay Sta Teresita
Jun. 3, 2003	SI, PNP	Community outreach in Barangay Sta Teresita
Jun. 9, 2003	SI	Presentation on domestic violence against women in Barangay Cutcut
Sept. 6, 2003	SI, PNP	Presentation on sex trafficking and prostitution for Catholic Women's League
Sept. 24, 2003	SI	Handicraft training for prostituted women at WHWC
Dec. 10–13, 2003	PNP, SI	GST and HIV/AIDS training to PNP representatives
Jan. 10, 2004	SI	Basic computer training at WHWC
Jan. 20, 2004	SI	Merienda get-together for prostituted women at WHWC
Feb. 11, 2004	SI	Community outreach in Barangay Cutcut

Date	Partner	Topic
Mar. 18, 2004	All	Ceremony to mark plans to begin construction of women's shelter at PNP Women's Desk head office
Mar. 23, 2004	SI	Bingo social held for prostituted women at WHWC
Mar. 25, 2004	SI, WEDPRO, Judges	SI presents awards to (Judge) Ofelia T. Pinto and Purificacion Gilbore for "Making a Difference for Women"
Mar. 26, 2004	Judges, SI, PNP	Meeting to discuss problems in the area
Mar. 2004	SI	Spiritual retreat for prostituted women at WHWC

Notes

1 "You've Got to Do Something"

1. See Boyer, *Scholarship Reconsidered*; idem, "The Scholarship of Engagement"; Rice, "Beyond "Scholarship Reconsidered"; ASHE-ERIC Higher Education Report, *A Broader View of Scholarship through Boyer's Four Domains*; Van de Ven, *Engaged Scholarship*; Yapa, "Public Scholarship in the Postmodern University"; Colbeck and Wharton Michael, "The Public Scholarship"; Barker, "The Scholarship of Engagement"; Weis et al., "A Call for Civically Engaged Educational Policy-Related Scholarship."

2. Yapa, "Public Scholarship in the Postmodern University," 73.

3. See Enloe, *Does Khaki Become You?*

4. Keeble and Ralston, "Discourses and Feminist Dilemmas," 147.

5. Nussbaum, *Women and Human Development*; Singer, *One World*; Pogge, *World Poverty and Human Rights*; Appiah, *Cosmopolitanism*.

6. Evans, *Tidal Wave*, 4.

7. Park, "Research, Teaching, and Service."

8. Mayberry, *Teaching What You're Not*, 3.

9. Johnson et al., "No Middle Ground?" 97.

2 The Problem of Analysis Paralysis

1. Landolt, "Famous Five Are No Heroines."

2. Yedlin, "To Some, It's the Infamous Five"; Sharpe et al., *The Persons Case*.

3. Yedlin, "To Some, It's the Infamous Five."

4. These terms are used by a number of authors, including the following. For "paralysis," see Duran, *Worlds of Knowing*; Saunders, *Feminist Post-Development Thought*; Ali, *Infidel*; Lurie, *Unsettled Subjects*; Whitworth, *Feminism and International Relations*; for "impasse," see Fraser and Naples, "To Interpret the World and to Change It"; Parpart, "Lessons from the Field"; Lurie et al., "Restoring Feminist Politics to Poststructurals Critique," Pieterse, "After Post-Development"; Okin et al., *Is Multiculturalism Bad for Women?*; Fraser, *Justice Interruptus*; for "crisis," see Webster, "The Politics of Sex and Gender"; Benhabib, *Feminist Contentions*; Alcoff, "The Problem of Speaking for Others"; for "rift," see Mohanty, *Feminism without Borders*, 300.

5. Fraser, "To Interpret the World and to Change It," 1104.

6. Okin, "Feminism, Women's Human Rights and Cultural Differences," 36–37.

7. Saunders, *Feminist Post-Development Thought*, 19.

8. Spivak, "Can the Subaltern Speak?"; Spivak, Landry, and MacLean, *The Spivak Reader*; Spivak, *A Critique of Postcolonial Reason*; Hedges et al., "Martha C. Nussbaum and Her Critics"; Torres, Russo, and Mohanty, *Third World Women and the Politics of Feminism*; Narayan, *Dislocating Cultures*; Narayan and Harding, *Decentering the Center*; Beck-Gernsheim, Butler, and Puigvert, *Women and Social Transformation*; Sharpe and Spivak, "A Conversation with Gayatri Chakravorty Spivak"; Ahmed, "Declarations of Whiteness.

9. Beck-Gernsheim, Butler, and Puigvert, *Women and Social Transformation*, 77, emphasis added.

10. Sievers, "There Is Evil," *Los Angeles Times*, June 12, 2005.

11. Alcoff, "The Problem of Speaking for Others," 5.

12. Ibid., 26.

13. Jaggar, "Globalizing Feminist Ethics," in Narayan and Harding, *Decentering the Center*, 5.

14. Ralston, "Upstream in the Mainstream."

15. Alcoff, "The Problem of Speaking for Others," 6, emphasis added.

16. Jaggar, "Globalizing Feminist Ethics," 3, emphasis added.

17. Narayan, *Dislocating Cultures*, 226.

18. In Spivak, "Can the Subaltern Speak."

19. Spelman, *Inessential Woman*; hooks, *Ain't I a Woman?*; Collins, "The Social Construction of Black Feminist Thought"; Harding, *The Science Question in Feminism*.

20. Hartsock, "The Feminist Standpoint"; Harding, *The Science Question in Feminism*, 271; idem, *Feminism and Methodology*; idem, *The Feminist Standpoint Theory Reader*.

21. Sommers, *Who Stole Feminism?*; Patai and Koertge, *Professing Feminism*.

22. Gardner, *Changing Minds*, 125–26.

23. Duran, *Worlds of Knowing*, 6.

24. McLaughlin, "Beyond 'Separate Spheres,'" 339, 341.

25. Judith Butler, in Beck-Gernsheim, Butler, and Puigvert, *Women and Social Transformation*, 6, 1.

26. Ibid., 83, 84,

27. Ibid., 94.

28. Hedges et al., "Martha C. Nussbaum and Her Critics."

29. Whitworth, *Feminism and International Relations*, 23.

30. Judith Butler, in Beck-Gernsheim, Butler, and Puigvert, *Women and Social Transformation*, 10, 15.

31. Ibid., 22, 27, 23, 17.

32. Webster, "The Politics of Sex and Gender," 8, 9, 18.

33. McLaughlin, "Beyond 'Separate Spheres,'" 341.

34. Duran, *Worlds of Knowing*, 8.

35. Sylvester, "Development Studies and Postcolonial Studies," 703.

36. Stienstra, "Cutting to Gender," 239.

37. Kapoor, "Hyper-Self-Reflexive Development?" 629.

38. Sharpe and Spivak, "A Conversation with Gayatri Chakravorty Spivak," 615.

39. Ibid., 616.

40. Ibid., 623.

41. Spivak, *A Critique of Postcolonial Reason*, 386, 407.

42. Ibid., 388.

43. Ibid., 386.

44. Kapoor, "Hyper-Self-Reflexive Development?" 635.

45. Spivak, *A Critique of Postcolonial Reason*, 415.

46. Kapoor, "Hyper-Self-Reflexive Development?" 632.

47. Stienstra, "Cutting to Gender," 233–44.

48. Weinstein, *Social and Cultural Change*, 233–34.

49. Ibid., 235.

50. Okin et al., *Is Multiculturalism Bad for Women?* 123.

51. Moghissi, *Feminism and Islamic Fundamentalism*, vii, 8.

52. Ibid., 5.

53. Ibid., 6, 87.

54. Ibid., 61.

55. Ibid., 96.

56. Billson and Fluehr-Lobban, *Female Well-being*, 387.

57. Sommers, "The Subjection of Islamic Women and the Fecklessness of American Feminism."

58. Ali, *Infidel*, 348–49.

59. Sommers, "The Subjection of Islamic Women and the Fecklessness of American Feminism."

60. Duran, *Worlds of Knowing*, 7, 9.

61. Ibid., 48.

3 Philosophical Issues of Prostitution

1. Barry, *Female Sexual Slavery*; idem, "The Underground Economic System of Pimping"; idem, *The Prostitution of Sexuality*; Leidholdt and Raymond, *The Sexual Liberals and the Attack on Feminism*; Asia Watch and Women's Rights Project, *A Modern Form of Slavery*; Delacoste and Alexander, *Sex Work*; Kempadoo and Doezema, *Global Sex Workers*; Nagle, *Whores and Other Feminists*; Weitzer, *Sex for Sale*.

2. Human Rights Watch, "The Philippines, Unprotected," 33.

3. Flowers, *The Prostitution of Women and Girls*, 146.

4. Working Group on Prostitution, *Report and Recommendations in Respect of Legislation, Policy and Practices concerning Prostitution-Related Activities*.

5. AWAN, "Aboriginal Women's Action Network Statement Against the Plans for Vancouver Brothel," December 13, 2007. Available online.

6. Ibid.

7. Canadian Advisory Council on the Status of Women, *Prostitution in Canada*, 84.

8. Ofreneo and Ofreneo, "Prostitution in the Philippines," 117.

9. Ex-Prostitutes Against Legislated Sexual Servitude, "Plans for Vancouver Brothel: No!" Email to Par-L Auto Digest (2007).

10. Aronson, "Seeking a Consolidated Feminist Voice for Prostitution in the U.S.," 370–71.

11. Raymond et al., *Comparative Study of Women Trafficked in the Migration Process*.

12. Working Group on Prostitution, *Report and Recommendations in Respect of Legislation, Policy and Practices concerning Prostitution-Related Activities*.

13. Weitzer, *Sex for Sale*, 160.

14. Marieke van Doorninck, quoted in Brewis and Linstead, "Managing the Sex Industry," 322.

15. Shrage, "Prostitution and the Case for Decriminalization," 42.

16. Nagle, *Whores and Other Feminists*; Delacoste and Alexander, *Sex Work*; Chapkis, *Live Sex Acts*; McElroy, *XXX*; Silver, *The Girl in Scarlet Heels*.

17. Chassin, "Experiential People?" Email to Par-L Auto Digest (2007).

18. Esther Shannon, "Experiential People?" Email to Par-L Auto Digest (2007).

19. Doezema, "Loose Women or Lost Women?" 23.

20. Doezema, "Ouch!" 17.

21. Shrage, "Prostitution and the Case for Decriminalization," 43.

22. Brewis and Linstead, "Managing the Sex Industry," 322.

23. Job Cohen, quoted in Sterling, "Dutch Try to Dim Red Light Tourism."

24. Shannon, "Experiential People?"

25. Barry, "The Underground Economic System of Pimping," 117–27.

26. Shrage, *Moral Dilemmas of Feminism*; Seidman, *Embattled Eros*.

27. Lee and WEDPRO, *From Carriers to Communities*, 4.

28. Ibid., 10.

29. West and Austrin, "Markets and Politics," 138.

30. Chapkis, *Live Sex Acts*.

31. See Overall, "What's Wrong with Prostitution?"

32. Barry, "The Underground Economic System of Pimping."

33. Ibid., 119.

34. WEDPRO, *From Manila, Angeles, and Olongapo to Cebu and Davao*, 6.

35. Ofreneo and Ofreneo, "Prostitution in the Philippines," 105.

36. Lim, *The Sex Sector*, 212.

37. Ibid.

38. CATW-AP, "Women Empowering Women."

39. See Ringdal, *Love for Sale*; Roberts, *Whores in History*; Shrage, *Moral Dilemmas of Feminism*.

40. Overall, *What's Wrong with Prostitution?* 717, 721.

41. See Kuo, *Prostitution Policy*, 138.

42. Davidson, "The Rights and Wrongs of Prostitution," 84.

43. Ibid., 93.

44. Ibid.

45. Perkins, *Sex Work and Sex Workers in Australia*.

4 Explanations for Prostitution in the Philippines

1. Enloe, *Does Khaki Become You?*; ibid., *Bananas, Beaches, and Bases*.

2. Lim, *The Sex Sector*, 1.

3. Ibid.; Brown, *Sex Slaves*; the catwinternational.org website.

4. Ofreneo and Ofreneo, "Prostitution in the Philippines," 100.

5. Roces, "Beauty Queens, Moral Guardian, *Inang Bayan*, and Militant Nun."

6. Abinales and Amoroso, *State and Society in the Philippines*, 58–59.

7. Dolan and Library of Congress Federal Research Library, *Philippines, a Country Study*, 98.

8. Ofreneo and Ofreneo, "Prostitution in the Philippines," 100.

9. Ibid., 100.

10. Ibid., 101.

11. Kwiatkowski, *Struggling with Development*; Osborne, *Southeast Asia*.

12. Ofreneo and Ofreneo, "Prostitution in the Philippines," 105.

13. Abinales, *State and Society in the Philippines*; Osborne, *Southeast Asia*.

14. Abinales, *State and Society in the Philippines*; Zaide, *The Philippines*; Osborne, *Southeast Asia*.

15. Zaide, *The Philippines*, 58–59.

16. Ibid., 59.

17. Pettman, "Body Politics," 102.

18. Mee-Udon and Itarat, "Women in Thailand," 292.

19. Ibid., 286.

20. Roces, "The Militant Nun as Political Activist and Feminist in Martial Law Philippines," 137.

21. Ibid.

22. Overall, "What's Wrong with Prostitution? 720.

23. Ofreneo and Ofreneo, "Prostitution in the Philippines," 105.

24. Ibid.

25. Pettman, "Body Politics," 102.

26. Human Rights Watch, "The Philippines, Unprotected," 13.

27. Ibid., 18.

28. Ibid., 43.

29. Roces, "The Militant Nun as Political Activist and Feminist in Martial Law Philippines," 138.

30. Ibid., 149.

31. Ibid., 152–53.

32. Ibid., 137.

33. Ibid.

34. Zaide, *The Philippines*, 302–3.

35. Nagel, *Race, Ethnicity, and Sexuality*, 10.

36. Anderson, *The Spectre of Comparisons*, 225.

37. Ibid., 212.

38. Rafael, *White Love and Other Events in Filipino History*, 206–7.

39. McMichael, *Development and Social Change*, 162–64.

40. Tyner, "Migrant Labour and the Politics of Scale," 136.

41. Sassen, "The Excesses of Globalization and the Feminisation of Survival," 102.

42. Wonders and Michalowski, "Bodies, Borders, and Sex Tourism in a Globalized World, 548.

43. Ibid., 551.

44. See Manning, "The Philippines in Crisis," 271.

45. Enloe, *Bananas, Beaches, and Bases*, 87.

46. Leonard Davis, *Revolutionary Struggle in the Philippines*, 93.

47. Miralao, Carlos, and Santos, *Women Entertainers in Angeles and Olongapo*, 2.

48. Enloe, *Bananas, Beaches, and Bases*, 84.

49. Ibid., 196.

50. Peterson and Runyan, *Global Gender Issues*; Beckman and D'Amico, *Women, Gender, and World Politics*; Tickner, *Gender in International Relations*.

51. Enloe, *The Morning After*, 151.

52. Lee and WEDPRO, *From Carriers to Communities*, 9, emphasis added.

53. Miralao, *Women Entertainers in Angeles and Olongapo*, 3.

54. Enloe, "It Takes Two," 23–24.

5 Sex Tourism in Angeles City

1. See Ofreneo and Ofreneo, "Prostitution in the Philippines," 107.

2. Ibid., 104–5.

3. Flowers, *The Prostitution of Women and Girls*; O'Neill and Barberet, "Victimization and the Social Organization of Prostitution in England and Spain"; Nanette Davis, "From Victims to Survivors."

4. Flowers, *The Prostitution of Women and Girls*, 127; Ofreneo, *Prostitution in the Philippines*, 105.

5. Human Rights Watch, "The Philippines, Unprotected," 1–68.

6. See Goodall, *The Comfort of Sin*; McKeganey and Barnard, *Sex Work on the Streets*; Flowers, *The Prostitution of Women and Girls*; Martin Monto, "Why Men Seek Out Prostitutes."

7. Monto, "Why Men Seek Out Prostitutes," 77.

8. Ibid., 80.

9. Ibid., 81.

10. Oppermann, *Sex Tourism and Prostitution*.

11. Davidson, *Prostitution, Power, and Freedom*, 172.

12. Seabrook, *Travels in the Skin Trade*.

13. Davidson, "British Sex Tourists in Thailand."

14. Davidson, *Prostitution, Power, and Freedom*, 176.

15. Ibid., 172.

16. Ibid., 170.

17. See, for example, Davidson, *Prostitution, Power, and Freedom*; Bishop and Robinson, *Night Market*; Seabrook, *Travels in the Skin Trade*; Ryan and Hall, *Sex Tourism*.

18. Shrage, *Moral Dilemmas of Feminism*, 152.

19. Davidson, *Prostitution, Power, and Freedom*, 174.

20. Seabrook, *Travels in the Skin Trade*, 4.

6 Making a Difference

1. Billson and Fluehr-Lobban, *Female Well-Being*, 59.

2. Keeble and Ralston, "Discourses and Feminist Dilemmas"; Dobrowolsky, *The Politics of Pragmatism*; Ralston, "Upstream in the Mainstream; Phillips, *Feminism and Politics*; Torres, Russo, and Mohanty, *Third World Women and the Politics of Feminism*; Adamson, Briskin, and McPhail, *Feminist Organizing for Change*.

3. Sztompka, *The Sociology of Social Change*, 291.

4. Grillo, "Anti-Essentialiam and Intersectionality," 32.

5. Moore, *Social Change*; LaPiere, *Social Change*; Moore and Cook, *Readings on Social Change*; Lauer, *Perspectives on Social Change*; Sztompka, *The Sociology of Social Change*.

6. Lauer, *Perspectives on Social Change*, 147.

7. Sztompka, *The Sociology of Social Change*, 28.

8. Weinstein, *Social and Cultural Change*, 310–11.

9. Sztompka, *The Sociology of Social Change*, 240.

10. Lauer, *Perspectives on Social Change*, 243.

11. Ibid., 250–51.

12. Ibid., 203.

13. Weinstein, *Social and Cultural Change*, 320.

14. Baumgardner and Richards, *Grassroots*, xvii.

15. Ibid., xviii.

16. Appiah, *Cosmopolitanism*; Gladwell, *The Tipping Point*.

17. Kanter and Stein, *A Tale of "O."*

18. Chait, "The Right's Wrong Books."

19. Tomlinson, *Globalization and Culture*, 204.

20. Scarry, "The Difficulty of Imagining Other People," 104–5.

21. Gardner, *Changing Minds*, 62.

22. Ibid., 62, 65, 129, 195.

23. Keeble and Ralston, "Discourses and Feminist Dilemmas."

24. Gardner, *Changing Minds*, 81.

25. Lind, "Feminist Post-Development Thought," 227.

26. Duran, *Worlds of Knowing*, 18.

27. Robert D. Putnam, *Democracies in Flux*.

7 No Conclusions, Just "Continued Somethings"

1. Gardner, *Changing Minds*, 30.

2. Ibid., 46.

3. Mohanty, *Feminism without Borders*, 209–11.

4. Ibid., 4, 7.

5. Ibid., 31–33.

6. Mohanty, "Under Western Eyes" (rev.), in Mohanty, *Feminism without Borders*.

7. Fraser and Naples, "To Interpret the World and to Change It," 1103, 1107.

8. Fraser, *Justice Interruptus*, 187; see also Fraser and Honneth. *Redistribution or Recognition*.

9. Fraser, "To Interpret the World and to Change It," 1108, 1110–11, 1111.

10. Ibid., 1112.

11. Ibid., 1120.

12. Ibid., 1122.

13. McLaughlin, "Beyond 'Separate Spheres,'" 327, 343, 344, 349.

14. Kapoor, "Hyper-Self-Reflexive Development?" 640–43.

15. Webster, "The Politics of Sex and Gender," 16.

16. Stone-Mediatore, "Chandra Mohanty and the Revaluing of 'Experience,'" 126.

17. Webster, "The Politics of Sex and Gender," 1–22.

18. Duran, *Worlds of Knowing*, 256.

19. Billson and Fluehr-Lobban, *Female Well-being*, 29.

20. Ibid., 41.

21. Ibid., 389.

22. Alcoff, "What Should White People Do?" 263.

23. Ahmed, "Declarations of Whiteness." Also available on the borderlands .net.au website.

24. hooks, *Ain't I a Woman?*; Kimberle Crenshaw, "Mapping the Margins: Intersectionality, Identity Politics and Violence against Women of Color," *Stanford Law Review* 43, no. 6 (1991): 1241–99.

25. Joyce Trebilcot, quoted in Alcoff, "The Problem of Speaking for Others," 5.

26. Cormier, "Ever Not Quite," 74.

27. Gardner, *Changing Minds*, 211–12.

28. Narayan, "The Project of Feminist Epistemology," 759.

29. Ibid., 760.

30. Ibid., 761.

31. Ibid., 762, 761.

32. Mandle, "How Political Is the Personal?"

33. Spivak, Landry, and MacLean, *The Spivak Reader*, 297.

34. Ibid., 297.

35. Lugones, "Playfulness, 'World-Travelling,' and Loving Perception," 73, 75, 79.

36. Bailey, "Locating Traitorous Identities," 295.

37. Ibid., 292–93.

38. Kr4løkke and Sørensen, *Gender Communication Theories and Analyses*, 20–21.

39. Yuval-Davis, "Human/Women's Rights and Feminist Transversal Politics," 283.

40. Kathy Davis, *The Making of Our Bodies, Ourselves*, 132.

41. Ibid., 205.

42. Ibid., 208.

43. Kruks, *Retrieving Experience*, 173.

44. Kruks, "Simone De Beauvoir and the Politics of Privilege," 191.

45. Ibid., 183, 184, 186.

46. Ibid., 196.

47. Kathy Davis, *The Making of Our Bodies, Ourselves*, 11.

48. Appiah, *Cosmopolitanism*, xv.

49. Nussbaum, *For Love of Country*; Benhabib et al., *Another Cosmopolitanism*.

50. Bailey, "Locating Traitorous Identities," 293.

51. Dallaire and Beardsley, *Shake Hands with the Devil*, 522.

52. Tomlinson, *Globalization and Culture*, 188.

53. McConnell, "Don't Neglect the Little Platoons," 82.

54. Putnam, "Must We Choose between Patriotism and Universal Reason?" 92.

55. Scarry, "The Difficulty of Imagining Other People," 103.

56. Himmelfarb, "The Illusions of Cosmopolitanism," 76–77.

57. Tomlinson, *Globalization and Culture*, 185.

58. Weinstein, *Social and Cultural Change*, 322.
59. Tomlinson, *Globalization and Culture*, 183.
60. Ibid., 197.
61. Kessler, "Globalization," 939–40.
62. Nussbaum, *For Love of Country*, 132.
63. Ibid., 138–39.
64. Appiah, "Cosmopolitan Patriots," 21.
65. Hart, "Trial Timeout to Remember Slain Men."
66. Lugones and Spelman, "Have We Got a Theory for You!"

Bibliography

Abinales, P. N., and Donna J. Amoroso. *State and Society in the Philippines*. State and Society in East Asia. Lanham, Md.: Rowman and Littlefield Publishers, 2005.

AWAN (Aboriginal Women's Action Network). "Aboriginal Women's Action Network Statement Against the Plans for Vancouver Brothel," December 13, 2007. Available online.

Adamson, Nancy, Linda Briskin, and Margaret McPhail. *Feminist Organizing for Change: The Contemporary Women's Movement in Canada*. Toronto: Oxford University Press, 1988.

Ahmed, Sara. "Declarations of Whiteness: The Non-Performativity of Anti-Racism." *Borderlands e-Journal* 3, no. 2 (2004). Available on the borderlands.net.au website.

Alcoff, Linda. "The Problem of Speaking for Others." *Cultural Critique* 20 (Winter 1991): 5–32.

———. "What Should White People Do?" In Narayan and Harding, *Decentering the Center*, 262–82.

Alexander, M. Jacqui, and Chandra Talpade Mohanty, eds. *Feminist Genealogies, Colonial Legacies, Democratic Futures*. New York: Routledge, 1997.

Ali, Ayaan Hirsi. *Infidel*. New York: Free Press, 2007.

Anderson, Benedict R. O'G. *The Spectre of Comparisons: Nationalism, Southeast Asia, and the World*. London: Verso, 1998.

Appiah, Kwame Anthony. *Cosmopolitanism: Ethics in a World of Strangers*. Issues of Our Time. New York: W. W. Norton and Co., 2006.

———. "Cosmopolitan Patriots." In Nussbaum, *For Love of Country*, 21–29.

Aronson, Gregg. "Seeking a Consolidated Feminist Voice for Prostitution in the U.S." *Rutgers Journal of Law and Urban Policy* 3, no. 3 (2006): 357–88.

ASHE-ERIC Higher Education Report. *A Broader View of Scholarship through Boyer's Four Domains*. Vol. 29 (2002).

Asia Watch and Women's Rights Project. *A Modern Form of Slavery: Trafficking of Burmese Women and Girls into Brothels in Thailand*. New York: Human Rights Watch, 1993.

Bailey, Alison. "Locating Traitorous Identities: Toward a Privilege Cognizant White Character." In Narayan and Harding, *Decentering the Center*, 283–98.

Bailey, Alison, and Chris J. Cuomo, eds. *The Feminist Philosophy Reader*. Boston: McGraw-Hill, 2007.

Barker, Derek. "The Scholarship of Engagement: A Taxonomy of Five Emerging Practices." *Journal of Higher Education Outreach and Engagement* 9, no. 2 (2004): 123–37.

Barry, Kathleen. *Female Sexual Slavery.* Englewood Cliffs, N.J.: Prentice-Hall, 1979.

———. *The Prostitution of Sexuality.* New York: New York University Press, 1995.

———. "The Underground Economic System of Pimping." *Journal of International Affairs* 35, no. 1 (1981): 117–127.

Baumgardner, Jennifer, and Amy Richards. *Grassroots: A Field Guide for Feminist Activism.* New York: Farrar, Straus and Giroux, 2005.

Beck-Gernsheim, Elizabeth, Judith Butler, and Lidia Puigvert. *Women and Social Transformation.* Counterpoints, vol. 242. New York: P. Lang, 2003.

Beckman, Peter R., and Francine D'Amico, eds. *Women, Gender, and World Politics: Perspectives, Policies, and Prospects.* Westport, Conn.: Bergin and Garvey, 1994.

Bell, Laurie, and Ontario Public Interest Research Group. *Good Girls/Bad Girls: Feminists and Sex Trade Workers Face to Face.* Seattle, Wash.: Seal Press, 1987.

Benhabib, Seyla. *Feminist Contentions: A Philosophical Exchange.* New York: Routledge, 1995.

Benhabib, Seyla, Jeremy Waldron, Bonnie Honig, Will Kymlicka, and Robert Post. *Another Cosmopolitanism.* The Berkeley Tanner Lectures. Oxford: Oxford University Press, 2006.

Billson, Janet Mancini, and Carolyn Fluehr-Lobban, eds. *Female Well-being: Toward a Global Theory of Social Change.* London: Zed Books, 2005.

Bishop, Ryan, and Lillian S. Robinson. "In the Night Market: Tourism, Sex, and Commerce in Contemporary Thailand." *Women's Studies Quarterly* 27, no. 1 (1999): 32.

———. *Night Market: Sexual Cultures and the Thai Economic Miracle.* New York: Routledge, 1998.

Boyer, Ernest L. "The Scholarship of Engagement." *Journal of Public Service and Outreach* 1, no. 1 (1996): 11–20.

———. *Scholarship Reconsidered: Priorities of the Professoriate.* Princeton, N.J.: Carnegie Foundation for the Advancement of Teaching, 1990.

Brewis, Joanna, and Stephen Linstead. "Managing the Sex Industry." *Culture and Organization* 8, no. 4 (2002): 307–26.

Brock, Deborah R. *Making Work, Making Trouble: Prostitution as a Social Problem.* Toronto: University of Toronto Press, 1998.

Brock, Rita Nakashima, and Susan Brooks Thistlethwaite. *Casting Stones: Prostitution and Liberation in Asia and the United States.* Minneapolis: Fortress Press, 1996.

Brown, T. Louise. *Sex Slaves: The Trafficking of Women in Asia.* London: Virago, 2000.

Canadian Advisory Council on the Status of Women. *Prostitution in Canada.* Ottawa: Canadian Advisory Council on the Status of Women, 1984.

Carpenter, Belinda J. *Re-Thinking Prostitution: Feminism, Sex, and the Self.* Eruptions. Vol. 6. New York: P. Lang, 2000.

CATW-AP. "Women Empowering Women: Proceedings of the Human Rights Conference on the Trafficking of Asian Women." Quezon City, Philippines, Ateneo de Manila University, 1993.

Chait, Jonathan. "The Right's Wrong Books." *Los Angeles Times*, June 3, 2005, sec. B13.

Chapkis, W. *Live Sex Acts: Women Performing Erotic Labor*. New York: Routledge, 1997.

Chassin, Tori. "Experiential People?" 2007 PAR-L Automatic Digest.

Colbeck, Carol L., and Patty Wharton Michael. "The Public Scholarship: Reintegrating Boyer's Four Domains." *New Directions for Institutional Research* 2006, no. 129 (Spring 2006): 7–19.

Collins, Patricia Hill. *Black Feminist Thought: Knowledge, Consciousness, and the Politics of Empowerment*. Perspectives on Gender. Vol. 2. New York: Routledge, 1991.

———. "The Social Construction of Black Feminist Thought." *Signs: Journal of Women in Culture and Society* 14, no. 4 (1989).

Cormier, Harvey. "Ever Not Quite: Unfinished Theories, Unfinished Societies, and Pragmatism." In *Race and Epistemologies of Ignorance*, ed. Shannon Sullivan and Nancy Tuana, 59–76. Albany: State University of New York Press, 2007.

Crenshaw, Kimberle. "Mapping the Margins: Intersectionality, Identity Politics, and Violence against Women of Color." *Stanford Law Review* 43, no. 6 (1991): 1241–99.

Dallaire, Roméo A., and Brent Beardsley. *Shake Hands with the Devil: The Failure of Humanity in Rwanda*. Toronto: Random House Canada, 2003.

Davidson, Julia O'Connell. "British Sex Tourists in Thailand." Unpublished paper for the Women's Studies Network conference, UK, July 9–10, 1994.

———. *Prostitution, Power, and Freedom*. Ann Arbor: University of Michigan Press, 1998.

———. "The Rights and Wrongs of Prostitution." *Hypatia* 17, no. 2 (2002): 84–98.

Davis, Kathy. *The Making of Our Bodies, Ourselves: How Feminism Travels across Borders*. Next Wave. Durham, N.C.: Duke University Press, 2007.

Davis, Leonard. *Revolutionary Struggle in the Philippines*. Basingstoke: Macmillan, 1989.

Davis, Nanette. "From Victims to Survivors: Working with Recovering Street Prostitutes." In Weitzer, *Sex for Sale*, 139–55.

Delacoste, Frédérique, and Priscilla Alexander, eds. *Sex Work: Writings by Women in the Sex Industry*. Pittsburgh, Penn.: Cleis Press, 1987.

Dobrowolsky, Alexandra Z. *The Politics of Pragmatism: Women, Representation, and Constitutionalism in Canada*. Oxford: Oxford University Press, 2000.

Doezema, Jo. "Loose Women or Lost Women? The Re-Emergence of the Myth of White Slavery in Contemporary Discourses of Trafficking in Women." *Gender Issues* 18, no. 1 (Winter 2000): 23–50.

———. "Ouch!" *Feminist Review* no. 67 (Spring 2001): 16–38.

Dolan, Ronald E., and Library of Congress Federal Research Library. *Philippines, a Country Study*. Area Handbook Series. 4th ed. Vol. 550–72. Washington, DC: Federal Research Division, Library of Congress, 1993.

Duran, Jane. *Worlds of Knowing: Global Feminist Epistemologies*. New York: Routledge, 2001.

Enloe, Cynthia H. *Bananas, Beaches, and Bases: Making Feminist Sense of International Politics*. London: Pandora, 1989.

———. *Does Khaki Become You? The Militarisation of Women's Lives*. London: Pluto Press, 1983.

———. "It Takes Two." In Sturdevant and Stoltzus, *Let the Good Times Roll*, 22–27.

———. *The Morning After: Sexual Politics at the End of the Cold War*. Berkeley and Los Angeles: University of California Press, 1993.

Evans, Sara M. *Tidal Wave: How Women Changed America at Century's End*. New York: Free Press, 2003.

Ex-Prostitutes Against Legislated Sexual Servitude. "Plans for Vancouver Brothel: No!" 2007 PAR-L Automatic Digest.

Ferree, Myra Marx, and Aili Mari Tripp, eds. *Global Feminism: Transnational Women's Activism, Organizing, and Human Rights*. New York: New York University Press, 2006.

Flowers, Ronald B. *The Prostitution of Women and Girls*. Jefferson, N.C.: McFarland and Co., 1998.

Fraser, Nancy. *Justice Interruptus: Critical Reflections on the "Postsocialist" Condition*. New York: Routlege, 1997.

Fraser, Nancy, and Axel Honneth. *Redistribution or Recognition? A Political-Philosophical Exchange*. London: Verso, 2003.

Fraser, Nancy, and Nancy A. Naples. "To Interpret the World and to Change It: An Interview with Nancy Fraser." *Signs: Journal of Women in Culture and Society* 29, no. 4 (Summer 2004): 1103–24.

Gardner, Howard. *Changing Minds: The Art and Science of Changing Our Own and Other People's Minds*. Leadership for the Common Good. Boston: Harvard Business School Press, 2004.

Garry, Ann, and Marilyn Pearsall, eds. *Women, Knowledge, and Reality: Explorations in Feminist Philosophy*. 2nd ed. New York: Routledge, 1996.

Gladwell, Malcolm. *The Tipping Point: How Little Things Can Make a Big Difference*. New York: Little Brown and Co., 2002.

Glassick, Charles E., Mary Taylor Huber, and Gene I. Maeroff. *Scholarship Assessed: Evaluation of the Professoriate*. A Special Report. San Francisco, Calif.: Jossey-Bass, 1996.

Goodall, Richard. *The Comfort of Sin: Prostitutes and Prostitution in the 1990s*. Folkestone, Kent, England: Renaissance Books, 1995.

Grillo, Trina. "Anti-Essentialism and Intersectionality: Tools to Dismantle the Master's House." In *Theorizing Feminisms: A Reader*, ed. Elizabeth Hackett and Sally Haslanger, 30–40. New York: Oxford University Press, 2006.

Hackett, Elizabeth, and Sally Anne Haslanger, eds. *Theorizing Feminisms: A Reader*. New York: Oxford University Press, 2006.

Halifax Social Planning Dept. and Stepping Stone. *Stepping Stone Street Services for Women, Youth and Men: 1994 Program Evaluation Report.* Halifax, N.S.: Social Planning Dept., 1995.

Hall, John R., and Mary Jo Neitz. *Culture: Sociological Perspectives.* Englewood Cliffs, N.J.: Prentice Hall, 1993.

Harding, Sandra, ed. *The Feminist Standpoint Theory Reader: Intellectual and Political Controversies.* New York: Routledge, 2004.

———. *Feminism and Methodology: Social Science Issues.* Bloomington: Indiana University Press, 1987.

———. *The Science Question in Feminism.* Ithaca, N.Y.: Cornell University Press, 1986.

Hart, Lianne. "Trial Timeout to Remember Slain Men." *Los Angeles Times,* June 20, 2005, sec. A12.

Hartsock, Nancy C. M. "The Feminist Standpoint: Developing the Ground for a Specifically Feminist Historical Materialism." In *Discovering Reality,* ed. Merril Hintikka and Sandra Harding, 283–310. Boston: Reidel, 1983.

———. *Money, Sex, and Power: Toward a Feminist Historical Materialism.* Northeastern Series in Feminist Theory. Boston: Northeastern University Press, 1985.

Hedges, Warren, Gayatri Chakravorty Spivak, Seyla Benhabib, Nancy Fraser, Joan W. Scott, Drucilla Cornell, and Sara Murphy. "Martha C. Nussbaum and Her Critics: An Exchange." *New Republic* 220, no. 16 (1999): 43–45.

Himmelfarb, Gertrude. "The Illusions of Cosmopolitanism." In Nussbaum, *For Love of Country,* 72–77.

hooks, bell. *Ain't I a Woman? Black Women and Feminism.* Boston, Mass,: South End Press, 1981.

———. *Feminist Theory from Margin to Center.* Boston, Mass.: South End Press, 1984.

———. *Talking Back: Thinking Feminist, Thinking Black.* Toronto: Between the Lines, 1989.

Human Rights Watch. "The Philippines, Unprotected: Sex, Condoms, and the Human Right to Health." *Human Rights Watch* 16, no. 6 (2004): 1–68.

Jaggar, Alison M. "Globalizing Feminist Ethics." In Narayan and Harding, *Decentering the Center,* 1–25.

Jakobsen, Janet R. *Working Alliances and the Politics of Difference: Diversity and Feminist Ethics.* Bloomington: Indiana University Press, 1998.

Jeffreys, Sheila. *The Idea of Prostitution.* North Melbourne, Vic., Australia: Spinifex, 1997.

Jenness, Valerie. *Making It Work: The Prostitute's Rights Movement in Perspective.* Social Problems and Social Issues. New York: Aldine de Gruyter, 1993.

Johnson, J. Scott, Jennifer Kellen, Greg Seibert, and Celia Shaughnessy. "No Middle Ground? Men Teaching Feminism." In *Teaching What You're Not: Identity Politics in Higher Education,* ed. Katherine J. Mayberry, 85–103. New York: New York University Press, 1996.

Juan, San. *Women Empowering Women: Proceedings of the Human Rights Conference on the Trafficking of Asian Women*. Metro Manila: Coalition Against Trafficking in Women-Asia, 1993.

Kanter, Rosabeth Moss, and Barry Stein. *A Tale of "O": On Being Different in an Organization*. New York: Harper and Row, 1980.

Kapoor, Ilan. "Hyper-Self-Reflexive Development? Spivak on Representing the Third World 'Other.'" *Third World Quarterly* 25, no. 4 (2004): 627–47.

Keeble, Edna, and Meredith L. Ralston. "Discourses and Feminist Dilemmas: Trafficking, Prostitution and the Sex Trade in the Philippines." In *Feminist Perspectives on Canadian Foreign Policy*, ed. Claire Turenne Sjolander, Heather A. Smith, and Deborah Stienstra, 136–54. Toronto: Oxford University Press, 2003.

Kempadoo, Kamala, and Jo Doezema, eds. *Global Sex Workers: Rights, Resistance, and Redefinition*. New York: Routledge, 1998.

Kessler, Clive S. "Globalization: Another False Universalism?" *Third World Quarterly* 21, no. 6 (2000): 931–42.

Krølokke, Charlotte, and Ann Scott Sørensen. *Gender Communication Theories and Analyses: From Silence to Performance*. Thousand Oaks, Calif.: Sage Publications, 2006.

Kruks, Sonia. *Retrieving Experience: Subjectivity and Recognition in Feminist Politics*. Ithaca, N.Y.: Cornell University Press, 2001.

———. "Simone De Beauvoir and the Politics of Privilege." *Hypatia* 20, no. 1 (Winter 2005): 178–205.

Kuo, Lenore. *Prostitution Policy: Revolutionizing Practice through a Gendered Perspective*. New York: New York University Press, 2002.

Kwiatkowski, Lynn M. *Struggling with Development: The Politics of Hunger and Gender in the Philippines*. Boulder, Colo.: Westview Press, 1998.

Landolt, C. Gwendolyn. "Famous Five Are No Heroines." *REAL Women of Canada Newsletter* (January/February 1998). Available on the realwomenca.com website.

LaPiere, Richard T. *Social Change*. McGraw-Hill Series in Sociology. New York: McGraw-Hill, 1965.

Lauer, Robert H. *Perspectives on Social Change*. Boston: Allyn and Bacon, 1973.

Law, Lisa. *Sex Work in Southeast Asia: The Place of Desire in a Time of AIDS*. Routledge Pacific Rim Geographies. Vol. 2. London: Routledge, 2000.

Lee, Lynn, and WEDPRO. *From Carriers to Communities: Alternative Employment, Economic Livelihood and Human Resource Development for Women in the Entertainment Industry*. Manila: WEDPRO, 1992.

Leidholdt, Dorchen, and Janice G. Raymond, eds. *The Sexual Liberals and the Attack on Feminism*. New York: Pergamon Press, 1990.

Lim, Lin Lean, ed. *The Sex Sector: The Economic and Social Bases of Prostitution in Southeast Asia*. Geneva: International Labour Office, 1998.

Lind, Amy. "Feminist Post-Development Thought: 'Women in Development' and Gendered Paradoxes of Survival in Bolivia." *Women's Studies Quarterly* 31, no. 3 (2003): 227–46.

Lugones, Maria C. "Playfulness, 'World-Travelling,' and Loving Perception." In Bailey and Cuomo, *The Feminist Philosophy Reader*, 69–80.

Lugones, Maria C., and Elizabeth V. Spelman. "Have We Got a Theory for You! Feminist Theory, Cultural Imperialism and the Demand for 'the Woman's Voice.'" *Women's Studies International Forum* 6, no. 6 (1983): 573–81.

Lurie, Susan. *Unsettled Subjects: Restoring Feminist Politics to Poststructuralist Critique*. Durham, N.C.: Duke University Press, 1997.

Lurie, Susan, Ann Cvetkovich, Jane Gallop, Tania Modleski, and Hortense Spillers. "Restoring Feminist Politics to Poststructurals Critique." *Feminist Studies* 27, no. 3 (Fall 2001): 679–708.

Mandle, Joan D. "How Political Is the Personal? Identity Politics, Feminism and Social Change." Available on the userpages.umbc.edu website (WMST-L).

Manning, Robert. "The Philippines in Crisis." *Foreign Affairs* (Winter 1984/85): 392–410.

Marchand, Marianne H., and Jane L. Parpart, eds. *Feminism postmodernism development*. International Studies of Women and Place. London: Routledge, 1995.

Mayberry, Katherine J., ed. *Teaching What You're Not: Identity Politics in Higher Education*. New York: New York University Press, 1996.

McCann, Carole R., and Seung-Kyung Kim, eds. *Feminist Theory Reader: Local and Global Perspectives*. New York: Routledge, 2003.

McConnell, Michael C. "Don't Neglect the Little Platoons." In Nussbaum, *For Love of Country*, 78–84.

McElroy, Wendy. *XXX: A Woman's Right to Pornography*. New York: St. Martin's Press, 1995.

McKeganey, Neil P., and Marina Barnard. *Sex Work on the Streets: Prostitutes and Their Clients*. Buckingham, England: Open University Press, 1996.

McLaughlin, Lisa. "Beyond 'Separate Spheres': Feminism and the Cultural Studies/Political Economy Debate." *Journal of Communication Inquiry* 23, no. 4 (1999): 327–54.

McMichael, Philip. *Development and Social Change: A Global Perspective*. 2nd ed. Thousand Oaks, Calif.: Pine Forge, 2000.

Mee-Udon, Farung, and Ranee Itarat. "Women in Thailand: Changing the Paradigm of Female Well-being." In Billson and Fluehr-Lobban, *Female Well-being*, 285–308.

Mikula, Maja, ed. *Women, Activism and Social Change*. Routledge Research in Gender and Society. Vol. 11. London: Routledge, 2005.

Miralao, Virginia, Cecilia Carlos, and Aida Santos. *Women Entertainers in Angeles and Olongapo: A Survey Report*. Manila: WEDPRO and KALAYAAN, 1990.

Moghissi, Haideh. *Feminism and Islamic Fundamentalism: The Limits of Postmodern Analysis*. London: Zed Books, 1999.

Mohanty, Chandra Talpade. *Feminism without Borders: Decolonizing Theory, Practicing Solidarity*. Durham, N.C.: Duke University Press, 2003.

———. "Under Western Eyes." In Torres, Russo, and Mohanty, *Third World Women and the Politics of Feminism*.

Monto, Martin. "Why Men Seek Out Prostitutes." In Weitzer, *Sex for Sale*, 67–83.

Moore, Wilbert Ellis. *Social Change*. Foundations of Modern Sociology Series. Englewood Cliffs, N.J.: Prentice-Hall, 1963.

Moore, Wilbert Ellis, and Robert Manuel Cook. *Readings on Social Change*. Prentice-Hall Readings in Modern Sociology Series. Englewood Cliffs, N.J.: Prentice-Hall, 1967.

Nagel, Joane. *Race, Ethnicity, and Sexuality: Intimate Intersections, Forbidden Frontiers*. New York: Oxford University Press, 2003.

Nagle, Jill, ed. *Whores and Other Feminists*. New York: Routledge, 1997.

Narayan, Uma. "The Project of Feminist Epistemology: Perspectives from a Nonwestern Feminist." In Bailey and Cuomo, *The Feminist Philosophy Reader*, 756–65.

———. *Dislocating Cultures: Identities, Traditions, and Third-World Feminism*. New York: Routledge, 1997.

Narayan, Uma, and Sandra Harding. *Decentering the Center: Philosophy for a Multicultural, Postcolonial, and Feminist World*. A Hypatia Book. Bloomington: Indiana University Press, 2000.

Nova Scotia. Working Group on Youth Exploited for the Sex Trade and Nova Scotia. Dept. of the Solicitor General. *Report of the Working Group on Youth Exploited for the Sex Trade*. Halifax, N.S.: Dept. of the Solicitor General, 1993.

Nussbaum, Martha C. *For Love of Country: Debating the Limits of Patriotism*. Boston: Beacon Press, 1996.

———. "The Professor of Parody—the Hip, Defeatist Feminism of Judith Butler." *New Republic* (February 22, 1999).

———. *Sex and Social Justice*. New York: Oxford University Press, 1999.

———. "Women's Education: A Global Challenge." *Signs: Journal of Women in Culture and Society* 29, no. 2 (2004): 325–355.

———. *Women and Human Development: The Capabilities Approach*. John Robert Seeley Lectures. Cambridge: Cambridge University Press, 2000.

Odzer, Cleo. *Patpong Sisters: An American Woman's View of the Bangkok Sex World*. New York: Arcade Pub., 1994.

Ofreneo, Rene E., and Rosalind Pineda Ofreneo. "Prostitution in the Philippines." In Lim, *The Sex Sector*, 109–29.

Okin, Susan Moller. "Feminism, Women's Human Rights and Cultural Differences." In Narayan and Harding, *Decentering the Center*, 26–46.

Okin, Susan Moller, Joshua Cohen, Matthew Howard, and Martha C. Nussbaum. *Is Multiculturalism Bad for Women?* Princeton, N.J.: Princeton University Press, 1999.

O'Neill, Maggie, and Rosemary Barberet. "Victimization and the Social Organization of Prostitution in England and Spain." In Weitzer, *Sex for Sale*, 123–37.

Oppermann, Martin. *Sex Tourism and Prostitution: Aspects of Leisure, Recreation and Work*. Tourism Dynamics. Elmsford, N.Y.: Cognizant Communication Corp., 1998.

Osborne, Milton. *Southeast Asia: An Introductory History*. Thailand: Silkworm Books, 1997.

Overall, Christine. "What's Wrong with Prostitution? Evaluating Sex Work." *Signs: Journal of Women in Culture and Society* 17, no. 4 (1992): 705–24.

Park, Shelley M. "Research, Teaching, and Service." *Journal of Higher Education* 67, no. 1 (1996): 46–84.

Parpart, Jane L. "Lessons from the Field: Rethinking Power, Gender, and Post- (Post?) Development Perspective." In *Feminist Post-Development Thought: Rethinking Modernity, Post-Colonialism and Representation*, ed. Kriemild Saunders, 41–56. London: Zed Books, 2002.

Pasuk Phongpaichit, and International Labour Office. *From Peasant Girls to Bangkok Masseuses*. Women, Work, and Development. Vol. 2. Geneva: International Labour Office, 1982.

Patai, Daphne, and Noretta Koertge. *Professing Feminism: Cautionary Tales from the Strange World of Women's Studies*. New York: Basic Books, 1994.

Perkins, Roberta, ed. *Sex Work and Sex Workers in Australia*. Sydney: UNSW Press, 1994.

Peterson, V. Spike, and Anne Sisson Runyan. *Global Gender Issues*. Dilemmas in World Politics. 2nd ed. Boulder, Colo.: Westview Press, 1999.

Pettman, Jan Jindy. "Body Politics: International Sex Tourism." *Third World Quarterly* 18, no. 1 (1997): 93–108.

———. *Worlding Women: A Feminist International Politics*. London: Routledge, 1996.

Phillips, Anne, ed. *Feminism and Politics*. Oxford Readings in Feminism. New York: Oxford University Press, 1998.

Pieterse, Jan Nederveen. "After Post-Development." *Third World Quarterly* 21, no. 2 (2000): 175–91.

Pogge, Thomas Winfried Menko. *World Poverty and Human Rights: Cosmopolitan Responsibilities and Reforms*. Cambridge, U.K.: Polity, 2002.

Porter, Marilyn, and Alissa Trotz, eds. *Gender, Globalization, and Development*. Special issue, *Atlantis: A Women's Studies Journal* 26 (2002).

Putnam, Hilary. "Must We Choose between Patriotism and Universal Reason?" In Nussbaum, *For Love of Country*, 91–97.

Putnam, Robert D. *Democracies in Flux: The Evolution of Social Capital in Contemporary Society*. New York: Oxford University Press, 2002.

Rafael, Vicente L. *White Love and Other Events in Filipino History*. American Encounters/Global Interactions. Durham, N.C.: Duke University Press, 2000.

Ralston, Meredith L. "Upstream in the Mainstream: Strategies for Women's Organizing." *Canadian Woman Studies* 20, no. 3 (2000): 176–80.

Raymond, Janice G., Jean D'Cunha, Siti Ruhaini Dzuhayatin, Patricia Hynes, Zoraida Ramirez Rodriguez, and Aida Santos. *Comparative Study of Women Trafficked in the Migration Process*. Coalition Against Trafficking in Women-Asia, 2002. Available on the action.web.ca website.

Rice, R. Eugene. "Beyond 'Scholarship Reconsidered': Toward an Enlarged Vision of the Scholarly Work of Faculty Members." *New Directions for Teaching and Learning* no. 90 (2002).

Ringdal, Nils Johan. *Love for Sale: A World History of Prostitution* [Verdens vanskeligste yrke]. Translated by Richard Daly. New York: Grove Press, 2004.

Roberts, Nickie. *Whores in History: Prostitution in Western Society*. London: Grafton, 1993.

Roces, Mina. "Beauty Queens, Moral Guardian, *Inang Bayan*, and Militant Nun: Images of Female Power." Chapter 5 in *Women, Power, and Kinship Politics: Female Power in Post-War Philippines*. Pasig City: Anvil, 2000.

———. "The Militant Nun as Political Activist and Feminist in Martial Law Philippines." In *Women, Activism, and Social Change*, ed. Maja Mikula, 136–56. London: Routledge, 2005.

Roy, Parama. "At Home in the World? The Gendered Cartographies of Globality." *Feminist Studies* 27, no. 3 (Fall 2001): 709–732.

Ryan, Chris, and Colin Michael Hall. *Sex Tourism: Marginal People and Liminalities*. London: Routledge, 2001.

Santos, Aida. "Gathering the Dust: The Bases Issue in the Philippines." In Sturdevant and Stoltzfus, *Let the Good Times Roll*, 32–44.

Sassen, Sakia. "The Excesses of Globalizaton and the Feminisation of Survival." *Parallax* 7, no. 1 (2001): 100–110.

Saunders, Kriemild, ed. *Feminist Post-Development Thought: Rethinking Modernity, Postcolonialism and Representation*. London: Zed Books, 2002.

Scarry, Elaine. "The Difficulty of Imagining Other People." In Nussbaum, *For Love of Country*, 98–110.

Schelkle, W., W. Krauth, M. Kohli, and G. Elwert, eds. *Paradigms of Social Change: Modernization, Development, Transformation, Evolution*. New York: St. Martin's Press, 2000.

Seabrook, Jeremy. *Travels in the Skin Trade: Tourism and the Sex Industry*. 2nd ed. London: Pluto, 2001.

Seidman, Steven. *Embattled Eros: Sexual Politics and Ethics in Contemporary America*. New York: Routledge, 1992.

Sen, Krishna, and Maila Stivens. *Gender and Power in Affluent Asia*. New Rich in Asia Series. London: Routledge, 1998.

Servaes, Jan, Thomas L. Jacobson, and Shirley A. White, eds. *Participatory Communication for Social Change*. Communication and Human Values. New Delhi: Sage Publications, 1996.

Shannon, Esther. "Experiential People?" 2007 PAR-L Automatic Digest.

Sharpe, Jenny, and Gayatri Chakravorty Spivak. "A Conversation with Gayatri Chakravorty Spivak: Politics and the Imagination." *Signs: Journal of Women in Culture and Society* 28, no. 2 (Winter 2003): 609–623.

Sharpe, Robert J., Patricia I. McMahon, and Osgoode Society for Canadian Legal History. *The Persons Case: The Origins and Legacy of the Fight for Legal Personhood*. Toronto: Osgoode Society for Canadian Legal History by University of Toronto Press, 2007.

Shrage, Laurie. *Moral Dilemmas of Feminism: Prostitution, Adultery, and Abortion*. New York: Routledge, 1994.

———. "Prostitution and the Case for Decriminalization." *Dissent* 43, no. 2 (Spring 1996): 41–45.

Sievers, Leroy. "There Is Evil." *Los Angeles Times*, June 12, 2005.

Silliman, G. Sidney, and Lela Garner Noble, eds. *Organizing for Democracy: NGOs, Civil Society, and the Philippine State*. Manila: Ateneo do Manila UP, 1998.

Silver, Rachel. *The Girl in Scarlet Heels*. London: Arrow Books, 1994.

Singer, Peter. *One World: The Ethics of Globalization*. Terry Lectures. New Haven, Conn.: Yale University Press, 2002.

Skrobanek, Siriporn, Boonpakdee Nataya, and Chanthathiro Chutima. *The Traffic in Women: Human Realities of the International Sex Trade*. London: Zed Books, 1997.

Smith, Jackie G., Charles Chatfield, and Ron Pagnucco, eds. *Transnational Social Movements and Global Politics: Solidarity Beyond the State*. Syracuse Studies on Peace and Conflict Resolution. Syracuse, N.Y.: Syracuse University Press, 1997.

Sommers, Christina Hoff. "The Subjection of Islamic Women and the Fecklessness of American Feminism." *The Weekly Standard* 12, no. 34 (2007). Available on the weeklystandard.com website.

———. *Who Stole Feminism? How Women Have Betrayed Women*. New York: Touchstone, 1995.

Spector, Jessica, ed. *Prostitution and Pornography: Philosophical Debate about the Sex Industry*. Stanford, Calif.: Stanford University Press, 2006.

Spelman, Elizabeth V. *Fruits of Sorrow: Framing our Attention to Suffering*. Boston, Mass.: Beacon Press, 1997.

———. *Inessential Woman: Problems of Exclusion in Feminist Thought*. Boston: Beacon Press, 1988.

Spivak, Gayatri Chakravorty. "Can the Subaltern Speak? Speculations on Widow Sacrifices." *Wedge* 7, no. 8 (1985): 120–30.

———. *A Critique of Postcolonial Reason: Toward a History of the Vanishing Present*. Cambridge, Mass,: Harvard University Press, 1999.

Spivak, Gayatri Chakravorty, and Sarah Harasym. *The Post-Colonial Critic: Interviews, Strategies, Dialogues*. New York: Routledge, 1990.

Spivak, Gayatri Chakravorty, Donna Landry, and Gerald M. MacLean, eds. *The Spivak Reader: Selected Works of Gayatri Chakravorty Spivak*. New York: Routledge, 1996.

Sterling, Toby. "Dutch Try to Dim Red Light Tourism." *Halifax Chronicle-Herald*, December 18, 2007, sec. A8.

Stienstra, Deborah. "Cutting to Gender: Teaching Gender in International Relations." *International Studies Perspectives* 1, no. 3 (2000): 233–44.

Stone-Mediatore, Shari. "Chandra Mohanty and the Revaluing of 'Experience.'" *Hypatia: A Journal of Feminist Philosophy* 13, no. 2 (Spring 1998): 116–33.

Sturdevant, Saundra Pollock, and Brenda Stoltzfus. *Let the Good Times Roll: Prostitution and the U.S. Military in Asia*. New York: New Press, 1993.

Sylvester, Christine. "Development Studies and Postcolonial Studies: Disparate Tales of the 'Third World.'" *Third World Quarterly* 20, no. 4 (1999): 703–21.

Sztompka, Piotr. *The Sociology of Social Change*. Oxford, UK: Blackwell, 1994.

Taylor, Allegra. *Prostitution: What's Love Got to Do with It?* Guernsey, UK: Guernsey Press, 1991.

Thomas, Dorothy Q., Sidney Jones, Women's Rights Project, and Asia Watch Committee. *A Modern Form of Slavery: Trafficking of Burmese Women and Girls into Brothels in Thailand*. New York: Human Rights Watch, 1993.

Thorbek, Susanne, and Bandana Pattanaik, eds. *Transnational Prostitution: Changing Patterns in a Global Context*. London: Zed Books, 2002.

Tickner, J. Ann. *Gender in International Relations: Feminist Perspectives on Achieving Global Security*. New Directions in World Politics. New York: Columbia University Press, 1992.

Tomlinson, John. *Globalization and Culture*. Chicago: University of Chicago Press, 1999.

Torres, Amaryllis. *Profiles of Disadvantaged Children: Street Children in Six Philippine Cities*. Quezon City: University of the Philippines Press, 1996.

Torres, Lourdes, Ann Russo, and Chandra Talpade Mohanty, eds. *Third World Women and the Politics of Feminism*. Bloomington: Indiana University Press, 1991.

Truong, Thanh-Dam. *Sex, Money, and Morality: Prostitution and Tourism in Southeast Asia*. London: Zed Books, 1990.

Tyner, James. "Migrant Labour and the Politics of Scale: Gendering the Philippine State." *Asia Pacific Viewpoint* 42, no. 1 (2000): 131–54.

Van de Ven, Andrew H. *Engaged Scholarship: A Guide for Organizational and Social Research*. Oxford: Oxford University Press, 2007.

Webster, Fiona. "The Politics of Sex and Gender: Benhabib and Butler Debate Subjectivity." *Hypatia: A Journal of Feminist Philosophy* 15, no. 1 (2000): 1–22.

Weinstein, Jay A. *Social and Cultural Change: Social Science for a Dynamic World*. 2nd ed. Lanham, Md.: Rowman and Littlefield, 2005.

Weis, Lois, Yoshiko Nozaki, Robert Granfield, and Nils Olsen. "A Call for Civically Engaged Educational Policy-Related Scholarship." *Educational Policy* 21, no. 2 (2007): 426–33.

Weitzer, Ronald John. "Prostitution as a Form of Work." *Sociological Compass* 1, no. 1 (2007): 143–155.

Weitzer, Ronald John, ed. *Sex for Sale: Prostitution, Pornography, and the Sex Industry*. New York: Routledge, 2000.

West, Jackie, and Terry Austrin. "Markets and Politics: Public and Private Relations in the Case of Prostitution." *Sociological Review Monograph* 54, no. 1 (2006): 136–48.

Whitworth, Sandra. *Feminism and International Relations: Towards a Political Economy of Gender in Interstate and Non-Governmental Institutions*. Macmillan International Political Economy Series. Basingstoke: Macmillan, 1994.

Wichterich, Christa. *The Globalized Woman: Reports from a Future of Inequality* [Globalisierte Frau]. Translated by Patrick Camiller. North Melbourne, Australia: Spinifex Press, 2000.

WEDPRO. *Halfway through the Circle: The Lives of Eight Filipino Survivors of Prostitution and Sex Trafficking*. Manila: WEDPRO, 1998.

──────. *From Manila, Angeles, and Olongapo to Cebu and Davao: The Continuing Lives of Women in the Entertainment Industry*. Manila: WEDPRO, 1994.

Wonders, Nancy, and Raymond Michalowski. "Bodies, Borders, and Sex Tourism in a Globalized World: A Tale of Two Cities—Amsterdam and Havana." *Social Problems* 48, no. 4 (2001): 545–71.

Working Group on Prostitution. *Report and Recommendations in Respect of Legislation, Policy and Practices concerning Prostitution-Related Activities*. Government of Canada, December 1998.

Yapa, Lakshman. "Public Scholarship in the Postmodern University." *New Directions for Teaching and Learning* no. 105 (2006): 73–83.

Yedlin, Deborah. "To Some, It's the Infamous Five." *Globe and Mail* (October 19, 2004).

Yuval-Davis, Nira. *Gender and Nation*. Politics and Culture. London: Sage Publications, 1997.

──────. "Human/Women's Rights and Feminist Transversal Politics." In Feerree and Tripp, *Global Feminism*, 275–95.

Zaide, Sonia M. *The Philippines: A Unique Nation*. 2nd ed. Quezon City: All-Nations Publishing Co., 1999.

About the Authors

Meredith Ralston is a professor in the departments of Women's Studies and Political Studies at Mount Saint Vincent University in Halifax, Nova Scotia. She is also an award-winning filmmaker, and her latest film, entitled *Hope in Heaven* AKA *Selling Sex in Heaven* about sex tourism in the Philippines, is narrated by Kiefer Sutherland and is available through Kumarian Press.

Edna Keeble is a professor in the Department of Political Science at Saint Mary's University in Halifax. Her work has focused on issues of security, particular from a feminist perspective, and through the years she has sat on national boards advising the Canadian government on foreign policy, national security, and Canada-U.S. border matters. She has won three significant teaching awards and has been selected as the University's 2008–9 teaching scholar.

Index

abolitionist feminists, 60–62, 67–68

Aboriginal Women's Action Network (AWAN), 56

abortion, 13–14, 71, 106, 110–11, 146

abstinence, 82

academic feminism, 10, 13, 15, 24–26, 44–45, 168

adultery, 81–82

advocacy group, 4, 7, 17, 65, 139

African Americans, 11, 183

Ahmed, Sara, 172

Alcoff, Linda, 27–28, 171–73

Ali, Ayaan Hirsi, 45

Alinsky, Saul, 144

Almodavar, Norma Jean, 59

alternative livelihood, 135, 163–64

Americans, 5, 7, 56

    Angeles City economic development from, 77, 123

    as bar owners, 108

    colonization by, 20, 52, 83

    Filipino immigration to, 87

    Philippines departure by, 91, 98, 109

    privilege of, 27

    sex trade work authority of, 93

analysis paralysis, 9–10, 19, 23–46, 31

Anderson, Benedict, 86

Angeles City, 85. *See also* project, in Angeles City

    American economic development of, 77, 123

    Clark Air Force Base in, 4, 20, 77, 84, 90, 93–94, 99

    customers reasons to be in, 118–21

    health checks in, 21, 69, 93, 99, 110, 113

    military prostitution in, 6, 9, 16, 20–21, 63, 71, 77, 84, 89, 97–98, 115, 165

    sex tourism in, 9, 16, 20–21, 77, 89, 95, 97–125

    WEDPRO sex worker study in, 69

Angeles University Foundation (AUF), 7, 130

anti-feminist, Sommers as, 32, 45

anti-racism, 12, 167, 180

    activism, 172

    multiculturalism and, 24–25

    Spivak on, 175

anti-solicitation laws, 55, 69

Appiah, Kwame Anthony, 11, 179–80, 183

Aquino, Corazon, 91, 93–94

Association of Universities and Colleges of Canada (AUCC), 7, 130, 132

AUCC. *See* Association of Universities and Colleges of Canada

AUF. *See* Angeles University Foundation

Australia/Australians, 5, 109, 124

    abolitionist system of, 68

    as bar owners, 77, 108, 116, 119

    escort workers in, 72

    regulated prostitution in, 74

    sex-workers' rights groups in, 59–60

AWAN. *See* Aboriginal Women's Action Network

Bailey, Alison, 176

Bangkok, Empower Foundation of, 65

Bank of Canada, Famous Five on $50 bill by, 24

bar fines, 69, 99, 101, 107–8, 110, 115, 121

bar girls, 5–6, 21, 51, 95, 101–15, 123–24, 137, 140–42, 161–63, 179

    age and, 108

Hope in Heaven
A companion DVD to *Reluctant Bedfellows*

2007 Beyond Borders National Media Award
2005 Best Documentary, Big Bear International Film Festival

Mila works at Heaven, a little bar on "blowjob alley" in Angeles city, the Philippines. Once the site of the United States Clark Air Force Base, the city is now one of the busiest and sleaziest sex-tourist destination in Southeast Asia. Mila lives in tremendous hope that someday a customer will rescue her from Heaven and take her to America.

In the Philippines, prostitution is not just lucrative business—it's an industry. *Hope in Heaven*, by filmmaker Meredith Ralston, examines the country's sex trade and the young women it traps. Seen through the eyes of two idealistic female students and a male university professor, the film depicts two years of Mila's life and the people who befriend her. The poverty and squalor she lives in and her hope that one day a foreigner will rescue her are both poignant and heartbreaking.

> For a trailer of the film, see http://www.youtube.com/user/StylusPub

Suggested uses:
Professors of Development Studies, International Relations, and Women's Studies: Shows how globalization and the global sex trade affect individuals.

Non-profits and NGOs: A starting point for organizers to talk about how change happens.

Hope in Heaven DVD
Region: NTSC. Plays on all computers worldwide
978-1-56549-273 8, 43 minutes, $35.00
Includes educational performance rights

Also from Kumarian Press...

Women & Gender:

Women and the Politics of Place
Edited by Wendy Harcourt and Arturo Escobar

Cinderella or Cyberella? Empowering Women in the Knowledge Society
Edited by Nancy Hafkin and Sophia Huyer

War's Offensive on Women: The Humanitarian Challenge in Bosnia, Kosovo, and Afghanistan
Julie Mertus

New and Forthcoming:

Hollow Bodies: Institutional Responses to Sex Trafficking in Armenia, Bosnia, and India
Susan Dewey

Living Our Religions: Hindu and Muslim South Asian-American Women Narrate Their Experiences
Edited by Yvonne Klynman, Nicholas Kouppari, and Mohammed Mukhier

The World Bank and the Gods of Lending
Steve Berkman

Coping with Facts: A Skeptic's Guide to the Problem of Development
Adam Fforde

Visit Kumarian Press at **www.kpbooks.com** or
call **toll-free 800.232.0223** for a complete catalog.

green press INITIATIVE

Kumarian Press / Stylus Publishing is committed to preserving ancient forests and natural resources. We elected to print this title on 30% post consumer recycled paper, processed chlorine free. As a result, for this printing, we have saved:

4 Trees (40' tall and 6-8" diameter)
1,337 Gallons of Wastewater
3 million BTU's of Total Energy
172 Pounds of Solid Waste
322 Pounds of Greenhouse Gases

Kumarian Press / Stylus Publishing made this paper choice because our printer, Thomson-Shore, Inc., is a member of Green Press Initiative, a nonprofit program dedicated to supporting authors, publishers, and suppliers in their efforts to reduce their use of fiber obtained from endangered forests.

For more information, visit www.greenpressinitiative.org

Environmental impact estimates were made using the Environmental Defense Paper Calculator. For more information visit: www.papercalculator.org.

 Kumarian Press, located in Sterling, Virginia, is a forward-looking, scholarly press that promotes active international engagement and an awareness of global connectedness.